Gentilly

A NEW ORLEANS PLANTATION IN THE FRENCH ATLANTIC WORLD

1818–1851

LOUISIANA STATE UNIVERSITY PRESS BATON ROUGE

TRANSLATED
AND EDITED BY
Nathalie Dessens AND
Virginia Meacham Gould

Published with the assistance of The Noland Fund

Published by Louisiana State University Press
lsupress.org

Manufactured in the United States of America
First printing

Designer: Kaelin Chappell Broaddus
Typefaces: Adobe Caslon Pro, text; Geographica and Geographica Script, display
Printer and binder: Sheridan Books, Inc.

Jacket illustration: *Carte particulière du flevue St. Louis dix lieües au dessus de la Nouvelle Orléans* (detail), ca. 1723, Cartes Marines, Newberry Library, Chicago.

Library of Congress Cataloging-in-Publication Data

Names: Dorville, Auvignac, author. | Dessens, Nathalie, 1963– translator, editor. | Gould, Virginia Meacham, translator, editor.
Title: Gentilly : a New Orleans plantation in the French Atlantic world, 1818–1851 / translated and edited by Nathalie Dessens and Virginia Meacham Gould.
Description: Baton Rouge : Louisiana State University Press, [2025] | Includes bibliographical references and index.
Identifiers: LCCN 2024048600 (print) | LCCN 2024048601 (ebook) | ISBN 978-0-8071-8366-3 (cloth) | ISBN 978-0-8071-8455-4 (epub) | ISBN 978-0-8071-8456-1 (pdf)
Subjects: LCSH: Dorville, Auvignac. | Plantations—Louisiana—New Orleans Region—History—19th century—Sources. | Enslaved persons—Louisiana—New Orleans Region—Social conditions—History—19th century—Sources. | Plantation overseers—Correspondence. | France—Colonies—America—Social conditions. | LCGFT: Business correspondence.
Classification: LCC F379.N555 D67 2025 (print) | LCC F379.N555 (ebook) | DDC 976.3/3505—dc23/eng/20250113
LC record available at https://lccn.loc.gov/2024048600
LC ebook record available at https://lccn.loc.gov/2024048601

TO *Mado,*

WHO WAS WITH US FOR

A LONG PART OF THE WAY BUT

LEFT US BEFORE THE BOOK CAME TO LIGHT

CONTENTS

ILLUSTRATIONS

MAPS

PREFACE

When we first discussed publishing the Sainte-Gême letters that detail the history of the Gentilly plantation, we knew it would be a long process.[1] We recognized that living on different sides of the Atlantic Ocean would severely limit our time for face-to-face collaboration. But each of us had been traveling back and forth between Toulouse and New Orleans for years, so we knew we would have some time together to hash out any difficult questions or differences of opinion that would surely arise. Further, each of us had been researching and writing about New Orleans for decades, so we decided that our mutually shared love of the city and its history, together with email, would see us through. We have always believed that our different identities—South of France and South of the United States—as well as our specialization in different periods and aspects of New Orleans history would allow us to bring a richer understanding of New Orleans with its multinational, multicultural, and multiracial past, as well as its place within the history of the Atlantic World. With that said, over the past years, we have sent thousands of emails to each other, lingered over transmitted documents, and traveled back and forth between Toulouse and New Orleans, all the while moving our knowledge of the history of the plantation further and further along.

At first, we meant to simply transcribe, translate, and publish the letters

1. The originals are housed with The Historic New Orleans Collection at the Williams Research Center in New Orleans. They are only a part of the Ste-Gême Family Papers (MSS 100), acquired by the collection in the early 1970s from a descendant of the Sainte-Gême family, Mrs. Albin La Fonta. The collection contains 849 items that span the years 1799 to 1904.

that Auvignac Dorville, a New Orleans French Creole, direct descendant of the French who settled the area, and manager of the Gentilly plantation, sent to the Frenchman Baron Henri de Sainte-Gême and his family, the plantation owners who were living in France. We believed that the historical value of the published letters, which set forth the activities and finances of the plantation, would expand what is known about urban plantations and the lives of the individuals living and working there, and would even complicate the history of early New Orleans and its hinterland. The plantation, which was located on a long ridge of land four and a half miles from the French Quarter, was distinct from the city but closely tied to it. It produced goods for the city and perhaps more closely resembled a truck farm than any of the monocrop sugar and cotton plantations that fueled the economy of the city and its hinterland.[2] Indeed, slavery on this small urban plantation was a curious mixture of two types of bondage, in some ways similar to the large sugar and cotton plantations in Louisiana and across the Atlantic World, in others, to the distinct form of slavery typical of New Orleans and other urban slave centers in the Americas.[3]

After we progressed through the transcription and translation of the letters, we began searching through local archives so we could more fully locate the plantation in time and place. It was there, in the archival documents, that we were able to piece together a far richer, more complex history of the plantation and the enslaved and free people who lived and worked there. Our first "Oh wow" moment was when we learned that the plantation dated back to the founding years of New Orleans and that it had continued as a plantation, albeit a small one, until the mid-nineteenth century. Our next discovery was that the plantation, founded in the 1720s, was passed down from one family member to the next from its founding until it was sold in 1850. In other words, it stayed

2. As Cécile Vidal puts it, it was part of the "vast agro-urban zone in which the city lived in symbiosis with its rural environment." Vidal, *Louisiana,* 12.

3. Although slavery was primarily a rural, agricultural institution, bondspeople lived many different experiences. In the cities, the enslaved population mainly included domestics and skilled workers who generally had greater freedom of movement. The Gentilly bondspeople lived between two worlds, toiling on the plantation but spending time in the city. As the letters will show, they often went to town to sell plantation products at the market. Some of them, especially the women, stayed for even longer periods of time. They could be hired out for months, if not years, apprenticed, or sent to the city to ensure their infants were delivered safely. On Louisiana's large cotton and sugar plantations, see Follett, *Sugar Masters;* W. Johnson, *Rivers of Dark Dreams.* For more on urban slavery, see Wade, *Slavery in the Cities;* R. Johnson, *Slavery's Metropolis.* For an overview of urban slavery in New Orleans, see Gould, "'The House that Was Never a Home,'" 90–103.

within the family for a century and a quarter. Taken together, the letters written by Dorville to the Sainte-Gêmes, along with the documentation in the archives, inspired us to position the story of the Gentilly plantation within the social, cultural, economic, and political changes that swept through the Atlantic World during the 125 years that followed its foundation.

ACKNOWLEDGMENTS

THIS BOOK IS THE PRODUCT OF MANY YEARS OF RESEARCH. IT COULD NOT have been completed without the institutions and people who graciously helped us along the way. We are grateful that The Historic New Orleans Collection understood the value of the Sainte-Gême collection and acquired it. We are indebted to the staff of the Williams Research Center, which houses The Historic New Orleans Collection, and more particularly Daniel Hammer, who is now the president and CEO of the collection, Mary Lou Eichhorn, Jennifer Navarre, and Robert Ticknor. They were always extremely hospitable and helpful.

We are also grateful to those who helped us at the Louisiana Division of the New Orleans Public Library, in particular Greg Osborne, and at the Notarial Archives Research Center, especially Siva Blake, Sally Sinor, and Ina Fandrich.

We also want to acknowledge the Louisiana Historical Center at the Louisiana State Museum and all the institutions that have put their indexes—and sometimes their records—online, giving us access to documents that are scattered throughout the city of New Orleans and thus offering us the possibility to follow the history of the Gentilly plantation and those who lived on it over a span of a century and a half.

We could not have done this work without the historians who have gone before us, from the early historians of Louisiana like Marcel Giraud, Charles Gayarré, François Xavier Martin, Alcée Fortier, and Grace King, to the most recent scholars who have contributed much to the field, among whom are Thomas Ingersoll, Gwendolyn Midlo Hall, Richard Campanella, Shannon Lee Dawdy, Larry Powell, and many more.

Our thanks also go to Modesta Suárez for her help in translating some of the most obscure Spanish records and to Jim Bolner, Michèle Kaltemback, Sheryl Rahal, and David Speights for being our early readers.

We also want to express our gratitude to the reviewers for their insightful comments, which helped us improve the book.

And we are forever grateful to Patrick Besse and David Speights for standing by us over the years as we translated, researched, wrote, rewrote. They were especially supportive as we suffered through a string of deadlines and the hurry caused by the short moments we could spend working together.

Gentilly

The Gentilly Plantation

A HISTORY

Late on the evening of March 14, 1818, Jean Baptiste Auvignac Dorville, a New Orleans Creole, sent a brief letter of apology to the French baron Henri de Sainte-Gême.[1] Dorville had scribbled the letter from the Gentilly plantation just outside New Orleans. In this, his first and otherwise deferential note to Sainte-Gême, Dorville apologized for not coming into the port city: "I apologize, Monsieur Sainte-Gême, and beg you to forgive me for not coming to town to bid you farewell. I am still suffering from fever and do not have the strength. Before leaving the plantation, you honored me with your trust. I hope one day to be deserving of your esteem as well." When he wrote the obsequious note, he had just been hired by Sainte-Gême as the manager of the plantation.[2] When Sainte-Gême received it, he was at the port of New Orleans, waiting to board a ship that would take him and his Creole bride, Marguerite Delmas Dreux Sainte-Gême, and her two children, Marie Hermine and Henri Antoine Dreux, Sainte Gême's godson, to his ancestral home in France.[3]

1. Dorville was a French-descended Creole. He was not of African descent. For the definition of the many ways in which *Creole/creole* can be used, see Gould, "Creoles."

2. Procuration between Henri de Sainte-Gême and Auvignac Dorville, Narcisse Broutin, vol. 37 (1818), Records of the Superior Council of Louisiana, Louisiana State Museum (henceforth RSC), 63.

3. Respectively named Hermina and Edgar in the correspondence. As was the custom, Henri Dreux was named after his godfather, but when they lived together, it was probably easier to avoid having two Henris in the household. Further, using names other than birth or baptismal names was a common practice in the early nineteenth century. For instance, Henri de Sainte-Gême was known in France as Jean-François, though he chose to call himself by his second name in Louisiana. For a full treatise on Sainte-Gême, see Dessens, *Creole City,* especially pages 7–26.

Dorville's letter, as obeisant as it was, initiated a decades-long business alliance centered upon the plantation. It is evident from the message that upon the marriage of Sainte-Gême and Madame Marguerite Delmas Dreux, Sainte-Gême assumed control of the family and the ninety-year-old plantation his wife and her two children had inherited from Louis Leufroy Dreux.[4]

As the newly hired manager of the plantation, Dorville moved into the big house, accepting responsibility for its day-to-day operation, including its fields and pastures, poultry, livestock, and crops, and most importantly, its enslaved people. His note makes it clear that he was honored to have been hired by the prestigious Frenchman. What he could not have forseen was that his position as caretaker of the plantation would continue throughout most of his life. When he wrote that first note to Sainte-Gême, just after stepping into the role of manager, he was twenty-five years old.[5] When the plantation was sold to John McDonogh in 1850, he was fifty-eight years old.[6] Even after the sale, he continued as manager for another five years, until he moved to his house on Esplanade Street in New Orleans's city center.[7] In or around 1870, he moved to his farm, which was just outside the city of New Orleans, in Saint Bernard Parish. He remained there until his death in 1876.[8] Throughout those

4. According to Louisiana law and the Code Napoléon, property brought into the family by the wife was considered the property of the husband. As for the property of the children, it was held in trust for them, but at their deaths it reverted to the mother if she was still alive. When the plantation was sold, in 1850, the owners mentioned in the act of sale were Marguerite de Sainte-Gême née Delmas, "by virtue of the rights resulting from the communities that have successively existed between her and her two husbands, and her capacity as heir to Henry Dreux junior, and her four children named below as the sole heirs of Mr. Jean François Henri de Saintegême, their father, who had all the rights of Madame Marie-Hermina Dreux, their uterine sister, on the properties concerned, according to the contract reported to us of June 16, 1828, duly recorded." Document registered by Jean-François Labatut, Notarial Act, St. Gaudens, May 17, 1850.

5. Jean Baptiste Lamolère D'Orville was born on September 4, 1792. His father and mother were François Lamolère D'Orville and Marie Marthe Pascalis de La Barre. Archives of the Archdiocese of New Orleans, Sacramental Records, Baptisms, September 4, 1792, Louisiana State Museum. Further references to the sacramental records will be indicated as AANO.

6. John McDonogh purchased the plantation in 1850 but died a few months later. In his last will and testament, he left the plantation to the city of New Orleans. Upon the settlement of the will, the city formed a committee to manage the plantation. Shortly thereafter, the committee hired Dorville to continue to manage the plantation, though that arrangement only continued for five years. In the last letter he penned from Gentilly, on October 26, 1855, Dorville informed Anatole Sainte-Gême, Sainte-Gême's son, that he was leaving.

7. New Orleans City Directory, 1861 and 1866, New Orleans Public Library.

8. Census of the United States, Saint Bernard Parish, 1860 and 1870, Records of Probate, New Orleans Public Library, Louisiana Division (henceforth NOPL).

later years, long after he left the Gentilly plantation, he remained committed to the Saint-Gême family, as is evidenced by his continuing correspondence. His responsibility to the Dreuxs ended only upon the death of Marguerite Delmas Dreux Sainte-Gême in 1873, when he acted as the local attorney for the probate of her estate.[9]

Despite the many letters, reports, and balance sheets Dorville sent to Sainte-Gême, he remains something of a mystery. It was rare for him to mention himself or his family in his letters. We know from other sources that he was descended from a long line of well-to-do planters, which is where he learned plantation management.[10] What he does mention several times in his letters is that he fathered a daughter named Irma, by an unnamed enslaved woman belonging to Sainte-Gême. While there is no evidence that he freed Irma, he remained committed to watching over her.[11] What he failed to note is that he married twice. In 1867, he married Celestine Couville, a woman of color. Auvignac and Celestine named their two legitimate sons Pierre and Anatole.[12] They were both described as mulattoes in the 1870 United States census. In 1873, when he was eighty-one years old, he married Mercedes Desbrosses; she too was a woman of color, a practice not unknown in the racially fluid world of New Orleans.[13]

9. The probate records of Marguerite Sainte-Gême can be found in the Records of Probate, NOPL.

10. Auvignac Dorville was descended from Francisco Joseph Lamolère, native of Paris, Chevalier of the Order of St. Louis, infantry captain in the service of His Most Christian Majesty. Auvignac's mother was Maria Marthe DelaBarre. Her father was a former cavalry officer in the service of His Most Christian Majesty, and the permanent regidor and aguazil mayor of the province of Louisiana. One of Dorville's brothers, François, inherited his family's plantation, evidently leaving Auvignac and his brother to seek employment elsewhere. For more on the Lamolère Dorville family, see AANO, Marriages, June 14, 1785; Baptisms, June 6, 1756, January 24, 1791, September 15, 1800, July 7, 1805.

11. See, for instance, the letter Dorville wrote to Sainte-Gême dated September 7, 1818. Also Gould, "'If I Can't Have My Rights,'' 179–201.

12. According to the 1850 United States census of New Orleans, Auvignac Dorville was living at the Gentilly plantation with his two sons, Pierre (age eleven) and Anatole (eight). Census rolls, NOPL.

13. Marriage of Dorville and Desbrosses, May 27, 1873. Marriage Index, 1846–1890, NOPL. On white men in early Louisiana fathering children by enslaved women, see Spear, *Race, Sex, and Social Order,* 61–69. Spear also examines the illegality of white men marrying free women of color in early New Orleans (29–99). Though the practice was illegal, it was not uncommon. Also see Vidal, *Caribbean New Orleans,* 248, 266–284. For an early work on interracial liaisons, particularly in the nineteenth century, see Gould, "In Full Enjoyment of Their Freedom." Also see Clark, *The Strange History*; Wegmann, *An American Color.*

Over the decades, when Dorville wrote to the Sainte-Gêmes from Gentilly, he focused on the plantation and its slaves as well as the ever-growing Sainte-Gême family and their French and Louisianan friends. His reports and letters remind us that nineteenth-century New Orleans was defined by the world of plantation slavery, a world that was located in a series of economic, political, and cultural networks. What is also valuable about his letters is that they shed light on the workings of a nineteenth-century suburban plantation, founded by the Frenchmen Pierre and Mathurin Dreux in early French Louisiana before it passed through generations of their descendants and well before Dorville became manager. In those ways, Dorville broadens our understanding of the Atlantic World in the ages of slavery, emancipation, and nascent capitalism. Over and over again, his letters offer a view of the political economy that fueled New Orleans and the symbiotic relationship that evolved between the port town and its immediate hinterland. And even though the letters are written in the nineteenth century, they invite us back to the plantation's colonial past, where we can see the processes that went into the formation of the plantation economy that developed jointly with the urban economy and yet remained distinct from it. Here we explore the formation of the plantation during the early years of the colonization of Louisiana, following its evolution through the French and Spanish colonial years and into the early decades of the nineteenth century, when it fell under the control of Henri de Sainte-Gême.

To understand the particular and peculiar nature of the Gentilly plantation, we first look back to the formation of the terrain that supported the evolution of a plantation on the edge of what would become one of the major cities of the United States. The geographically young terrestrial landscape that would become lower Louisiana began to take shape about five thousand years ago. As the Mississippi River changed course, it deposited sediment, which eventually separated the lower Mississippi River valley from the open waters of the Gulf. The alluvial deposits created a geographic wilderness of brackish water that surrounded and sometimes submerged the natural levees, ridges, and terrain that is now known as the Greater New Orleans area. The ancient labyrinth that lay behind New Orleans, which is now Gentilly and Lake Pontchartrain, was eventually bisected by natural bayous created between 600 BCE and 1000 CE, when the last main distributary of the river—the Metairie-

Gentilly distributary—was gradually choked off from the present river.[14] By 1400, the Metairie-Gentilly distributary had become two sluggish bayous that cut across the back of town—east to west—and intersected Bayou St. John, which in turn flowed into Lake Pontchartrain. The bayous were skirted by natural levees, or ridges, that were at points wide enough for settlements and high enough to avoid all but the worst of flooding.

Centuries before the French arrived, the ridges, made up of sand, silt, and mud held together by vast expanses of cane, served as footpaths and campgrounds for roving bands of Indigenous peoples. Cypress, magnolia, pecan, oak, and willow, among other native trees, bushes, grasses, and mosses, grew along the ridge. Soon after, the French began their effort to plant a town on the crescent of the river, and for the next 150 years the ridge was claimed as a plantation, first by the Dreux brothers, who named it l'habitation [plantation] de Gentilly. Today, it is difficult to imagine that the Gentilly plantation was ever there. It is a maze of concrete roads and parking lots, houses, banks, drugstores, fast-food joints, shopping malls, and universities protected by canals and tall concrete barriers—levees—that control flooding from Lake Pontchartrain and the canals that crisscross the area. The exact location of the old plantation house built in the early years of the eighteenth century, and the one that replaced it in the nineteenth century, is most probably buried under Interstate 610 where it crosses Gentilly Boulevard.

The first Europeans to take note of the improbable landscape that would become New Orleans and its hinterland, including the Gentilly bayou and ridge, were the Canadian brothers and adventurers Pierre Le Moyne d'Iberville and Jean Baptiste le Moyne de Bienville. In 1698, Louis XIV and the French minister of marine Jérôme Phêlypeaux, Comte de Pontchartrain, sent Iberville to find and explore the Mississippi River. The goal was purely geopolitical. Iberville was sent to "select a good site that can be defended with a few men, and block entry to the river by other nations."[15] In early 1699, he and his brother, Bienville, began searching for the river along the northern Gulf. By March, they had entered the mouth of the river. According to Iberville's journal, they soon met a local Indian who guided them through inlets, bays, swamps, and marshes in and around the river, and even showed them a shortcut to the coast. Later, Iberville reflected in

14. Dawdy, *Building the Devil's Empire,* 74–77; Freiberg, *Bayou St. John, 1699–1803,* 19–20; Campanella, *Bienville's Dilemma,* 77, 84–85.

15. Campanella, *Bienville's Dilemma,* 103–104. Also see Morris, "Impenetrable but Easy," 103–104.

his journal that the Indians (sauvages) had "made maps of the whole country" for him.[16] A few days later, while exploring the river with an Indian guide, he spotted the future site of New Orleans. On March 9, he noted in his journal that the guide had pointed out a portage from the river to the lake. The portage was known to the Indians as Bayou Choupic. Bienville later renamed it Bayou Saint-Jean (later anglicized to Bayou St. John) after his favorite saint.[17]

Months later, Bienville and a few of his companions returned to Lake Pontchartrain and Bayou St. John. In his journal, Iberville described the bayou as "1 league long, and half the distance being full of water and mud up to the knees, the other half fairly good, part of it being a country of canes and fine woods, suitable to live in."[18] They recognized that the backdoor portage from the river to the lake would provide the strategic location they had been seeking. Then he spotted the Metairie-Gentilly ridge. He wrote that, after traveling some distance upstream, he and his crew reached a place where the land on either side of the bayou was higher. It was there, he noted, that he had found a primitive bridge over a short stretch of water, which linked Bayou St. John to Bayou Sauvage (Gentilly).[19]

After Iberville's untimely death in Cuba in 1706, Bienville grew obsessed with the idea that a settlement on the levee on the crescent of the river would provide a position to defend the Mississippi River and the American interior. The location also offered a deepwater port and a viable route to Mobile, Biloxi, the Gulf of Mexico, the Caribbean, and the wider Atlantic World.[20] Its hinterland was ideal for the development of an agricultural economy. Yet despite Bienville's commitment to the site, seventeen years would slip by before John Law's Company of the West presented the anxious Bienville with the opportunity to site New Orleans at the crescent on the river.[21]

In March 1718, Bienville began to clear the ground for the settlement of New Orleans. Ten weeks later he sent a brief report to the French navy stating

16. LeMoyne d'Iberville, *Iberville's Gulf Journals,* 60, 71; Campanella, *Bienville's Dilemma,* 107.

17. Kidder, "'Making the City Inevitable,'" 20.

18. LeMoyne d'Iberville, *Iberville's Gulf Journals,* 111–112.

19. Giraud, *Histoire de la Louisiane Française,* 3:7–21.

20. Campanella, *Bienville's Dilemma,* 110.

21. Bienville to the Navy Council, June 12, 1718, in Rowland and Sanders, *Mississippi Provincial Archives,* 225–228. By December 23, 1717, the newly formed Company of the West had made its final decision to allow Bienville to locate a settlement on the crescent of the river. For the best description of John Law's settlement, see Powell, *Accidental City,* 23–32.

that he and his men were working on the establishment of New Orleans.[22] Otherwise, he was silent on the subject. There is, however, another account, written by Jonathan Darby, an Englishman who was, as unlikely as it seems, one of the town's earliest settlers. In his memoir written in the 1750s, he described the founding of New Orleans. Monsieur de Bienville, he wrote, "arrived with six vessels loaded with provisions and men. Of the men, thirty were convicts reclassified as workmen, six were carpenters, and four were Canadians. Also accompanying Bienville was Monsieur Pailloux, commander of the future settlement, Monsieur Chassin, Intendant of Commerce, and Monsieur Dreux." Darby added that "Monsieur Bienville cut the first cane and Chassin, Pailloux, and Dreux the second." The goal was to open a passageway through the dense canebrake that would stretch from the river to the lake. The first and second cutting of the cane by Bienville, Pailloux, Chassin, and Dreux was more than likely symbolic, at least for Bienville.[23]

The Dreux who cleared the cane with Bienville was Pierre. His younger brother, Mathurin, arrived about a year later.[24] The records are almost entirely silent on Pierre and Mathurin before they arrived in New Orleans. The sacramental records archived at the Archdiocese of New Orleans reveal that the brothers hailed from Savigné-sur-Lathan, Anjou-Touraine, in the Loire Valley region of France. They told the priest registering the record that their father, Louis Dreux, was a tanner, a burgher, which amounted to a man of the middle class. Nothing is known about their mother, Françoise Harant. Over time, Pierre and Mathurin grew from respectable middle-class Frenchmen to be prosperous and influential, tied by their position as planters to New Orleans's elite, a feat that would have been denied to them in France.[25]

The Dreuxs were drawn to New Orleans by the opportunity afforded them by vast land grants promised by the Duke of Orléans, regent of France, during the childhood of Louis XV, and the Scottish John Law, a close friend of the duke and a man later to be known as a schemer. Had the brothers migrated to

22. Bienville to the Navy Council, June 12, 1718, in Rowland and Sanders, *Mississippi Provincial Archives,* 222–228.

23. Jonathan Darby was a neighbor and friend of Pierre and Mathurin Dreux. Darby left a memoir that was later published. Darby, "Account of Jonathan Darby," 201.

24. Mathurin Dreux arrived on the fluyt *Le Philippe* on January 25, 1719. Census of New Orleans and its Environs, November 24, 1721, Archives Nationales d'Outre-Mer, Aix-en-Provence, 464; Conrad, *First Families of Louisiana,* vii.

25. AANO, Marriages, November 17, 1732.

Louisiana earlier, they would have found that the first French outposts at Fort Maurepas (Old Biloxi, 1699) and Fort Louis de la Louisiane (Mobile, 1702) were primarily military outposts. The few settlers lured there had been encouraged to plant gardens, though their attempts were more futile than not. Those first settlers were unequipped to cultivate the sandy soil that was quickly overworked. The dearth of laborers fit for the heavy work of clearing and planting also hindered prosperity. Even the wildlife around the two forts had grown scarce as hungry settlers overhunted the woods.

What was different about New Orleans was that it was surrounded by fertile terrain. Its rich alluvial soil supported thick strands of trees and underbrush, which sustained an abundance of wildlife. Writing in his journal years before New Orleans was carved from the crawfish-teeming mud of the crescent along the river, Iberville unwittingly described the fecundity of the soil. "Both banks of the river, almost the entire distance above the sea, are so thickly covered with canes of every size . . . that one cannot walk through them."[26] In his journal, completed in 1723, André Penicault, an inhabitant of Old Mobile, wrote that he thought that if the excessive growth of trees that filled the landscape were cleared away, the "country of Louisiana would be a terrestrial paradise, with the agriculture that would be developed there."[27] Bienville also reported that there was an abundance of wild game, enough to feed the early settlers. He found herds of buffalo and cattle grazing on the levees along the river. In other words, he understood that settlers around the future site of New Orleans would not want for food. In his mind, New Orleans was ripe for settlement.[28]

Bienville understood that in order to have a town and an agro-economy, he needed colonists and laborers. In 1719, he addressed the problem with the Company of the Indies (earlier known as the Company of the West), whereupon the company promised to reinvigorate Louisiana's meager population by sending six thousand European settlers and up to three thousand enslaved Africans. The tactics the company devised to meet the quota of Europeans included recruiting all segments of the populace. The least fortunate of the mostly French immigrants were *forcés,* or forced laborers, men and women scooped off the streets of French cities or out of orphanages, poorhouses, and prisons to be exiled to the colony. *Engagés,* or indentures, were sent with concession holders. Sailors and soldiers were sent to protect the colony. Those who stayed after being discharged

26. LeMoyne d'Iberville, *Iberville's Gulf Journal,* March 7, 1699, 56.
27. McWilliams, *Fleur de Lys and Calumet,* 20.
28. Morris, "Impenetrable but Easy," 26–28.

were issued small concessions or farms after marrying and promising to stay and cultivate the land. France's military officers and its notables were ceded land grants or large concessions, though they too were obligated to remain in the colony to clear and work the land.[29]

Even as Pierre Dreux aided in clearing cane for the future settlement, well-connected settlers were being granted large concessions of fertile ground that lay along the river. The first large concessions went to Bienville and the king.[30] After securing those concessions, he granted the Canadian Chauvin brothers, Joseph Chauvin Delery, Nicolas Chauvin La Frénière, and Louis Chauvin Beaulieu, large concessions on the relatively high and fertile land at the Tchoupitoulas Coast, which lay upriver from the settlement. Claude Joseph Dubreuil, the Frenchman, was also granted a concession at Tchoupitoulas. His wife, Marie Payen Dubreuil, and the Chauvins, who were Canadians, were Bienville's cousins.[31] They were the founding elites of the colony.

Since the Dreuxs were not ceded land on the river, it seems that they were not related to Bienville, nor were they as "elite" as the Dubreuils and Chauvins. Instead of hundreds of arpents on the river, they were granted a small but fertile concession on the banks of Bayou St. John, as well as a small lot on the levee (Rue du Quai) of the slowly emerging settlement.[32] It is not that those concessions were not valuable. They were. But since the brothers were not related to Bienville, the size and location of their first lots suggest that they were awarded them in return for their service to him. It also appears that Pierre Dreux aided Adrien de Pauger, an engineer and the town planner, in designing and laying out the town since Pauger, in his last will and testament, left his concession on the west bank to him. However, it also appears that Bienville voided the transfer to Pierre, claiming that the concession was never Pauger's to leave.

Those first small land grants on Bayou St. John apparently did not satisfy

29. Powell, *Accidental City,* 68–73; Ingersoll, *Mammon and Manon,* 6–9, 12, 41; Hall, *Africans in Colonial Louisiana,* 29–35; Giraud, *Histoire de la Louisiane française,* 3:252. For the women forced to Louisiana as brides, see Gould, "Bienville's Brides," 389–408.

30. The long lot, or ribbon lot, was a unit of land division common in France. The lots were typically lined up along waterways, a system that had originated in Canada. Iberville laid claim to an extensive stretch of land between Riviere du Chien on Mobile Bay and Pascagoula. He also laid claim to several large concessions in Mobile and New Orleans.

31. Allain, "Not Worth a Straw," 65–66; Giraud, *History of French Louisiana,* 274, 350.

32. One arpent is about 180 feet, or about 60 meters. The lots located along Bayou St. John were first settled by Mobilians looking for fertile soil. Rowland and Sanders, *Mississippi Provincial Archives,* 55; Giraud, *History of Louisiana,* 327; de Villiers, "A History of the Foundation of New Orleans," 168.

LAC PONTCHARTRAIN

Entrée du Bayou

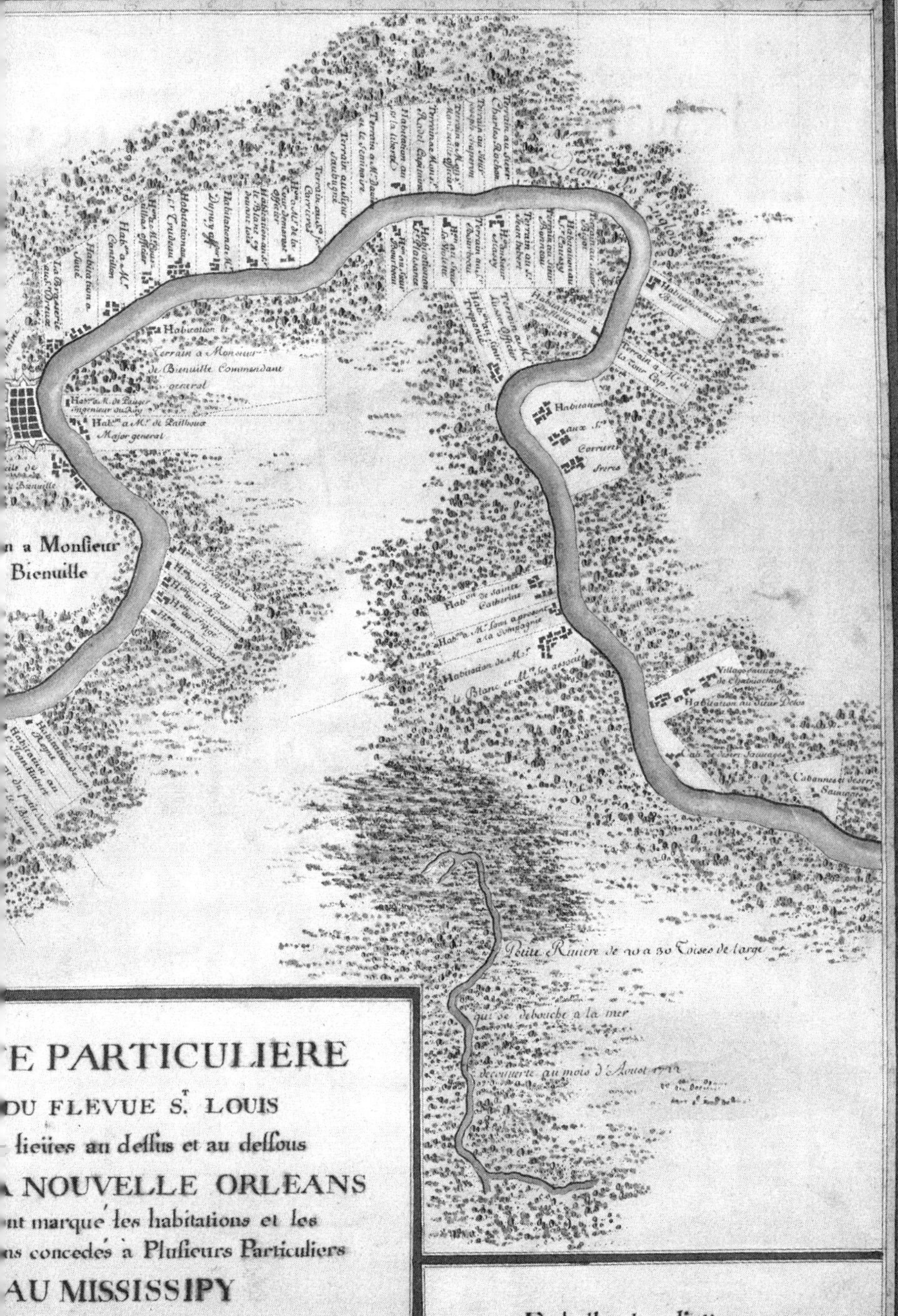
E PARTICULIERE
DU FLEVUE S.T LOUIS
lieües au dessus et au dessous
A NOUVELLE ORLEANS
nt marqué les habitations et les
ns concedés à Plusieurs Particuliers
AU MISSISSIPY
Echelle de 2 lieües
Petite Riviere de 10 a 30 Toises de large
qui se debouche a la mer
decouverte au mois d'Aoust
Habitation et Terrain a Monsieur de Bienuille Commendant general
n a Monsieur
Bienuille

the acquisitive nature of the Dreuxs. In 1720, they made their first move, selling their lots on Bayou St. John, although they kept their lot and house on the Rue du Quai. Of course they kept their town house. After all, the town was the social, intellectual, economic, and religious center of the colony. It was where the colonists met to worship, socialize with their peers, and exchange gossip.[33]

The Dreuxs did not immigrate to New Orleans to be town dwellers. They traveled to Louisiana in search of economic potential. In 1719 or 1720, with the profits they earned from the sale of their lots on Bayou St. John and with a steep mortgage of 12,500 livres held by Sieurs Chauvin and de la Garde, they purchased a long lot on the Mississippi River, next to the emerging city. The long lots in Louisiana mirrored those in Canada. They mostly measured four arpents on the river by forty arpents deep. By English measure, the lot purchased by the Dreuxs was not inconsiderable. Its river frontage measured approximately eight hundred feet wide and eight thousand feet deep. In other words, it stretched nearly a mile and a half into the swamps that lay behind New Orleans. Its back boundary bordered on the front edge of the Bayou Sauvage (Gentilly) swamp, or what would eventually be the eastern boundary of the Gentilly plantation.[34]

The Dreuxs' long lot, located on the waterfront, downriver and next to the muggy, stinking, mosquito-ridden town, provided them with a unique commercial opportunity. It was as if they looked into the future and saw Bourbon Street. Instead of dedicating themselves entirely to plantation slavery, they built a brewery, a bar, and a fancy eating establishment on the riverfront portion of their concession. Their beverages were especially popular with the thirsty settlers, soldiers, and sailors who rotated in and out of town, and it was a popular

33. Freiberg, *Bayou St. John*, 42. The long lot was originally co-owned by Sieur Chauvin and Sieur de la Garde, who purchased the property on speculation. Since Chauvin, cousin of Bienville, was the director of the Chaumont concession in Pascagoula, it is most likely that he and Chauvin obtained their lot from Bienville. However, anyone owning property during the French period was required to live on it, and neither Chauvin nor de la Garde did. Some of the records of the Superior Council concerning the sale of the property are missing, but those that are extant indicate that Chauvin and de la Garde sold the riverside long lot to the Dreuxs.

34. The footage is based on the English measurement of linear feet. At first, the Dreux plantation was known as Chantilly, but as time went by it became Gentilly. It seems probable that the Dreuxs named it after the Gentilly neighborhood near Paris.

MAP ON PREVIOUS PAGES

Carte particulière du flevue St. Louis dix lieües au dessus de la Nouvelle Orléans . . . (ca. 1723), showing French long lots along the Mississippi River. Ayer MS, map 30, sheet 80, Cartes Marines, Newberry Library, Chicago.

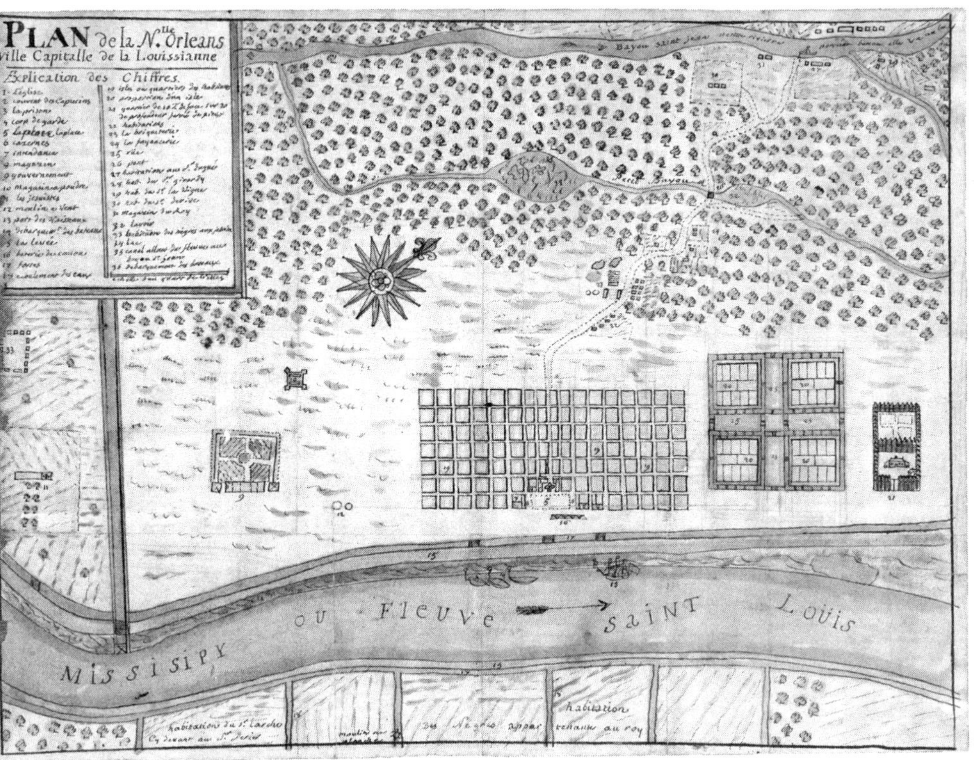

Plan de la Nlle. Orleans, ville capitalle de la Louissianne (1747), by Dumont de Montigny, showing the city of New Orleans and the plantations along the Petit Bayou and Bayou St. John. Ayer MS 257, map 7, Newberry Library, Chicago.

watering hole and bakery with the locals.[35] La Brasserie, as they named it, proved to be the most popular place in town—and the most profitable. In his memoir, Marc-Antoine Caillot described the brewery: "At a quarter of a league downriver, there is a brew house that functions as a place of recreation for taking promenades, and at this place you can also drink this beer that is brewed with roasted maize, also known as Turkish wheat. It is not one of the best, but when

35. It is possible that Bienville suggested they build and operate a brewery. Bienville's eldest brother, Charles Le Moyne, owned and operated a brewery in Canada, outside of Montreal. King Louis XIV commended Charles for having a fine brewery and a mill that were very useful to the colony. Louis Pilié's 1847 Plan of New Orleans shows that Pierre Dreux was in partnership with Jean de la Garde as early as 1723. The partnership was dissolved in 1724. RSC, June 19, 1725, July 11, 1725. Also see *Tronquidy vs. Dreux Frères,* awarding Tronquidy 250 francs and 10 sous for 835 pounds of bread they failed to supply.

wine is lacking it is good. This place has the feel of an open-air Café in Paris where countless numbers of people go to have fun."[36]

Pierre and Mathurin were not only New Orleans's first brewers but also were among its first planters. The brothers planted sections of their acreage and utilized the rest, the lowlands that extended back from the river and into the swamps, as pasturage for their cattle and horses and hunting. Only scattered records of the crops the Dreuxs cultivated have survived. We know they planted corn and secured a contract to supply the government with corn for the troops. They also pastured cattle and horses on sections of the long lot. And if they followed custom, they planted indigo for the international trade and corn, rice, squash, and beans for local consumption and trade. By 1721, they had accumulated five horses, more horses than anyone else in the colony. They owned the plantation on the river that included the brewery, La Brasserie, and their townhouse on the Rue du Quai. Their plantation on the river was eventually dubbed La Brasserie. They also held eight enslaved Africans.[37] The evidence is that they had begun working the Gentilly Ridge by 1720. At that point, the long, fertile strip of land that ran along Bayou Sauvage was not theirs, but it lay behind La Brasserie and perpendicular to their riverfront plantation. This was the strip of property that would become known as the Gentilly plantation.[38]

Despite, and perhaps because of, their many ventures, the Dreuxs quickly fell into debt, a state not unlike that of so many of their Louisiana neighbors. Before 1721, Pierre and Mathurin had purchased enslaved Africans from the Company of the Indies. No doubt the Dreuxs, like most other colonists, mortgaged their

36. Caillot, *Company Man,* 83. Also see the map *Carte particulière du flevue St. Louis dix lieües au dessus de la Nouvelle Orleans* (ca. 1723), reproduced in this volume.

37. Maduell, *Census Tables,* 16–27. In comparison to other concessionaires in the area, they were not the most prosperous. Monsieur Bienville had far more property and claimed thirty-six indentures and slaves. The others who seem to have been more prosperous were the concessionaires at Tchoupitoulas. Messieurs Dulude and Deconoire held ninety-three laborers; the Chauvin brothers, who were relatives of Bienville, held more than three hundred enslaved laborers; and Claude Joseph Dubreuil, whose wife was also one of Bienville's family members, worked forty-seven enslaved people.

38. In a dispute over a right-of-way to the trail that wound its way alongside Bayou Sauvage (later Bayou Gentilly), two colonists, Livet and Soubaigné, who were appealing on behalf of the Gentilly settlers, argued that there had always been a public road, which had been restored five years before by the Dreuxs. The testimony places the Dreuxs at Gentilly as early as 1720. In volume 4 of *New Orleans Architecture,* Christovich et al. state that Mathurin or Pierre Dreux had begun to acquire property as early as 1719. See also RSC, March 28, 1725, June 14, 1725.

slaves through the company; the favorable terms of the company's mortgage policy would have been advantageous for the Dreuxs. But the mortgage for the long lot on the river, which was originally held by Sieur Chauvin and Jean de la Garde, was not favorable.[39] A dispute over the debt between the Dreuxs and de la Garde began on May 5, 1725, when de la Garde requested that the Superior Council summon the brothers to answer his claim demanding payment for the riverfront concession. The case dragged on for two years, though in the end the Dreuxs continued to own and operate the brewery and plantation until Pierre's death.[40]

In 1724, the same year that financial trouble struck, Mathurin and Pierre requested the Company of the Indies grant them a concession on the ridge at Gentilly. A court document suggests that they had been squatting on the property since 1719 or 1720. They were officially awarded the concession in 1726.[41] The plantation, north to south, lay between Lake Pontchartrain and the property that lay back of the brewery and the other plantations downriver of New Orleans. Bayou St. John was the plantation's westerly boundary. Decades would pass before its easternmost boundary was defined. During those early years, French administrators did not always determine exact boundaries. So at first it appears that it extended back toward today's Chef Menteur Boulevard.[42] The requested plantation would, in future years, be thought of as back-of-town, back-swamp, the woods, and the *prairies tremblantes.*[43] As for the plantation house, an estimate places it near the present-day exchange at Interstate 610 and Gentilly Boulevard.

39. Jean de la Garde was the manager of the Chaumont plantation at Pascagoula, Mississippi.

40. According to de la Garde, the Dreuxs had breached their contract with him when they failed to pay the two thousand livres that were due. On May 23, 1725, the Superior Council found, by default, for de la Garde, ordering the Dreuxs to pay the two thousand livres they owed and another five thousand when it fell due. About two weeks later, on June 9, the Dreuxs filed a counterclaim. The judgment is illegible. However, it appears that they paid their outstanding debt. Two years later, on March 10, 1727, they were again summoned before the Superior Council for failure to pay the remaining 6,910 livres, 16 sols, 6 deniers for the plantation. At that hearing, de la Garde requested that the counsel foreclose on the mortgage. Documents for the final judgment are no longer extant, but the Dreuxs kept the property.

41. Christovich et al., *New Orleans Architecture,* 15–16.

42. Other boundary disputes heard by the Superior Council imply that early colonial administrators did not affix rigid boundaries to many of the concessions. The Gentilly plantation was briefly known as the Chantilly plantation, a happenstance that has inspired decades of debate over the name of the plantation and its meaning.

43. Campanella, *Bienville's Dilemma,* 81.

Besides planting, cultivating, harvesting, hunting, and brewing and selling beer, the Dreuxs were lumberers, brickmakers, builders, and bakers. During the early years of settlement, most of the houses and buildings of New Orleanians were constructed of cypress wood, with crushed oyster shells used for mortar and bricks. Recognizing that the heavily wooded areas of the long lot on the river and the Gentilly ridge offered them a nearly endless supply of enormous oaks on the high ground and cypress in the swamps, they harvested and sold timber, crafting it into planks, boards, beams, and cypress tiles necessary for the construction of housing, administrative buildings, and fortifications by colonial builders and engineers.[44] The entrepreneurial brothers also turned to building and selling furniture and boats, owned and operated a lumber mill and a brick manufactory, and imported wheat from the northern reaches of the river, where the weather was more amenable for its cultivation.[45] In July 1729, they brought the colonist Jean-Daniel Kolly before the Superior Council, explaining that he owed them for the 1,700 pounds of *farine* (flour) they had sold him in 1721, 1722, and 1723. It is impossible to believe that they did not bake and sell bread, since colonists were continually complaining about the corn-based bread they were consuming, and in addition to flour they imported sugar, which they sold or used to bake galettes (flat, crusty cakes).[46] Thus, it appears that in addition to importing farine and sugar to sell, they also were operating a bakery on the premises of their brewery.[47] Most of what they produced was sold locally or north up the Mississippi River, or it would have been illicitly traded with ports that were scattered along the Gulf Coast or across the Caribbean. The one piece of evidence for products shipped legally to France was the fifteen bundles of deerskins they sent to France aboard *L'Éléphant* in 1745.[48] Otherwise, much of their produce was sold locally or transported to other Gulf ports.

44. RSC, November 18, 1723.

45. Christovich et al., *New Orleans Architecture,* 15–16.

46. Receipt for items they sold to St. Julien, RSC, November 18, 1723. On December 4, 1723, they sold a boat to Bordier and Blanchard. For debt on the boat, see RSC, January 15, 1725. On March 4, 1725, in a case before the Superior Council, Dreux argues that Paul Barré, a Canadian, owed him 374 pounds of flour that he had contracted for on October 9, 1723. Then, on June 19, 1725, Sieur de Tronquidy claimed that the Dreux brothers owed him 835 pounds of bread. On their bread business, see RSC, February 7, 1727. It is possible that they were operating a retail store. See RSC, October 26, 1726. On selling beer, see RSC, December 11, 1728.

47. According to the Superior Council record of January 9, 1729, the Dreuxs were described as *boulangers,* or bakers.

48. The records of the French fluyt *L'Eléphant* can be found at Archives Nationales d'Outre-Mer, C13A, 28, fol. 342.

Lumber, clay, beer, corn, and cattle appear to have been their most profitable ventures. Corn was the most dependable crop—it was adaptable and could withstand inundation several times a season. The productivity of corn on the Gentilly plantation can be seen in a contract dated October 19, 1744, in which Mathurin agreed with colonial officials to furnish enough corn to supply the government. It was not the first time he agreed to feed the officers and soldiers of the area.[49]

The sprawling, isolated plains of the Gentilly plantation were also easily converted to pasturage. In 1739, Pierre and several of his neighbors complained to the Superior Council that Monsieur Mathieu and his slaves were stealing their cattle. According to Mathurin Dreux, Mathieu had stolen one of his cows and a bull, both from Havana Grand stock imported from Cuba.[50] Eventually, Pierre and Mathurin owned hundreds of cattle. In 1769, long after Pierre had died, Mathurin brought a complaint to the Superior Council accusing Monsieur Brazillier and his slaves of hunting his cattle. He further stated that he had previously owned seven hundred to eight hundred cattle but that Monsieur Brazillier and his slaves had so depleted his herd that he only had sixty cattle remaining.[51]

Another method of accumulating wealth and status was through smuggling. Louisianians turned to extralegal trade and smuggling with ports scattered across the Gulf Coast and the Caribbean. From the founding of the colony, as a consequence of isolation and imperial negligence, many Louisianians turned to extralegal trade. During the 1720s the pirate Jean Beranger boasted that New Orleans was well situated for smuggling and privateering. The proximity of Louisiana to the Spanish, he wrote, assured a good trade. He then bragged that he had aided in the survival of Louisiana's colonists by running a corsair between Martinique and the French ports on the Gulf of Mexico.[52]

Evidently no one was immune from suspicion. Bienville was investigated twice for privateering. One early colonist suspected of a salt smuggling attempt was the Superior Council member Jacques Fazende, the father of René Fazende, the future son-in-law of Mathurin and Claudine Françoise Dreux. Jacques Fazende was not the only New Orleanian involved in the plot. The Superior Council record mentions—in a vague sort of way—that the plot also

49. RSC, October 19, 1744.

50. RSC, March 29, 1739. Pierre won the case. Mathieu was ordered to pay for the cow and the bull.

51. RSC, January 14, 1769.

52. Pirates and privateers operated between New Orleans, Jamaica, Veracruz, and Cuba. Dessens, *From Saint-Domingue to New Orleans,* 82–84; Dawdy, *Building the Devil's Empire,* 115.

included other New Orleanians.[53] Mathurin Dreux was not named in any of the investigations of smuggling during the colonial period. Nevertheless, it is impossible for us to believe that he did not participate. His wealth and his position within the merchant-planter elite suggest it. Still more convincing was the location of the Gentilly plantation. On one end, closest to town, the bayou emptied into Bayou St. John where it intersected with the rear of the Indian Market, which was convenient as a transfer point. On the other end, it dumped into waterways that emptied into the Gulf. The plantation was thus perfectly situated for smuggling goods in and out of the area without detection. And Jonathan Darby, Pierre Dreux's neighbor at La Brasserie, remembered that between 1745 and 1750 Louisiana's commerce had prospered because of the Spanish money in circulation as a consequence of privateering. Many ships, he added, sailed in from a variety of ports to share in the benefits of the commerce. Jonathan Darby agreed with Beranger that it was the illegal contraband that supported the colony.[54]

Smugglers sailing to the shores of the northern Gulf off-loaded their cargo onto flatboats and other shallow draft vessels before navigating the network of bays, lakes, and bayous that lay southeast of New Orleans. From there, contraband was transported to Bayou St. John then passed eastward toward the remote levees of Bayou Gentilly and the back of the Indian Market, where it was off-loaded. Writing in his journal in 1766, Captain Harry Gordon noted that there was "all manner of smuggling" in the area around Bayou St. John.[55] Smugglers marketed their goods to eager New Orleanians. Marketable goods—especially wine, eau-de-vie (a clear, fruity brandy), clothing, hats, flour, cattle, and other sought-after European goods—were smuggled in, while timber, milled lumber, tar, pitch, clay, tobacco, and indigo were smuggled out. Of course, it is impossible to identify individual smugglers, like the Dreuxs, in and around colonial New Orleans, since smuggling naturally depends on secrecy.[56]

Whether they were smugglers or not, a few years after Pierre and Mathurin stepped ashore in New Orleans they would have been counted among the largest landholders in the region. According to the American State Papers, pub-

53. Dawdy, *Building the Devil's Empire,* 21. Jacques Antoine de Fazende was the same generation as Mathurin Dreux. He was a member of the Superior Council during the 1720s. His son René Jean Gabriel Fazende was born in Louisiana in 1726 and married Françoise Charlotte Dreux in 1745.

54. Darby, "Account of Jonathan Darby," 201; Dawdy, *Building the Devil's Empire,* 119.

55. Gordon, "New Orleans and Bayou Saint John in 1766," 464–489; Dawdy, *Building the Devil's Empire,* 112.

56. Dawdy, *Building the Devil's Empire,* 117.

lished nearly a century after the founding of the plantation, the Dreuxs had accumulated more than 173 arpents of land during their lifetimes.[57] To be sure, they can be counted among the aspiring planter class that viewed agriculture and animal husbandry as opportunities that would allow them to adopt the lifestyle of feudal lords, which would have been an impossibility for them in France.[58] If nothing else the Dreuxs were resourceful; they were go-getters, and they had a plan when they immigrated to New Orleans. Like so many others, they imagined themselves as planters before they stepped onto the muddy shores of the Mississippi River. Yet it is too far-fetched to imagine that the Dreuxs had the knowledge, the skill, or the energy to clear fields, cultivate crops, manufacture furniture, brew beer, bake bread, harvest lumber, operate a sawmill, or manufacture bricks. For those labor-intensive tasks, they needed laborers, and labor in Louisiana is best understood within the context of the French empire in the Americas.

Four classes of labor had been established in the French Atlantic well before Louisiana was founded: enslaved Native Americans, *forçats* (criminals and impoverished laborers forced to the New World), indentured engagés, and enslaved Africans. The Dreuxs employed individuals from at least three of these categories. Their first laborers were most likely Native Americans. The French encouraged Indian enslavement long before the Dreuxs purchased their Indian laborers. For a century, between 1630 and 1760, the French in North America pursued two opposing Indian policies. Through diplomacy they negotiated far-reaching systems of Indian alliances. At the same time, in a counterintuitive move, they encouraged settlers to coerce Indigenous men, women, and children into slavery.[59] A census of Biloxi, Mobile, and New Orleans in November 1721 counts 780 people living in and around the settlements. Of those, 161 were enslaved Native Americans.[60] In 1721, the Dreuxs owned two Natives. They also owned two in 1727.[61] They were more than likely the same two souls, who have gone nameless in the records.

The Dreuxs did not hire *forçats* as laborers. Instead, in the early years they employed engagés, or lower-class artisans, laborers, and peasants. In the 1630s,

57. Morris, "Impenetrable but Easy," 28; *American State Papers*, 6:672.

58. Dawdy, *Building the Devil's Empire*, 170.

59. Rushforth, "'A Little Flesh We Offer You,'" 777–808.

60. Maduell, *Census Tables*, 16–27. For more on the Gulf South Native Americans, see Usner, *American Indians in the Lower Mississippi Valley*; Usner, *Indians, Settlers, and Slaves*; and Usner, *American Indians in Early New Orleans*. Also see White, *Wild Frenchmen and Frenchified Indians*.

61. RSC, June 7–10, 1728.

France had begun to entice its expendable populace to cross the Atlantic to settle and work in its islands, Canada, and Louisiana. The engagés exchanged three years of hard labor for what they believed would be a better life in the New World.[62] In 1721, there were 178 engagés in Louisiana. The Dreuxs employed two; both worked at the brewery. They also employed two—perhaps the same ones—in 1726. Some sources suggest that the Dreuxs' engagés were brewers. Nonetheless, by 1727, one engagé had either died or had moved on to establish his own brewery. By 1731, they had adjusted their workforce and there were no engagés working at the brewery or at Gentilly. It is possible that one of them continued to work for them, though not as an engagé. Those who had traveled to Louisiana in the early years would have worked their way out of debt by 1731. Further, engagés were too independent-minded, too demanding, and too undisciplined to remain in the employ of others. The system of indentured labor envisioned by French authorities was a failure. Once they served their terms, fulfilled their duties, they were free to compete with the property-owning class. Instead of engagés, then, colonists insisted on Africans as laborers.

It cannot be a surprise that Louisiana's concessionaires looked to the centuries-old system of African slavery as they searched for a reliable supply of permanent laborers. In the view of Louisiana's officials and concessionaires, Louisiana was only going to prosper if France supplied an adequate supply of bound laborers, but officials in France were not easily convinced that Louisianans should receive shipments of enslaved Africans. They argued that the colony needed to prove its worth before they would divert any of the slave trade from the profitable plantations of Martinique and Saint-Domingue. By 1719, the officials relented, after recognizing that cattle, corn, and rice not only sustained the settlers of Louisiana; those products also could provide the foundation for a profitable export trade.[63] The first two shipments of enslaved Africans reached Louisiana in 1719. By 1721, enslaved Africans in and around New Orleans numbered 533. In a report dated November 24, 1721, Diron D'Artaguette pointed out that it was necessary to send many slaves to Louisiana, which he claimed would not do well unless a sufficient number of slaves was sent. They are "more suited than whites for the working of the land," he wrote, adding that "no other constraint than that of clothing them in winter" was necessary.[64]

62. Giraud, *Histoire de la Louisiane,* 3:221–251; Eccles, *France in America,* 157–158.

63. Morris, "Impenetrable but Easy," 33.

64. Louisiane, Recensements, 41, Louisiana State Museum; Archives Nationales d'Outre-Mer, G1, 464. Also see Mertas, Daget, and Daget, *Répertoire des expéditions négrières.* Their work influ-

During its first decade, the slave trade to Louisiana was robust. From 1721 to 1727 the trade increased from 533 to 1,561 enslaved Africans. In all of Louisiana, by the official end of the slave trade in 1731, the number of Louisiana's enslaved Africans amounted to nearly six thousand people.[65] In 1731, in lower Louisiana, enslaved Africans outnumbered the French by 3,352 to 1,095.[66] African slavery had quickly become the dominant form of labor organization, and concomitantly the basis of the economy and social fabric of the colony.[67] By 1763, enslaved Africans and their Creole offspring outnumbered the French by 4,539 to 2,966.[68] By then, colonists were firmly convinced that African slavery, and only African slavery, assured their own survival and advanced their interests.[69]

Louisiana's enslaved settlers cultivated the land they had cleared. They herded livestock, planted and cultivated crops, and constructed levees and buildings. Africans not only were obligated to provide labor for their owners but also were requisitioned by officials to aid in the construction of the colony's warehouses, levees, and canals. Even so, no matter how much labor they provided, it was never enough. Though Europeans and Creoles had an insatiable need for more, after 1731 their pleas went unanswered by officials, who refused to divert slaves away from the hugely profitable West Indies. There were never enough slaves to satisfy colonial artisans, farmers, or planters, which left them perpetually aggrieved.[70]

The Dreuxs were among the early Louisiana settlers to own Africans, and through the exploitation and commodification of the bodies of enslaved people they gained a kind of New World power, assets, and influence.[71] Indeed, it was only through slaveholding that enslavers found the power that would make them

---

enced Hall's *Africans in Colonial Louisiana,* the seminal work on slavery in Louisiana. Also see the Trans-Atlantic Slave Trade Database, https://www.slavevoyages.org/voyage/database.

65. Dawdy, *Building the Devil's Empire,* 7.

66. Hall, *Africans in Colonial Louisiana,* 35.

67. McGowan, "Creation of a Slave Society," 43–45; Ingersoll, *Mammon and Manon,* 95; Berlin, *Many Thousands Gone,* 96–99.

68. The latter number does not include soldiers. White, *Voices of the Enslaved,* 7; Vidal, *Caribbean New Orleans,* 121.

69. McGowan, "Creation of a Slave Society," 3; Hall, *Africans in Colonial Louisiana,* 71, 86; Berlin, *Many Thousands Gone,* 195; Spear, *Race, Sex, and Social Order,* 56–58.

70. Hall, *Africans in Colonial Louisiana,* 161

71. Baptist, *The Half Has Never Been Told.* Giraud discusses the migration to Louisiana of the middling classes, to which the Dreuxs belonged. He describes their expectations and their demands on the Company of the West. Giraud, *Histoire de la Louisiane Française* 3:154–220. See also Dawdy, *Building the Devil's Empire,* 162, 183–184.

rich, and the Company of the Indies afforded them the bodies that would enrich them. According to company records, the purchase price of a bondsman or woman was 660 livres, also called *pièce d'Inde,* per African. Purchasers had three years to pay. The payments were made in equal parts from the date of delivery. The sum of the debt was due in payments of tobacco or rice, calculated by the directors, who judged payment by the quality of the inhabitants' lands. Besides payment to the company for their enslaved Africans, it was incumbent upon the settlers to prove that they could feed their slaves and keep them healthy.[72]

The Dreuxs were joined by other concessionaires scrambling for Africans, and with income from the popular brewery, they were positioned to guarantee payments. No available information shows when the Dreuxs purchased their first Africans. However, by 1721 they owned eight men and women who either toiled at the brewery or in the fields and pastures around and behind it. By 1726, as they began the process of transforming their Gentilly concession into a plantation, they had purchased another African. Two were employed at La Brasserie. Seven labored on the back-of-town ridge that would slowly transform into the Gentilly plantation. By 1731, there were twenty Africans laboring for the Dreuxs. Three—two children and one adult—were at La Brasserie, while the other seventeen were to be found at Gentilly. Of those, ten were adults and seven were children.[73]

Other than raw numbers, there is a paucity of information on the identities and activities of the enslaved people the Dreuxs owned before the official end of the slave trade in 1731. We know from Gwendolyn Midlo Hall's groundbreaking work that, except for one ship from Angola, the slaves imported into Louisiana from 1719 to 1731 were transported from West Africa. Of those, sixteen slave ships transported the majority of enslaved laborers from Senegambia. They were from the Bambara, Ibo, Mandinga, and Wolof nations. One ship transported the recently enslaved from Angola. Six slave ships sailed from Whydah (also known as Ouidah or Juda, present-day Benin) with enslaved men and women aboard. Two slave ships arrived after the end of the official slave trade. In 1743, Claude Joseph Dubreuil financed a slave trading voyage from Senegambia. Another slave ship arrived from Angola in 1758. It appears that the Dreuxs purchased slaves at every opportunity.[74]

72. Morris, "Impenetrable but Easy," 33; Wilson, "Plantation of the Company of the Indies," 163–164.

73. Maduell, *Census Tables,* 115.

74. Hall, *Africans in Colonial Louisiana,* 175.

The majority of the eight enslaved Africans owned by the Dreuxs before 1721 had most likely been transported from Whydah, the commercial center of the Bight of Benin, which in those years was one of the largest slave trading ports in West Africa.[75] In the late seventeenth century, the coastal nation of Whydah was reputedly visited by as many as fifty slavers a year, and it was capable of supplying one thousand slaves every month. During this period, Whydah became known as the Slave Coast. Some enslaved Africans were Whydans, or they were captured when Whydans launched raids inland in order to secure captives.[76]

In all, 450 enslaved people with extensive agricultural skills were forcibly transported from the port at Whydah to Louisiana. Like Louisiana, the economy of the Whydah region was based on agriculture, herding, and internal and external trade. Its soil was extremely rich. In the early eighteenth century, William Snelgrave, a slave captain, described the economic conditions of Whydah. According to him, the soil was so very rich and "well cultivated by the inhabitants, it looked like an entire garden." His description suggests that enslaved Whydans would have brought with them the knowledge to cultivate corn, rice, peas, and melons, and to raise poultry and cattle.[77]

The predominance of Whydans in Louisiana did not persist more than a handful of years. From 1720 to 1731 the French transported the majority of slaves (4,000 out of 5,987) from the slave trading ports of Saint-Louis and Gorée Island in the Senegambian region of Africa (today's Senegal). The region was described as rich and productive. The Senegal River, like the Mississippi, regularly overflooded its banks, leaving behind a large area of rich and productive soil. Like the Africans from Whydah, the people of Senegambia were well-versed in the cultivation of rice, tobacco, indigo, peas, corn, and melons. According to André Brue, the director of the Senegal concession, gangs worked the fields, planting, cultivating, and harvesting. Islands in the middle of the river provided pasturage for cattle, goats, sheep, and fowl. It was a scene that was repeated in Louisiana.[78] The two regions, Whydah and Senegambia, included many language groups, though they shared two: mutually intelligible Mande and West

75. Hall, *Africans in Colonial Louisiana,* 60.

76. Adkins, *A Voyage to Guinea,* 119–122; Hall, *Africans in Colonial Louisiana,* 21–55. In her chapter on Senegambia during the slave trade, Hall details the arrival of different groups of Africans and how they reestablished themselves in Louisiana. For an interesting collection of essays on the similarities and dissimilarities between Louisiana and Saint-Louis, Senegal, see Clark, Vidal, and Thioub, *New Orleans, Louisiana, and Saint-Louis, Senegal.*

77. Law, "Original Manuscript," 367–372.

78. Hall, *Africans in Colonial Louisiana,* 35–36; Labat, *Nouvelle relation de l'Afrique occidentale.*

Atlantic. The Bambara and the Whydans shared some cultural concepts. Both were hierarchical, both were patriarchal, and each clung to their traditional religions, which shared similarities. Hall argues that over time the slaves brought from Senegambia—mostly Bambara who spoke Mande—predominated in the formation of Louisiana's Afro-Creole culture.[79]

The situating of ethnically similar African groups on the small number of lower Louisiana concessions facilitated the adaptation and preservation of African cultural autonomy. African continuities and the formation of a unique Afro-Creole culture in French colonial Louisiana were facilitated by family formation and kinship networks. In Louisiana, enslaved Creole children grew up in tightly knit nuclear families. Mothers and fathers—sometimes married, sometimes not—were present to usher their children into adulthood. Children could be sold away from their parents but not until the age of fourteen. Parental unions were protected by law and by custom.[80] In his *Histoire de Louisiane,* Giraud notes the importance of the family in lower Louisiana. Nothing, he argued, secured Blacks to a concession better than having children there.[81]

Louisiana's earliest documents do not allow for a close study of the Dreux slaves or of their continuity on the plantation, though there is evidence that their enslaved labor force grew throughout the French period. Some of the increase would have been natural, though there is also scattered evidence that Mathurin slowly added to his slave force. We can ascertain that he purchased slaves as his neighbors perished and their estates were auctioned off. In 1740, he purchased a three-year-old enslaved Indian named Jara from the estate of Louis Pellerin. The child was not sold with his mother. In 1745, Mathurin purchased three slaves from the estate of Dartagnan. They were described as a mulatto man named Mory, a man named Mousa or Moses, who was described as an Indian, and an unnamed woman described as an octoroon and the wife of Mousa. The record also states that Mousa's wife was from the coast of Congo.[82] In 1758, Mathurin purchased two men who had been aboard the British ship the *Judith* when it was captured by the French fluytes *L'Opal* and *La Fortune.*[83] A year later, in

79. Hall, *Africans in Colonial Louisiana,* 29; Mintz, *Caribbean Transformations,* 11–12, 27–28; Vidal, *Caribbean New Orleans,* 464–481.

80. Hall, *Africans in Colonial Louisiana,* 159.

81. Giraud, *Histoire de Louisiane Française,* 1:340–351; Hall, *Africans in Colonial Louisiana,* 29–55.

82. "Afro-Louisiana History and Genealogy, 1719–1820," https://www.ibiblio.org/laslave.

83. Archives Nationales d'Outre-Mer, C13A, 40, fol. 189, cited in Hall, *Africans in Colonial Louisiana,* 160.

1758, Mathurin purchased twenty-three slaves from the Morisette estate. With that purchase, he doubled his labor force. By 1763, Mathurin had accumulated forty-six slaves. One, a man, was described as an Indian. Of the others, twenty-three were African men, ten were African women, eight were African boys, and four were African girls. The number of slaves on the Gentilly plantation did not equal that of some of the other plantations, especially those along the Tchoupitoulas Coast, where hundreds of slaves toiled on plantations.[84]

The records tell us nothing about the natural increase in the early enslaved population. What they do say is that, like many other colonists, Mathurin encouraged his enslaved people to live in family units. After all, with the end of the official slave trade to Louisiana in 1731, he would have benefited from the stability family ties offered to the enslaved and the natural increase that would augment his and his family's wealth. The trend in Louisiana during the French period was to support the formation of the slave family, a strategy that paid off. In 1741, writing to the Ministry of the Colonies in Paris, Commissary Edmé Gatien Salmon noticed that there were no new slaves arriving in the colony and that many of the old slaves were dying off. He then elaborated:

> This species survives almost entirely by procreation which has taken place. In effect, among the approximately 4,000 blacks of all types and ages, two-thirds are Creole. That is a difference between this country and the French West Indies islands where there is a very little natural reproduction among slaves. It is certain that if a cargo of 250 Black adult men and women would come here every year, little by little the result would be a very considerable quantity of slaves in few years.[85]

Of the slaves Mathurin purchased in 1745, twenty were sold to him in family groups. Mathurin purchased Bazaza and Magdalaine with their children Philippe and François. Baptiste and Fanchon were purchased together with their children Fanchonette, Louis, Marie, and Angelique. A significant number of the enslaved

84. "Afro-Louisiana History and Genealogy, 1719–1820." Before the death of Gwendolyn Midlo Hall, this database, which she compiled, was deposited on the internet in several places. Hall also published the database on CDs that are available at The Historic New Orleans Collection and the New Orleans Public Library, Louisiana Division. Many of the CDs were sold to scholars and genealogists.

85. Salmon to the Ministry of the Colonies, New Orleans, April 25, 1741, Archives Nationales d'Outre-Mer, C13A 26, fols. 138–139.

people who inhabited the slave cabins on the Dreux plantation over the years more than likely lived in some sort of family, whether real or fictional. That fact alone, however, does not suggest that life was anything other than acceptance of servitude, of survival rather than death. It was a choice made in the sufferings of their day-to-day lives. Edward Baptist argues that individual enslaved people, finding their pre-slavery lives "killed off," were forced to choose between a scrabble for "individualistic subsistence" or solidarity. By choosing solidarity, he argues, they were able to build an alternative story to the enslavers' power.

The brutal day-to-day power that underpinned slavery was evident on the Dreux plantation. In 1764, the twenty-five-year-old enslaved African Marguerite was arrested for running away and was brought before the Superior Court in New Orleans. She claimed that she ran away because three weeks earlier

> her master and mistress always beat her, that when she fell sick her mistress came to see her after 4 days and said "Mademoiselle is playing at being ill, is she?" and right then beat her with a stick, made her work and clear the courtyard, and threatened that if she did not work, she would call the slaves to take her to the public square to give her a hundred lashes of the whip.

The mistress was Françoise Claudine Dreux, wife of Guy Soniac Duffosset, daughter of Mathurin and his wife, Claudine Françoise Hugot Dreux, founders of the plantation. Like mother, like daughter. The Superior Council convicted Marguerite of running away, sentenced her to have her ears cut and to be branded with a fleur-de-lis on her right shoulder.[86] Then, the worst punishment of all, she was returned to her mistress.

While we cannot track the generational shifts of the eighteenth-century enslaved population, we can track that of their enslavers, the Dreuxs. During the latter years of the French period, records of slave purchases suggest that the Mathurin Dreux family was beginning to experience a generational shift. In 1758, two of Mathurin's sons, François Pierre and Guy, purchased three enslaved Africans who had been aboard a British prize ship seized by the French. As the colonial period advanced, his sons followed in his footsteps. In 1763, when Mathurin was entering old age, his son François Pierre held ten enslaved people. Seven were men, three were women. Another son, Louis, held seven slaves, five

86. RSC, October 23, 1764. Also quoted in White, *Voices of the Enslaved,* 1–5.

men and two women. In 1766, François Pierre purchased twelve slaves from the Arnaud estate, most were grouped in families.[87]

As Africans labored to transform the wilderness into plantations, the Dreuxs rose within the ranks of Louisiana's quasi nobility and along the way imbued themselves with a local uniqueness, a new identity, and finally an aristocrat-like prestige.[88] We could have simply viewed the success of Pierre and Mathurin through the lens of their plantations and their enslaved people. But that would have ignored the many ways in which they set out to refashion their identities as elites. If the parents of Pierre and Mathurin Dreux are any indicator, their social positions in France, before they migrated to New Orleans, had been middle class. Certainly, they were not among the criminals or impoverished citizens who rambled through the countryside in France before being swept up and forcibly deported to Louisiana. Neither were they engagés. They were not military. Nor were they members of the petty nobility. Their father, Louis Dreux, was middle class, a bourgeois.[89] There is, however, one hint that suggests the source of their aspirations. Their father's father, Urbain Dreux, had been inducted into the Ordre royal et militaire de Saint-Louis, a dynastic order created by Louis XIV to recognize military officers for their exceptional service.[90] As a grandson of a knight of the ordre, Mathurin surely felt entitled to an elite status, even a title. In an isolated colony like French Louisiana, assuming airs and adopting a title was more usual than not. Some colonists dropped the tag *dit,* meaning "so-called," before their surnames and instead adopted the more honorific *de*—the particle implying ownership of a landed estate or a hereditary bloodline. The

87. RSC, March 3 and March 24, 1766. In February 1767, François Pierre ceded three slaves, a mother and two children, to Jean Hazeur.

88. Massey, *Spatial Divisions.*

89. AANO, Marriages, November 17, 1732. Louis Dreux was born in 1666 and died in 1726. Église Catholique Saint-Pierre, Savigné-sur-Lathan, Indre et Loire, Archives Départementales d'Indre-et-Loire, Baptêmes, Mariages, Sépultures, 246–247. He is described as a tanner, which at that time in France would be a middling occupation. For more on the Dreux family, see Starr, "In Search of Royalty,"125–128.

90. The Ordre royal et militaire de Saint Louis was founded in 1693. Members were recognized by the Cross of Saint Louis. The honor was not necessarily for nobility. Instead, it was awarded for more than ten years of military service as an officer in the army. Starr, "In Search of Royalty," 125–128.

Canadian Chauvin brothers of the Tchoupitoulas Coast added *de* and second names to their surnames. In Louisiana, they were known as Joseph Chauvin de Léry, Nicolas Chauvin de La Frénière, and Louis Chauvin de Beaulieu.[91] As for the Dreuxs, one brother adopted a byname while the other did not. During his relatively short lifetime, Pierre Dreux evidently did not. Instead, he merely assumed the honorific title of *sieur*, which in Louisiana was not uncommon and which separated him from the legions of ordinary colonists who had no label at all. Maybe Pierre should have given his brewery and plantation another name, as he could hardly have dubbed himself Pierre Dreux, sieur de la Brasserie.

Mathurin did add a title to his name. During the early years after naming his plantation Gentilly, he caught the status bug. By the early 1720s, Mathurin had promoted himself to the Louisiana nobility; he was Mathurin Dreux, sieur de Gentilly. Mathurin definitely belonged to the ranks of self-promoters and social climbers, and he was successful at it.[92] Both brothers began with little or nothing, a condition that did not stop them from clawing their way to the top. They were in Louisiana for only a few years before they counted themselves among *les grands*—the "French bureaucrats, noble military officers, large landholders, wholesale merchants, and missionaries, where social hierarchy, based in wealth and kinship emerged, which was antithetical to the structured lineage of old regime nobility."[93] Mathurin's title stuck. It was still in use by his descendants in the nineteenth century.

Upon arriving in the colony with little more than raw ambition, the Dreuxs set out to refashion their identities.[94] As Thomas Ingersoll writes, after arriving in the colony, Louisiana planters "could see a vast expanses of rich soil along the river, a patrimony for landed dynasties."[95] The Dreuxs allied themselves with Bienville, Adrien de Pauger, and Antoine-Simon Le Page du Pratz, all deemed to be among the founders of New Orleans.[96] A notation on the Carondolet map identifies Mathurin as the *avocat* (lawyer) for the ethnographer, historian, and naturalist Le Page du Pratz.[97] Pierre Dreux was favored by Pauger, the French engineer and cartographer who is best known for his design of the streets of

91. Powell, *Accidental City*, 106.

92. Dawdy, *Building the Devil's Empire*, 3, 19, 171.

93. Dawdy, *Building the Devil's Empire*, 28.

94. Dawdy, "Scoundrels, Whores, and Gentlemen," 137–138.

95. Ingersoll, *Mammon and Manon*, 38.

96. Dawdy, *Building the Devil's Empire*, 3.

97. The map was drawn for Governor Carondelet in 1798 for the purpose of clarifying land titles before the digging of the Carondelet Canal.

early New Orleans. Was it Pierre who, working alongside Pauger, participated in laying out the settlement? Probably so. Pauger in fact willed his plantation at Pointe Saint-Antoine (now Algiers Point) to Pierre in 1726.[98]

After establishing themselves as well-to-do merchants and planters, Pierre and Mathurin were soon counting themselves among the more trusted members of New Orleans's society. It was not unusual for them to serve as curators of the estates of their deceased neighbors and tutors to their children.[99] They served as officers in the colonial militia and were often asked to serve as arbitrators in matters of the Superior Council.[100] As some of its more devout members, they actively participated in the rituals of the Church. Both brothers and their wives stood as godparents to the infants of other colonists and witnesses to their marriages and each married in the Church. Pierre had no children, though he acted as godfather to his brother's children. The brothers saw to the catechesis and baptism of their slaves. Mathurin was a *marguillier* (church warden) and an administrator of the poorhouse.[101] Both were trusted allies of the community, the court, and the church. Within a short time, they were counted among *les grands* of the colonists.[102]

In order to further their social positions, they married the daughters of other colonial elites. On November 17, 1732, at the age of thirty-two, Mathurin married Claudine Françoise Hugault (Hugot), a twenty-two-year-old native of Lyon, daughter of Françoise Harant, and step-daughter of Louis Morissette, director of concessions for the Company of the Indies. A few months later, on April 28, 1733, Mathurin's older brother, the thirty-eight-year-old Pierre, married Anne Marie Corbin Bachemin, the eighteen-year-old French-born daughter of Anne Marie Judith le Hardy and Jean Marie Corbin, Sieur de Bachemin. Anne Marie's father, Jean Corbin Bachemin, was a successful concessionaire on the Mississippi River.[103] With their marriages, Pierre and Mathurin further consolidated their positions within the ranks of New Orleans's emerging class of elites, a colonial

98. Cabildo Archives, 246. Bienville claimed the property was his and thus Dreux did not inherit Pauger's plantation. Rushforth, "'Next Stop, Honoré Beaugrand,'" 245–250.

99. RSC, October 7, 1735, August 5, 1752, June 21, 1758.

100. AANO, Marriages, November 17, 1732.

101. RSC, 1769. Also see RSC for the marriage contract between François Bernoudy and Anne Dreux, June 29, 1765; and marriage contract, Pierre François Dreux and Jeanne Marie Constance Hazeur, February 14, 1767. In the first contract, Mathurin signs as Dreux de Gentilly; in the latter contract, the son of Mathurin also served in the militia. For instance, see RSC, March 24, 1753.

102. RSC, October 7, 1735. Also see Vidal, *Caribbean New Orleans,* 248–252.

103. AANO, Marriages, November 17, 1732, April 28, 1733.

amalgam of bureaucrats, military officers, large concessionaires, missionaries, and employees of the trading companies.[104]

Their positions were further advanced by their wives' affiliation with the Congrégation des Enfants de Marie (Children of Mary), a French Catholic confraternity of devout women, organized with the aid of the Ursulines in New Orleans. The constitution of the organization reads that the members should profess to serve the Blessed Virgin, visit the sick, relieve the poor, and instruct their children and slaves in religion. They vowed to uphold high moral standards. The assemblage was not a sanctuary for the elite. Rather, it was a haven for the "habitually devout." It included women from differing ranges of wealth and social standing. And though the affiliation of either Claudine Françoise Hugault Dreux and Anne Marie Corbin Bachemin Dreux with the Enfants de Marie must be seen as an act of faith and dedication to morality, it was also a way for them to affiliate with the most devout women in New Orleans, without the presence of men. Their presence in the group offered them the opportunity to collaborate with the most influential women in town.[105]

The Dreuxs' identity as elites was remembered two centuries after they arrived in New Orleans. For instance, they appear in Grace King's *Creole Families of New Orleans.* Published in 1921, King's book focuses on the so-called elite Creoles of New Orleans. Her description of the Dreux brothers' attitude toward their positions within the social fabric of New Orleans is that the two brothers lived in a "style of stately independence" and maintained "an attitude of aristocratic supremacy over what was virtually their seigneurie Gentilly."[106] Though King was famous for embellishing her descriptions of New Orleans and its Creoles, she did not embellish the pretension of the Dreuxs. Nor was she alone in praising their status and successes.

---

104. Dawdy, *Building the Devil's Empire,* 29.

105. Clark, *Masterless Mistresses,* 79–81. Clark argues that the confraternity was inclusive, which it was, though the largest group of women were the wives of planters, administrators, officials, and merchants. These were the women who served almost exclusively as officers of the confraternity. The primary object of the group was devotion and piety; however, it is not far-fetched to imagine that the group dynamic served to further the status of its members.

106. King, *Creole Families of New Orleans*, 59–66. A seigneurie is a position of authority. In France it would refer to a feudal lordship or the domain of a feudal lord. King's use of the word "seigneurie" for the Dreux family implies that they viewed themselves—and were viewed by others—as lords of their domain, though legally, in Louisiana, it was of no importance. Pritchard, *In Search of Empire*, 78–83.

In 1743, after Pierre's death, his widow requested that Mathurin, the executor of the estate, give her consent to sell the river plantation and brewery.[107] No extant records exist to explain why the request was necessary.[108] It is probable that Pierre left a will, which is no longer extant, appointing Mathurin executor of his estate. But there is the question of ownership of La Brasserie. Early Superior Council records identify both brothers as owners. Nevertheless, at some point they evidently came to a financial arrangement, more than likely when they each married, to separate their interests. According to the marital laws embodied in the Coutume de Paris, Pierre's widow, Corbin Bachemin, would have inherited one half of La Brasserie and the Gentilly plantation. However, she only inherited La Brasserie. Corbin Bachemin, like most other widows in early Louisiana, remarried soon after she was widowed. On November 3, 1742, she married Pierre Voison. Six months later, with Mathurin's permission, she sold her part of La Brasserie, both the brewery and the plantation around it, to Claude Joseph Dubreuil, the most prosperous planter in Louisiana.[109]

From the 1730s to the 1760s, Mathurin and his wife, Claudine Françoise, began the process of transferring the Gentilly plantation, in twelve-arpent segments, to their children and their spouses.[110] The first twelve arpents were awarded to their oldest daughter, Claudine Françoise, upon her marriage to Guy Soniac (Saunhac) Dufossat, who was an officer in the French navy and an engineer.[111] In 1759, they ceded twelve arpents, valued at two thousand livres, to their fifteen-year-old daughter, Jeanne, upon her marriage to Robert Antoine Robin de Logny, a native of France, militia captain, planter, and future judge in St.

107. There is no death record for Pierre Dreux. Other documents make it clear that he died sometime between 1740 and 1742. He appeared in a court hearing in 1740. Records of the Superior Council, August 27, 1740.

108. Early French administrators were often negligent when defining boundaries or interests in property. The case of the Dreux brothers is a perfect example. Early Superior Council records imply that Mathurin owned La Brasserie with Pierre; however, other records imply that Pierre was the sole owner of La Brasserie. Mathurin was always identified as the sole owner of the Gentilly plantation, which had undefined boundaries until the area around it began to develop.

109. RSC, July 15, 1743. In 1712, when the French Crown awarded Antoine Crozat the charter to administer Louisiana, it decreed that the Coutume de Paris be implemented and that a Conseil Supérieur be established. J. Johnson, "La Coutume de Paris," 145–155.

110. Evidently their son Louis died early, though there is no extant record.

111. The marriage contract of François Pierre Dreux mentions the Gentilly property owned by Dufossat. The couple married in or around 1755. There is no extant marriage contract for Claudine Françoise, but other evidence verifies the gift.

John the Baptist Parish.[112] The next twelve arpents were gifted to Charlotte in 1760, when she married Jean René Gabriel Fazende, a scrivener.[113] In 1765, Anne Dreux, the youngest daughter of Mathurin and Claudine Françoise, received her twelve arpents when she entered into a marriage contract with François Bernoudy.[114] In 1767, Louis François Pierre Dreux, dit François, received his twelve arpents when he married Jeanne Marie Constance de Lorme Hazeur of Mobile. She was the daughter of Marie Joseph de Lusser of Mobile and François Marie Joseph Hazeur, infantry captain and knight of Saint-Louis.[115] The youngest child of Mathurin and Claudine Françoise, Guy Charles Dreux, married Pelagie Toutant Beauregard, the daughter of a wealthy New Orleans merchant, in 1777. Since Guy's father had died, his twelve arpents were granted by his mother.[116]

The Gentilly plantation had become a flourishing enterprise by the time Mathurin and Claudine Françoise Hugault Dreux began to transfer property to their Creole offspring. In general, Louisianans were profiting from the steady exportation of fur, lumber, pitch, tar, shingles, staves, corn, rice, dried beans, and peas to France and the French West Indies. Specifically, the Gentilly plantation prospered by the export of raw materials they could harvest from their vast holdings. The census of 1766 offers a sketch, albeit an incomplete one, of the plantation just before the Spanish took possession of the colony. At that time, Mathurin held eighty-one enslaved people, far more than most others in the colony. His eldest son, François, held another ten. Louis, his second son, held seven.[117] At that point, Guy was a mere nine years old, too young to own property, and more likely a grandson than a son.[118] The labor of their bondspeople enriched the second generation of Dreuxs. Yet even though Mathurin and Claudine Françoise had donated property to most of their children, only one of their daughters, Charlotte Dreux, and her husband, Jean René Gabriel Fazende,

112. RSC, February 17, 1759.

113. AANO, Marriages, February 20, 1759.

114. RSC, June 29, 1765.

115. AANO, Marriages, February 18, 1767; RSC, February 14, 1767.

116. It is likely that it was after Pélagie Beauregard's death, in 1787, that he married Geneviève Felicité Trudeau de Longueuil, the daughter of an officer of the Royal Reserve and the granddaughter of Claude Joseph Dubreuil, the wealthiest of the New Orleans planters. Between his two wives, he had nine children.

117. Census of 1766, Missouri State Archives.

118. Claudine Françoise Dreux was born in Saint Malo, Brittany, in 1710, which would have meant that she gave birth to Guy Dreux when she was fifty-six years old, which is highly unlikely. It appears that the grandmother would have claimed the child as hers.

lived on their share of the original plantation.[119] François Bernoudy, procurer for the king and treasurer of Mobile, was most probably still living in Mobile, and the prosperous and influential Robin de Logny and his wife were living on his plantation on the German Coast.[120] Even though the aging Mathurin and Claudine Françoise had ceded twelve-arpent wedges of the original Gentilly plantation to each of their children, they continued to retain more than one hundred arpents of Gentilly land.

By the 1760s, while the Dreux family was experiencing a generational shift, French officials viewed Louisiana as a thorn in their side.[121] In 1762, as the Dreux family prospered, Louis XV of France, wearied by the Seven Years' War, ceded Louisiana west of the Mississippi River to his cousin King Carlos III of Spain. A mere year later the cousin kings signed the Treaty of Paris of 1763, which officially and publicly ceded Louisiana to Spain, a move that worried Louisiana's colonists. Those fears were somewhat eased when the Spanish hesitated to occupy New Orleans. It was not until March 1766 that Charles III of Spain sent Antonio de Ulloa to Louisiana to govern the colony. Spain's policies, personified by Ulloa, threatened the local economy—or to put it another way, it interfered with the self-interest of the colonists. To make matters intolerable, the Spanish prohibited New Orleanians from any trade with France, depriving the infuriated Louisianians of French wine and other French goods.[122]

Three years crawled by before the newly appointed Governor Ulloa arrived in the colony. A man of fifty, thin and stooped, his physical appearance was nonthreatening, though the few New Orleans founders who were still living, and the Creole elite, viewed him with deep suspicion. His orders were to exert control over the colonists, whom he believed were nothing more than a handful of smugglers, factionalists, and insubordinates whose behavior bordered on sedition.[123] As the animosity between the governor and the populace grew, it added to the financial and governmental instability of the colony.[124]

It was untenable to Louisianians that Spain intended to interfere with the

119. René Fazende, the son of Jacques Fazende and Hélène De Morier Fazende, married Charlotte Dreux on April 14, 1760. AANO, Marriages, April 14, 1760.

120. Census of 1766, Missouri State Archives.

121. Powell, *Accidental City,* 127. Also see Price, *History of the French Tobacco Monopoly,* 329–360.

122. Hoffman, *History of Louisiana before 1813,* 107–111. Also see Whitaker, "Antonio De Ulloa," 155–194; Winston, "Cause and Results," 186.

123. Powell, *Accidental City,* 133, 136–137, 139.

124. Kolb, "New Orleans Revolt of 1768," 9–10, 16.

colony's discrete system of justice and to regulate trade, which some historians believe was based on smuggling. By the 1760s, New Orleanians had long responded to their decades-old isolation from France by devising their own policies, social order, and economy. It did not mean, however, that they did not think of themselves as French. Neither did it mean that they would think of themselves as Spanish. With news of a takeover by Spain, they vowed they would not stand by while the Spanish regulated trade, including assuming the right to eliminate illegal activities. Most scholars agree with Ulloa that Louisiana's colonists had become adept at smuggling, profiteering, and privateering.

On September 7, 1766, in order to thwart the Spanish, a group of elite planters and merchants voiced concern for their loss of "la liberté du commerce."[125] By October 29, 1768, New Orleanians affiliated with the powerful and long-standing colonial Superior Council, and many of their allies, revolted. Their intention was to achieve the transfer of Louisiana back to France, but the rebels overplayed their hands. Word of retribution came fast. Ulloa left New Orleans two days after the revolt, but only after he had accused a mob of Creole oligarchy of treason. Ulloa's accusations did not include all of the elite, however, and he praised those who did not side with the rebels. In his words, "The people of high station in life and generally those who formerly had been [militia] officers and were now retired, refused to join the party [of rebels], and those who replied with most moderation called those who were making the request rebels, scoundrels and agitators."[126]

Mathurin, perhaps joined by his Creole sons, was among the moderate elites who refused to participate in the insurrection, breaking with many of their friends and neighbors. Instead, the Dreuxs supported Ulloa, even going so far as to attend the elaborate social events Ulloa and his Peruvian wife held at their house three times a week. It is not far-fetched to imagine that the Dreuxs accepted the invitation in order to ingratiate themselves with the governor.[127] And the affiliation the Dreuxs and others formed with him might have worked, had Ulloa not retreated. The new council that Ulloa was forming was composed of several Spanish officials and a few inhabitants. François Marie, Chevalier de Reg-

125. Moore, *Revolt in Louisiana,* 55–58; Hoffman, *History of Louisiana,* 120–126.

126. Chandler, "Ulloa's Account," 417. Ulloa explains, "Those who entered into the conspiracy were the families that were related to La Frénière and the three militia captains of the city. All the rest, which was the greater number, was composed of the common folk of the city and of the nearby establishments of Germans and Acadians."

127. Gayarré, *History of Louisiana,* 3:137, 287.

gio, and Pierre-François Olivier de Vézin were to be appointed to the council.[128] Jacques-Auguste de la Chaise and Mathurin Dreux, captains of the militia, were named honorary members.[129] Mathurin Dreux and his sons perhaps understood that the Spanish trade policies Ulloa promoted would, in the end, prove beneficial to them and to the Gentilly plantation.

Ulloa retreated from New Orleans two days after the revolt, though the vacuum he left behind was short-lived. In August 1769, General Alejandro O'Reilly took possession of Louisiana for Spain. This time, taking no chances, Spain sent twenty-four ships and 2,600 troops to accompany its new governor. O'Reilly had two opposing goals: he intended to ensure the peaceful occupation of the colony and to retaliate against the rebels. Shortly after he arrived, he convened a brief trial and the rebels were court-martialed. Some were deported or condemned to prison. Others faced a firing squad. Word that the sentences had been carried out terrified New Orleans's white residents who knew the insurrectionists as their kin, friends, or leaders.[130]

There is no evidence that the Dreuxs were ever in collusion with the insurrectionists, though they had been affiliated with many of the rebels for generations. One leader of the insurrection, in particular, Nicolas Chauvin La Frénière Jr., was executed by a firing squad. He, like his father before him, was a close associate of the Dreuxs.[131] Nonetheless, the Dreuxs not only escaped the fate of their close allies and friends but also somehow seemed to understand that the Spanish would not hinder their economic efforts. Had they been conducting extralegal trade with the Spanish, like so many of their planter associates? Or were they given special privileges by Ulloa, like a few other planters and merchants?

Mathurin did not live long enough to realize the consequences of O'Reilly's policies. On January 7, 1772, sixty-three years after he migrated to New Or-

128. François Marie, Chevalier de Reggio, was an Italian nobleman who became an important government official in Louisiana. Pierre-François Olivier de Vézin was born in France but had lived for a time in Canada. After a failed enterprise in Canada, he returned to France and was then appointed by the king to the position of chief of the roads in Louisiana in 1742.

129. Gayarré, *History of Louisiana,* 3:87.

130. Hoffman, *History of Louisiana,* 131. Some historians have argued that the 1768 revolt was the first of many insurrections of the Creoles of the Atlantic World. See, for instance, Moore, *Revolt in Louisiana,* 35–37. See also Powell, *Accidental City,* 158–159; Texada, *Alejandro O'Reilly and the New Orleans Rebels,* 23–25; Ingersoll, *Mammon and Manon,* 147–180.

131. Martin, *History of Louisiana,* 193–204. Martin was the presiding judge of the Louisiana Supreme Court, and his history was first published in New Orleans in 1827. Its value is that Martin wrote it straight out of the sources and included references. See Ingersoll, *Mammon and Manon,* 148–180; Powell, *Accidental City,* 129–163; O'Neil, "Louisiana Manifesto of 1768," 247–289.

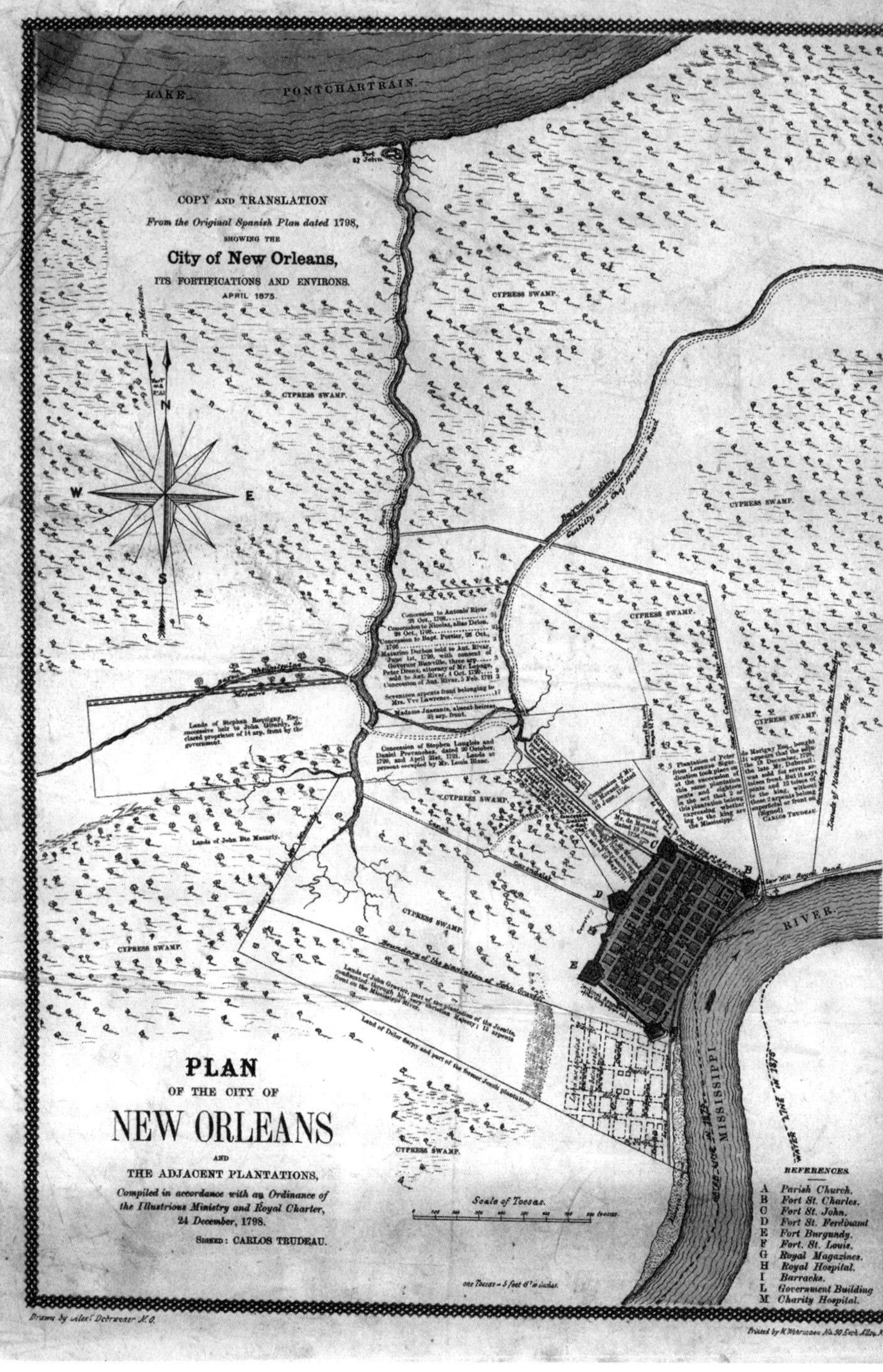

LAKE PONTCHARTRAIN.
COPY AND TRANSLATION
From the Original Spanish Plan dated 1798,
SHOWING THE
City of New Orleans,
ITS FORTIFICATIONS AND ENVIRONS.
APRIL 1875.
CYPRESS SWAMP.
N
S
W
E
Bayou Gentilly
Lands of John Bte Macarty.
RIVER.
MISSISSIPPI
PLAN
OF THE CITY OF
NEW ORLEANS
AND
THE ADJACENT PLANTATIONS,
Compiled in accordance with an Ordinance of
the Illustrious Ministry and Royal Charter,
24 December, 1798.
SIGNED: CARLOS TRUDEAU.
Scale of Toesas.
REFERENCES
A Parish Church.
B Fort St. Charles.
C Fort St. John.
D Fort St. Ferdinand
E Fort Burgundy.
F Fort. St. Louis.
G Royal Magazines.
H Royal Hospital.
I Barracks.
L Government Building
M Charity Hospital.

leans and three years after O'Reilly seized control of New Orleans, Mathurin summoned the notary Juan Garic to his bedside, where he dictated his will. He first declared that upon his death his slave Nicolas should be freed and that six arpents of land should be sold to Bernardo Bermudez, as he had promised. As for the Gentilly plantation, he stated that his wife, Claudine Françoise Hugault (Hugot) Dreux, should retain usufruct of the plantation until her death, at which time the plantation would pass in its entirety to his six children, who each would inherit an equal part.[132] With Mathurin's death in 1772, New Orleans lost one of its few surviving French founders. Claudine Françoise died in 1786, fourteen years after her husband and a year before the death of her oldest son, François Pierre Dreux.[133]

During the last decades of Spanish rule and into the early American period, François, Guy, and Louis Leufroy Dreux, three brothers who were the grandsons of Mathurin and Claudine Françoise Hugault, set out to reassemble much of the original Gentilly acreage. Louis Leufroy noted in his last will and testament, written in 1799, that he solely owned a segment of the Gentilly plantation that had been in production for seventy-nine years. He also claimed that he owned half of another Gentilly plantation. His brother François owned the other half. The second plantation measured twenty arpents and faced Bayou Gentilly. It included buildings, implements, and twenty-four enslaved people of both sexes and of different ages and conditions. The second plantation lay a half league (about 1.5 miles) away from the first and stretched along Bayou

132. Juan B. Garic archives, January 7, 1772, New Orleans Notarial Archives (henceforth NONA). The children of Mathurin and Claudine Françoise Dreux were Claudine Françoise (wife of Guy Soniat Dufossat), François Louis Pierre Mathurin (husband of Jeanne Marie Constance de Lorme), Jeanne Marie (wife of Robin de Logny), Françoise Claudine Charlotte (the wife of Jean René Gabriel Fazende), Louis, Anne Felicité (wife of François Marie Cesaire Bernoudy), and Guy (husband of Pelagia Beauregard).

133. Fernando Rodriguez, last will and testament, March 6, 1787, 226, NONA. His death is obscured in the records of the AANO, Funerals, March 1787. Thousands of notarial records have survived, but many were either destroyed or over time have become illegible.

MAP

***Plan of the City of New Orleans and Adjacent Plantations* (1798), by Carlos Trudeau, copied and translated from the original Spanish, indicating the concessions and naming the proprietors and sometimes the previous owners, as is the case of a land grant along Bayou St. John sold in 1720 by Pierre (Peter) Dreux. Library of Congress, Geography and Maps Division.**

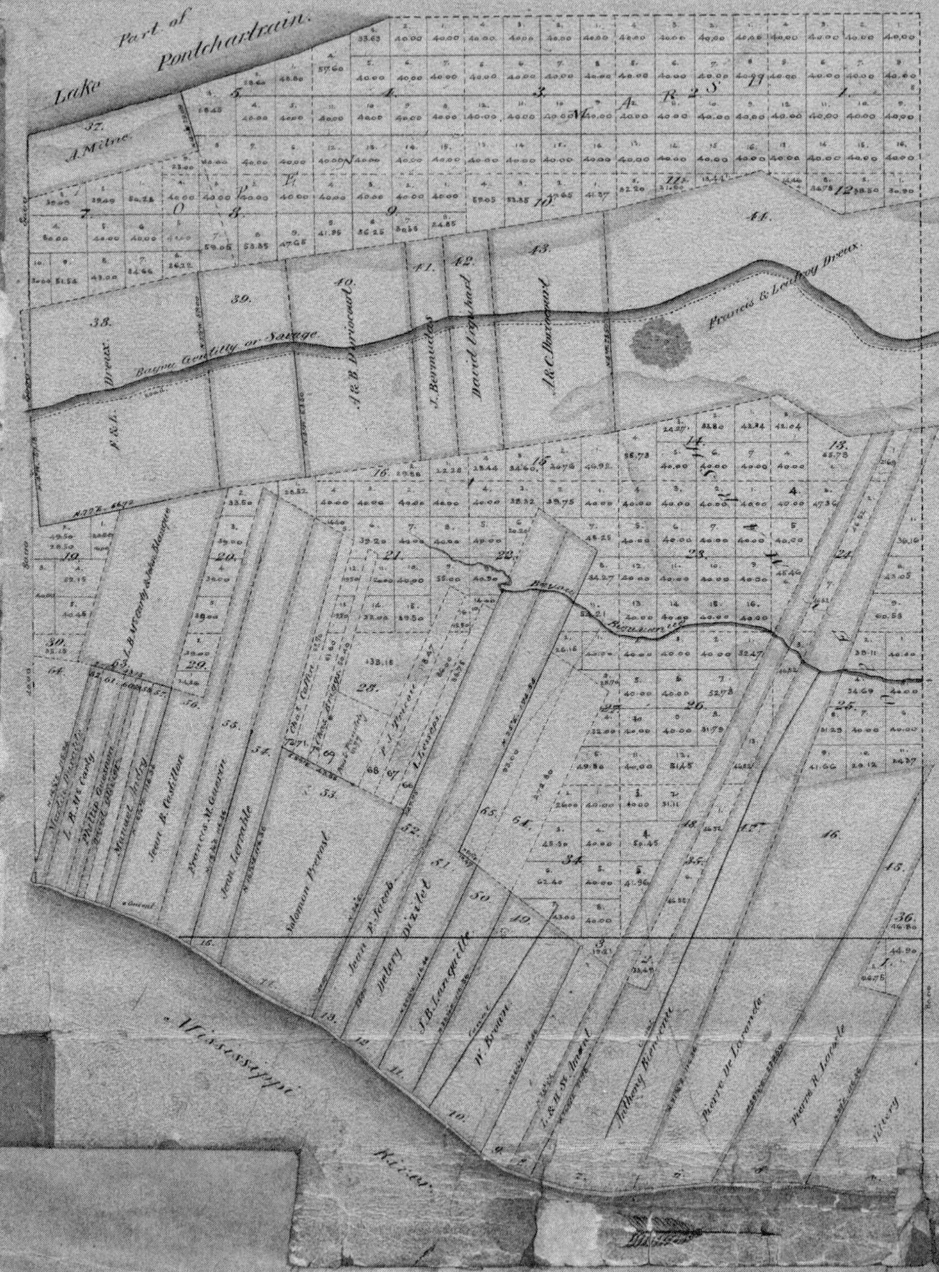
T. 12 & 13 S – R. 12 E.
South Eastern District La
Part of
Lake Pontchartrain.
A. Milne.
Bayou Gentilly or Savage.
David Urquhart
Salomon Prevost
Mississippi
River

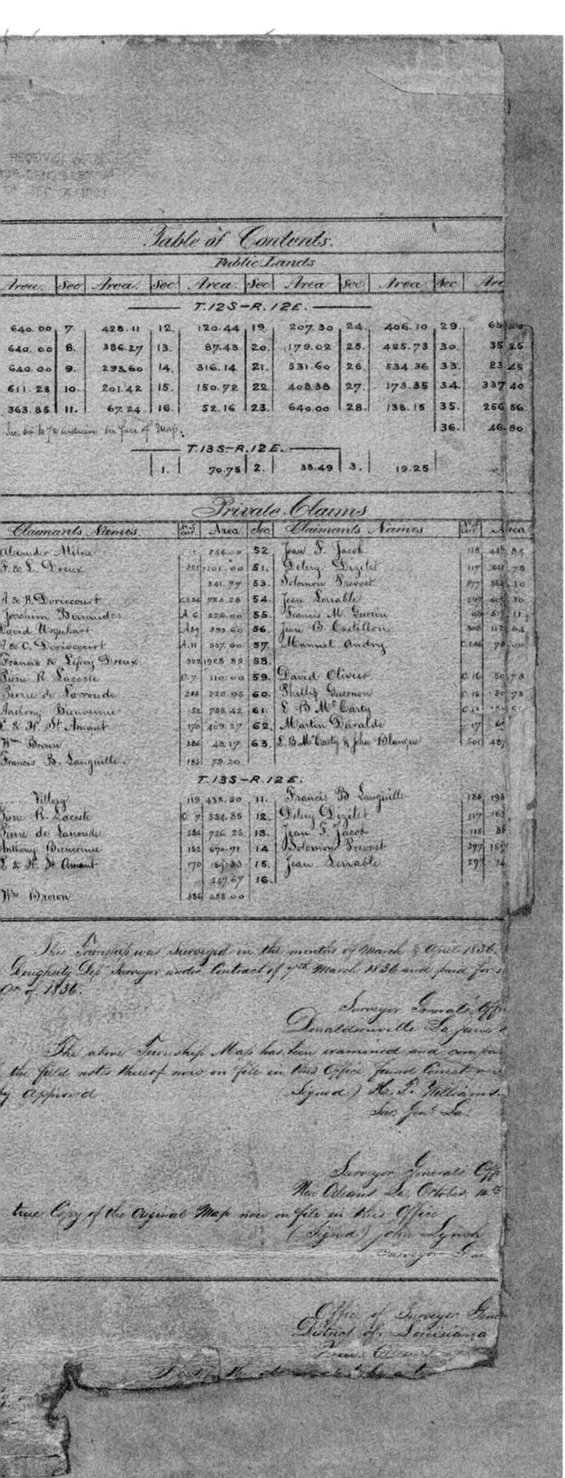

Table of Contents.

Public Lands

Area	Sec	Area	Sec	Area	Sec	Area	Sec	Area	Sec	Area
T.12S–R.12E.										
640.00	7.	428.11	12.	120.44	19.	207.30	24.	406.10	29.	65.[illegible]
640.00	8.	386.27	13.	87.48	20.	179.02	25.	425.73	30.	35.25
640.00	9.	293.60	14.	316.14	21.	531.60	26.	534.36	33.	23.45
611.23	10.	201.42	15.	150.72	22.	408.38	27.	173.35	34.	337.40
363.85	11.	67.24	16.	52.16	23.	640.00	28.	138.15	35.	256.56
									36.	46.80
T.13S–R.12E.										
			1.	70.75	2.	38.49	3.	19.25		

Private Claims

Claimants Names	No. of cert.	Area	Sec	Claimants Names	No. of cert.	Area
Alexander Milne	[illegible]	256.00	52	Jean F. Jacob	118	43[illegible].84
F. & L. Dreux	321	1101.00	51.	Deling Dizilet	117	341.78
		541.77	53.	Solomon Prevost	277	36[illegible].30
A. & B. Doriocourt	[illegible]	721.28	54.	Jean Lerable	297	40[illegible].30
Joachim Bermudas	A. 6	226.00	55.	Francis M. Guerin	95	51[illegible].11
David Urqahart	A. 39	393.60	56.	Jean B. Castillon	308	117.64
A. & C. Doriocourt	A. 11	557.60	57.	Manuel Andry	[illegible]	79.[illegible]
Francis & Lefroy Dreux	322	1928.89	58.			
Pierre R. Lacoste	C. 7	110.00	59.	David Olivier	C. 16	50.78
Pierre de Laronde	284	320.95	60.	Phillip Guesnon	C. 15	50.73
Anthony Bienvenue	152	735.42	61.	L. B. McCarty	C. 12	[illegible]
L. & H. St. Amant	170	409.27	62.	Martin Duralde	17	6[illegible]
Wm. Brown	386	48.17	63.	L. B. McCarty & John Blanque	501	48[illegible]
Francis B. Languille	185	79.20				
T.13S–R.12E.						
[illegible] Villery	119	438.80	11.	Francis B. Languille	185	193
Pierre R. Lacoste	C. 7	554.85	12.	Deling Dizilet	117	16[illegible]
Pierre de Laronde	284	726.25	13.	Jean F. Jacob	118	8[illegible]
Anthony Bienvenue	152	670.71	14.	Solomon Prevost	277	15[illegible]
L. & H. St. Amant	170	189.33	15.	Jean Lerable	297	74
		247.67	16.			
Wm. Brown	386	488.00				

This Township was surveyed in the months of March & April 1836, [illegible] Dougherty Dep. Surveyor under Contract of 7th March 1836 and paid for [illegible] Qr. of 1836.

Surveyor General's Off[ice]
Donaldsonville La. [illegible]

The above Township Map has been examined and compa[red with] the field notes thereof now on file in this Office, found correct an[d is hereb]y approved
(Signed) H. T. Williams
Sur. Genl. La.

Surveyor General's Off[ice]
New Orleans La. October [illegible]
[illegible] true Copy of the Original Map now on file in this Office
(Signed) John Lynch
Surveyor Gen[eral]

Office of Surveyor Gen[eral]
District of Louisiana
New Orleans [illegible]

This plat lists the properties along the Mississippi River and Bayou Gentilly/Sauvage. The map on the left indicates the two properties owned by Francis and Leufroy Dreux, located on both sides of the bayou, separated by four properties belonging to A. and B. Doriocourt, J. Bermudas, David Urguhart, and A. and C. Doriocourt. On the right, the table of contents indicates the section and area of the public lands and private claims, including the two Dreux brothers' properties. Louisiana State Land Records, Office of the Survey General, Baton Rouge.

Gentilly for one league. It also included buildings and mills.[134] According to Louis Leufroy's will, he and François had purchased this plantation from their widowed mother, Françoise Hazeur Dreux, wife of François Pierre Dreux, the oldest son of Mathurin and Claudine Françoise. Finally, he listed a plantation that was only land, without a mill, stating that he had purchased this plantation from his mother, Francisca Hazeur, for ten thousand pesos. He then revealed that he had paid 7,400 pesos to Don Luis Floretin and Doña Celeste Dreux, who also were heirs, for their share of the plantation.[135] Not everyone in the Dreux family had a desire to cultivate the family land, only the founders' three grandsons François, Leufroy, and Guy. Maybe they held onto their parts of the plantation out of sentiment. Its most likely that they believed that they could recapture the fortunes their grandfather and grandmother enjoyed.

At the dawn of the nineteenth century, two of Mathurin's grandsons were continuing to profit from the Gentilly plantation. The population of New Orleans was booming, with more mouths to feed in the city, and feeding the city was their heritage. Their cash crops were in high demand, as were their dairy and poultry products. The Dreuxs profited from the beef cattle and milk cows that had freely roamed the plains of the Gentilly ridge for nearly a century.[136]

In the early nineteenth-century years, the Gentilly plantation was nearly a century old. Mathurin's grandsons François and Louis Leufroy, and later Guy Dreux, as Creole heirs to the charter generation of Louisiana planters, continued the family tradition of planting. They also continued in the tradition of affirming their social positions by marrying into the elite planter merchant class, serving in the militia as officers, and participating in the many functions of the church. They also were so embedded in plantation slavery that decades later Guy's son Charles Didier Dreux would be the first Confederate field officer killed in the Civil War. The Creole descendants of the founding Dreuxs, the Dreuxs who had tamed the muddy wilderness of the Gentilly ridge to become members of the elite slaveholding class, would defend slavery to their deaths.

For their part, during the first years of the nineteenth century, the plantation's enslaved Africans and Creoles, many of them descendants of the founding

134. François and his brothers purchased this section of the plantation from their mother on February 8, 1778, as recorded in the Andres Almonaster y Roxas archives, NONA. In a document recorded in 1802, the mother of François and Louis Leufroy sold Louis Leufroy and François two plantations.

135. Narcisse Broutin archives, December 11, 1799, September 2, 1802, NONA.

136. Morris, "Impenetrable but Easy," 26–30.

generation of African slaves, continued their backbreaking labor, which allowed their owners to profit and thus maintain their social positions within the quasi aristocracy of New Orleans. But as the Gentilly bondspeople and their owners continued on in the style of their fathers and grandfathers, the political climate in Louisiana changed again. In October 1800, to the surprise of every Louisianian, Charles IV secretly retroceded Louisiana to Napoléon.[137] There is no direct evidence to demonstrate the Dreuxs' reaction to the retrocession, though it would appear that they welcomed it. Eberhard Faber writes that Laussat's first weeks in the city were a "swirl" of celebratory optimism. In March 1803, after stopping at the Gentilly plantation on his way to New Orleans, Pierre Clément Laussat wrote his impression of the plantation, later published in his *Memoirs.*[138] Laussat had been appointed colonial prefect of Louisiana in France in 1802. He wrote in his *Memoirs* that when he reached the Gentilly plantation, he was greeted with magnificent generosity. The plantation, he wrote, was well known as one of the finest between New Orleans and the sea.[139] It seems Laussat's voyage through the lakes and bayous had confused him, as the Gentilly plantation did not lie between New Orleans and the sea. Instead, it was north of the city, in the opposite direction from the sea, between the city and Lake Pontchartrain. Laussat wrote that sugar and cotton were cultivated on the plantation and that the plantation had a sawmill. This would have been the sawmill constructed nearly a century before. Evidently the Dreuxs were so welcoming to Laussat and his party that, after dining, they stayed the night. Laussat only reached New Orleans the next day. A few months later Laussat discovered, to his horror, that Napoléon had sold Louisiana to the United States.[140]

There were many oddities about the Louisiana Purchase. One was the surprising price, $15 million for more than 500 million acres. The vast territory was so sparsely inhabited that officials wondered about swapping most of it for West Florida, which was still in the hands of the Spanish. New Orleans was the one jewel in the purchase, and as Larry Powell asserts, "everyone with half a brain knew it."[141] The French possession of New Orleans, however, created a division

137. Kastor and Weil, *Empires of the Imagination,* 1–22.

138. Laussat, *Memoirs of My Life,* 16.

139. Faber, "Passion of the Prefect," 261–291.

140. Laussat, *Memoirs of my Life,* 16–17; Dubois, "Haitian Revolution," 93–113; Paquette, "Revolutionary Saint-Domingue," 204–225. Napoléon concluded his negotiation with Charles IV of Spain to exchange Louisiana for an Italian principality, though the Spanish kept control of Louisiana until 1803. Napoléon envisioned Louisiana as a breadbasket that would feed the enslaved in the Antilles.

141. Powell, *Accidental City,* 320.

between the *ancienne population,* Creoles, and the resident Americans, who welcomed the transfer of Louisiana to the United States. They were exultant. The *ancienne population,* on the other hand, presented American politicians with a problem: How would the multicultural inhabitants be handled? One bemused New Yorker wondered, "What shall we do with them?"[142]

Americans, however, were not alone in expressing their skepticism. New Orleanians were no less anxious about the purchase. Their mood at the lowering of the French flag on the Place d'Armes was sullen if not hostile. After all, Laussat had proclaimed that "all Louisianians are Frenchmen at heart," a sentiment that was music to the ears of the region's Creoles, who had no reason to doubt that they would once again be governed by France. Their greatest desire was the return of Louisiana to the motherland.

After the Purchase, other differences appeared. The old colonial elite were especially appalled to learn that most American officials believed they were corrupt. Americans also damned them for speaking French, or occasionally Spanish. Their religious beliefs, Catholicism, which included a certain style of worship and entertainment, also appalled the Americans, who were overwhelmingly Protestants. The other accusations aimed at the Creoles were that they were hedonists and royalists. In the minds of the Americans, Louisianans were not fit to participate in the democratic process. Eberhard Faber writes that "unionism, cosmopolitanism, and their association with federal power . . . put the generation of 1804 [Americans and Europeans] on a natural collision course with New Orleans's Creole oligarchy."[143]

The divisions between the old elite and their Creole supporters and the Anglos widened into a gulf when, in 1804, Creoles learned that their American leaders believed they were too multicultural, too attached to their provincial ways, too royalist, too hedonistic to be admitted into the union of states.[144] They were not only going to be deprived of statehood; the positions of patronage they had negotiated also were to be stripped from them. They even watched as their legal system was challenged. One "native" set forth the grievances of the old elite in a pamphlet published in 1804. He opined that Governor Claiborne had fallen from the clouds, without the least knowledge of the country or its inhabitants. English was overwhelmingly spoken by the Americans and a few Europeans

142. Powell, *Accidental City,* 317. For the quotation, see Kastor, *Nation's Crucible,* 49; Kukla, *A Wilderness So Immense,* 120–133.

143. Faber, *Building the Land of Dreams,* 132.

144. Powell, *Accidental City,* 323; Faber, *Building the Land of Dreams,* 195–204.

who were aggressively seeking their fortunes. The pamphlet also claimed that the assertive nature of the Americans exacerbated the tensions that separated them from Creoles like the Dreuxs. As far as the Creoles were concerned, the Americans were disrespectful, brash, and violent. New Orleanians described them as drunks and whorers. According to Faber, most of the American immigrants were young, away from their parents, and they misbehaved. The Creoles resented their manners, their customs, their very language, and their laws.[145] The animosity continued unabated until 1808, when the new legal code was drafted, amalgamating English common law with the legal traditions practiced in Louisiana. A further easing of the tensions developed as Creole elites were drawn into alliance with their American counterparts. Alliances between some of the monied Creoles and their American counterparts were bound to happen.[146]

Other Creoles were dispirited. The French Creoles did not feel allegiance to the United States. They dreaded the change in government, with its different language, customs, tastes, and prejudices.[147] On May 17, 1803, two weeks after the Purchase, as the Dreux family pondered what financial and social ills the transfer of Louisiana meant for their future, the forty-five-year-old planter Louis Leufroy Dreux, grandson of Mathurin, redefined his future. In a Catholic Mass held at St. Louis Cathedral, the self-described sieur de Gentilly married Marguerite Delmas, a sixteen-year-old French Creole.[148] Ten months later, the couple assured the continuation of the Dreux dynasty when they welcomed a daughter into their family, naming her Marie Hermine. She was followed, five years later, by a brother, Henri Antoine, who was fondly called Edgar.[149] He was named after his godfather, Henri de Sainte-Gême.

Louis Leufroy had his Gentilly plantation, his title, and his growing family, but after falling ill in the autumn of 1813 and knowing the end was near, he dictated a will. It was his second. He had executed the first in 1799.[150] His final

145. Fortier, *History of Louisiana,* 10; Faber, *Building the Land of Dreams,* 134–136.

146. Powell, *Accidental City,* 328. Also see Tregle, *Louisiana in the Age of Jackson,* 123–124.

147. Weil, "Purchase and the Making of French Louisiana," 303–313; Gayarré, *History of Louisiana,* 4:9–20; Beauchamp, *Instruments of Empire,* 1, 5, 8, 12–42. Also see Dessens, "Cultures plurielles et hybridation," 137–164.

148. AANO, Marriages, May 17, 1803. Marguerite's father, Jean Baptiste Delmas, was an immigrant from Provence. Her mother, Marie Magdelaine Raby, was a French Creole. Marguerite had been educated by the Ursulines. Beauchamp, *Instruments of Empire,* 80.

149. Throughout the correspondence between Dorville and Sainte-Gême, this is the name used by Dorville.

150. Louis Leufroy had executed a will on December 11, 1799, before he married or had children. In that will, he left his entire estate to his mother.

will, written in 1813, was a mere page and a half long. In it, he appointed his older brother, François, executor of his estate and tutor of his children. He proclaimed that his slave Martin was to be freed two years after his death, and in a sentence that might seem to be uncaring or spiteful, he granted his wife, Marguerite Delmas, ownership of the horse and cabriolet she had previously been using, as well as the furniture in his house. As Louis Leufroy understood, Louisiana's civil code of 1808 favored the community of acquets and gains, which provided that the products of reciprocal labor and industry of both husband and wife would become community property, owned by both husband and wife.[151] In short, his wife inherited 50 percent of any property accumulated during the marriage and his children inherited the remaining 50 percent. Any property was divided after all debts were paid by the executor. Yet, other than the furniture and the horse and cabriolet, Louis Leufroy failed to mention his wife. Instead, he merely stated that his *biens,* or goods, should go to his young children, Marie Hermine and Henri, and declared that they should be conserved in nature, which meant that he intended for his children to safeguard their inheritances from modifications or interference. Though the declaration was unusual for Louisiana, it was not atypical in France. Even today the phrase appears in France in successions, transactions, and exchanges. In his last will and testament, Louis Leufroy voiced his obsession with the past to his wife and children. By then Marie Hermine was ten years old and Henri was five.

On May 24, 1814, Jean Baptiste Marc Brierres, deputy registrar of the wills for the City of New Orleans, went to Gentilly and made a detailed inventory of Louis Leufroy's estate. That was four years before Dorville's correspondence with Sainte-Gême began.[152] The inventory states that, upon his death, Louis Leufroy still had two plantations, or a plantation divided into two pieces. One of the sections, estimated at ten thousand piastres, was located a league and a half, or about four and a half miles, from New Orleans.[153] It had thirty to thirty-two arpents facing each side of Bayou Gentilly and included the original plantation house, a kitchen, a dovecote, a cowshed, eleven slave cabins,

151. *A Digest of the Civil Laws Now in Force in the Territory of Orleans* (1808), also known as *Digest de la Loi Civile,* was written in 1808 by James Brown, Louis Moreau-Lislet, and Edward Livingston.

152. The inventory, translated into English, is reproduced in appendix 4.

153. Throughout the correspondence, Dorville uses dollars, gourdes, and piastres interchangeably.

and a building for carts. The "old half-timbered master house" seemed to be a relatively rudimentary lodging, in bad condition, raised seven feet off the ground. It had two rooms and a pantry and contained few pieces of furniture. The other section, estimated at four thousand piastres, was located one league farther, or about seven miles from New Orleans. It measured approximately seventy-five arpents, facing each bank of Bayou Gentilly, twenty arpents deep on each side, sixty arpents of which had been cleared. This second property did not include buildings.[154]

The estate, according to the 1814 inventory, was estimated in its entirety at 23,396.50 piastres and also included a large number of cattle, horses, mules, and sheep. The first plantation was a little over one mile in length; it was bound on the north by the cypress groves of Lake Pontchartrain and on the south by the Mississippi River. It spanned Bayou Gentilly and included about fifty cleared acres.[155] It would not have been considered a large productive unit. It is estimated that a significant part of it was either subject to flooding or was outright swampland. Nor was there an adequate number of enslaved people to cultivate large fields of the sugar or cotton crops that were fueling the rise of monocrop agriculture in the Mississippi River valley. Instead, for the most part, the profits derived from the plantation depended on the production of livestock, dairy products, and fruits and vegetables, some produced to be exported, the rest to be sold locally.

Before his death, Louis Leufroy held a workforce of twenty-one slaves. The enslaved workforce had diminished by half since his grandfather's heyday. Of the enslaved laborers, nine were men, ages eighteen to sixty. One was described as a maroon. Six of the enslaved were women between the ages of fourteen and forty-five. It seems that all of the women were of childbearing age, but there were only six children. Their ages ranged from one to ten. There were seven Creoles: Joseph and Bazile were each described as being 38 years old. Catherine was 45, Nérisse was 20, Amazilie was 18, Zaïre was either 13 or 14, and Colas was 10. One was described as a Creole. Seven were Africans: both 35-year-old Bacchus and 38-year-old Hector were identified as Manginga; Charles (18 or 19) as Senegal; César (60), Télémaque (60), and Azo (30, maroon) as Congo; and 24-year-old Catherine as Igbo. There were two Saint-

154. The inventory is an extraordinary source for the study of material culture.

155. The second piece of property was larger (about three miles in length and three-quarters of a mile in depth on both sides of the bayou), but only fifty acres had been cleared.

LAKE PONTCHARTRAIN
DIRECTORY
FOR PUBLIC BUILDINGS AND SQUARES
FOR FINDING LOCATIONS—SEE EXPLANATIONS ON STREET DIRECTORY.
ACADEMY OF MUSIC, St. Charles st.
ANNUNCIATION SQ., Annunciation st.
BOYS HOUSE OF REFUGE.
BIENVILLE DRAINING MACHINE.
CHAMBER OF COMMERCE, Common
CITY HALL, St. Charles street
CITY PARK, Metairie Road
CITY PARK, Sixth District
CLAIBORNE MARKET
CLAY SQUARE, Chippewa street
COLISEUM PLACE, Camp street
CONGO SQUARE, N. Rampart street
COTTON EXCHANGE, Gravier street
COURT HOUSES, Chartres Street
CRESCENT HALL, Canal Street
CLAY STATUE, Canal st.
CHARITY HOSPITAL, Common st.
DUBLIN AV. DRAINING MACHINE
DOUGLAS SQ., Washington St.
DRYADES MARKET
EXPOSITION HALL, St. Charles st.
FAIR GROUNDS
FILLMORE SQ.
FRENCH MARKET
FROGMORE, Crescent City Rifle Club
GLOBE THEATRE, Perdido st.
GRAIN ELEVATOR
GRUNEWALD HALL, Baronne st.
HOTEL DIEU, Common st.
JACKSON SQUARE
JACKSON R. R. PASSENGER DEPOT
JEFFERSON MARKET, Magazine st.
JOCKEY CLUB
LAFAYETTE SQ., St. Charles st.
LAWRENCE SQ., Napoleon Av.
LONDON AV. DRAINING MACHINE
LOUISIANA COTTON MANF'Y.
MELPOMENE DRAINING MACHINE
MAGAZINE MARKET
MASONIC HALL, St. Charles st.
MECHANICS INSTITUTE, Dryades st.
METAIRIE CEMETERY
MOBILE R. R. PASSENGER DEPOT
MORGAN'S R. R. DEPOT
NINTH STREET MARKET
OAKLAND PARK
ODD FELLOWS HALL
OPERA HOUSE, Bourbon st.
PARISH PRISON, Orleans st.
POYDRAS MARKET
RIDGE CEMETERIES
SECOND STREET MARKET
SMALL-POX HOSPITAL
SLAUGHTER HOUSE
SORAPARU MARKET
ST. BERNARD MARKET
ST. CHARLES THEATRE
ST. MARY'S MARKET
ST. PATRICK'S HALL
STATE HOUSE, St. Louis Hotel
TIVOLI CIRCLE—LEE PLACE
TREME MARKET
U. S. BARRACKS
U. S. MINT, Esplanade st.
U. S. CUSTOM HOUSE, Canal st.
UNIVERSITY OF LA., Common st.
VARIETIES THEATRE
WASHINGTON SQ., Elysian Fields
WATER WORKS RESERVOIRS
WESTWEGO, Texas R. R. Depot
CYPRESS SWA
METAIRIE RIDGE
CITY PARK
RACE COURSE
NEW ORLEANS ST. LOUIS AND CHICAGO R. R.
MISSISSIPPI
NAPOLEON AV.
MORGAN'S LOUISIANA & TEXAS R. R.

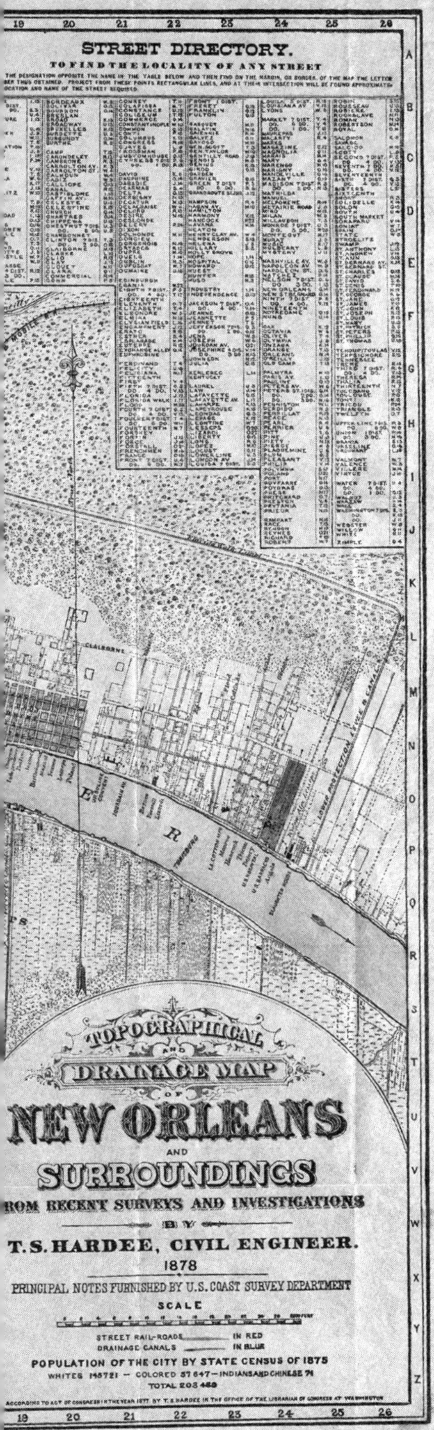

Topographical and Drainage Map of New Orleans and Surroundings (1877), by Thomas Sydenham Hardee, showing the expansion of New Orleans's urbanization three decades after the sale of the Gentilly plantation. Historic New Orleans Collection (00.34 a–b), Williams Research Center, New Orleans.

The River Missisippi
to the City of New Orleans
NEW ORLEANS
MISSISSIPPI RIVER
VI
VII
Missis

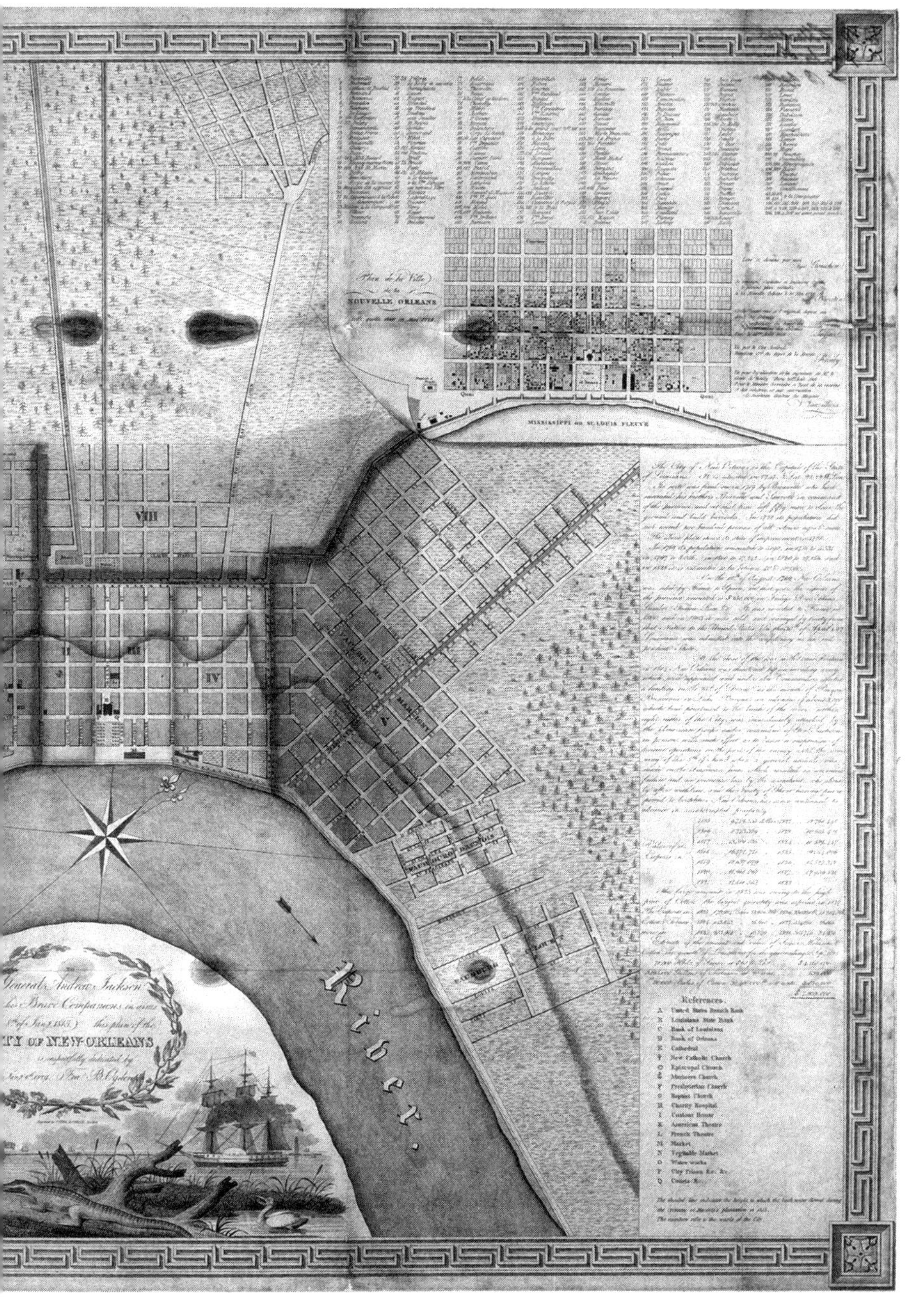

City of New Orleans (1829), by Francis B. Ogden. Historic New Orleans Collection, 1971.21 i–v, Williams Research Center, New Orleans.

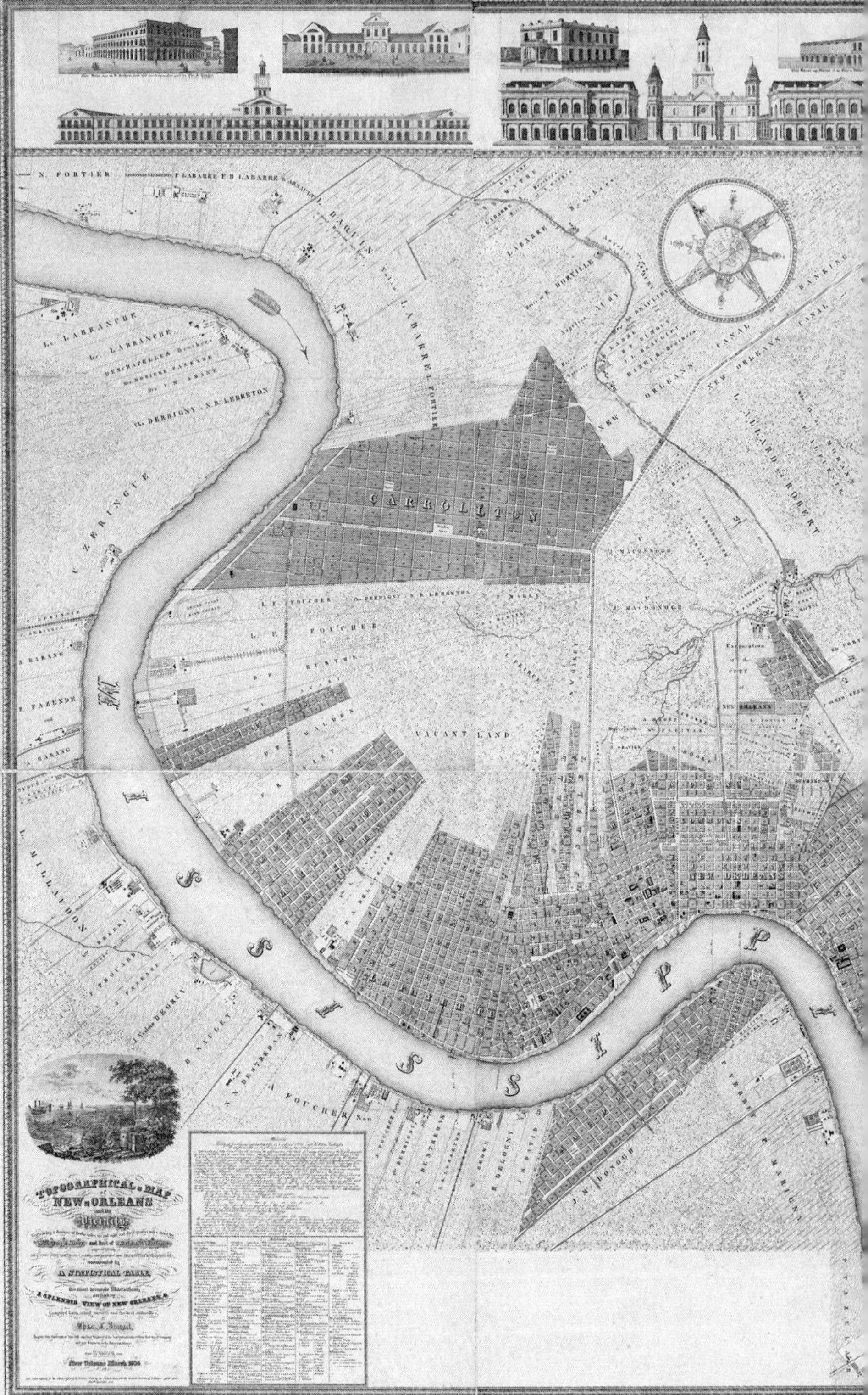

N. FORTIER
P. LABARRE
F. B. LABARRE
L. LABRANCHE
DESCHAPELLES Brothers
Vve DERBIGNY & N. B. LEBRETON
CARROLLTON
C. ZERINGUE
VACANT LAND
L. E. FOUCHER
NEW ORLEANS CANAL
NEW ORLEANS
MILLAUDON
A. FOUCHER
J. M. DONOGG
M I S S I S S I P P I
TOPOGRAPHICAL MAP
NEW ORLEANS
A STATISTICAL TABLE
A SPLENDID VIEW OF NEW ORLEANS
New Orleans March 1856

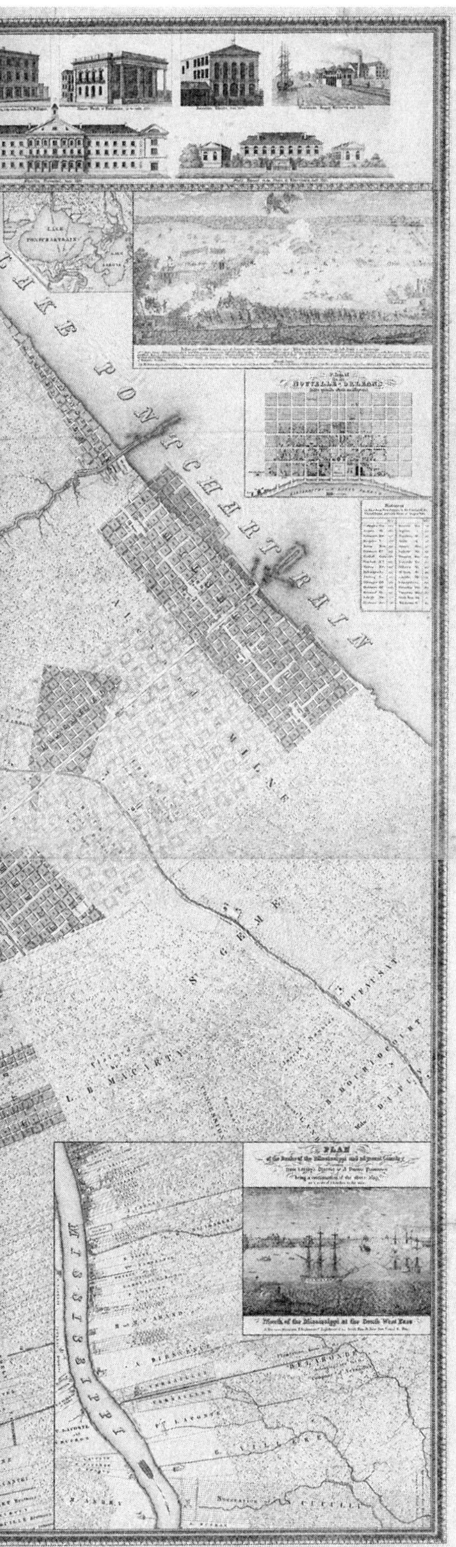

Topographical Map of New Orleans (1835), by Charles F. Zimpel, a detailed map of the city and its surroundings. Historic New Orleans Collection, 1955.19 a-f, Williams Research Center, New Orleans.

Domingue Creoles: Bazile (24 or 25) and Noisette (19, described as mulatto). The children can also be labeled as Creole, including Catherine's son, Augustin (7); Noisette's two children, described as quadroons, Valsin (4) and Herminaque (1); and two children given by Dreux to his children—Honoré, who was 5, was given to Henri, and Féliciane, who was 15 months, was given to Marie Hermine. The ethnicities of the enslaved were not as cohesive as in the French colonial period.

The inventory of Dreux's estate suggests that five of Louis Leufroy's slaves were field hands. Joseph and the older Bazile were described as suitable for all the work of a plantation. The younger Bazile, César, and Hector are listed as field slaves. It is safe to surmise that Charles, Nérisse, Amazilie, and Zaïre were not put to work in the fields. There are no specifics on Azor's duty, maybe because he had run away. Neither are there details on the tasks performed by the two Catherines and Noisette. Some of the women would have been domestics, others would have been marketers or leased out to other planters or city dwellers. There are no details on the remaining seven, although we learn that the younger Catherine was unskilled and that three of the enslaved had health conditions: the older Catherine had asthma; Azor, the maroon, suffered from a hernia; Télémaque had problems with his vision and was described as crippled. It is evident in Dorville's later letters to Sainte-Gême that he believed the aging workforce severely limited the profitability of the plantation.

In 1816, two years after her husband's death, Marguerite Delmas Dreux married the Frenchman and future baron Henri de Sainte-Gême, a friend of her deceased husband. Perhaps Louis Leufroy had asked his old friend to take care of his wife. And perhaps the marriage was advantageous for both Henri and Marguerite. Henri understood that he would benefit from the income of the plantation. Plus there might have been some exotic prestige associated with owning a plantation in the Americas. The marriage was certainly advantageous for Marguerite, as she moved her way up the social ladder. Her deceased husband, Louis Leufroy Dreux, sieur de Gentilly, had owned a plantation in the wilderness back of New Orleans and fancied himself a Louisiana aristocrat. Henri de Sainte-Gême, on the other hand, *was* an aristocrat, a French one. His family had a chateau in Southwestern France, where he would eventually assume the title of baron from his father. Marguerite swapped her role as a plantation mistress for that of a baroness.

We have wondered how Henri de Sainte-Gême, a newcomer to New Orleans, came to be so close to Louis Leufroy. Sainte-Gême had only arrived in

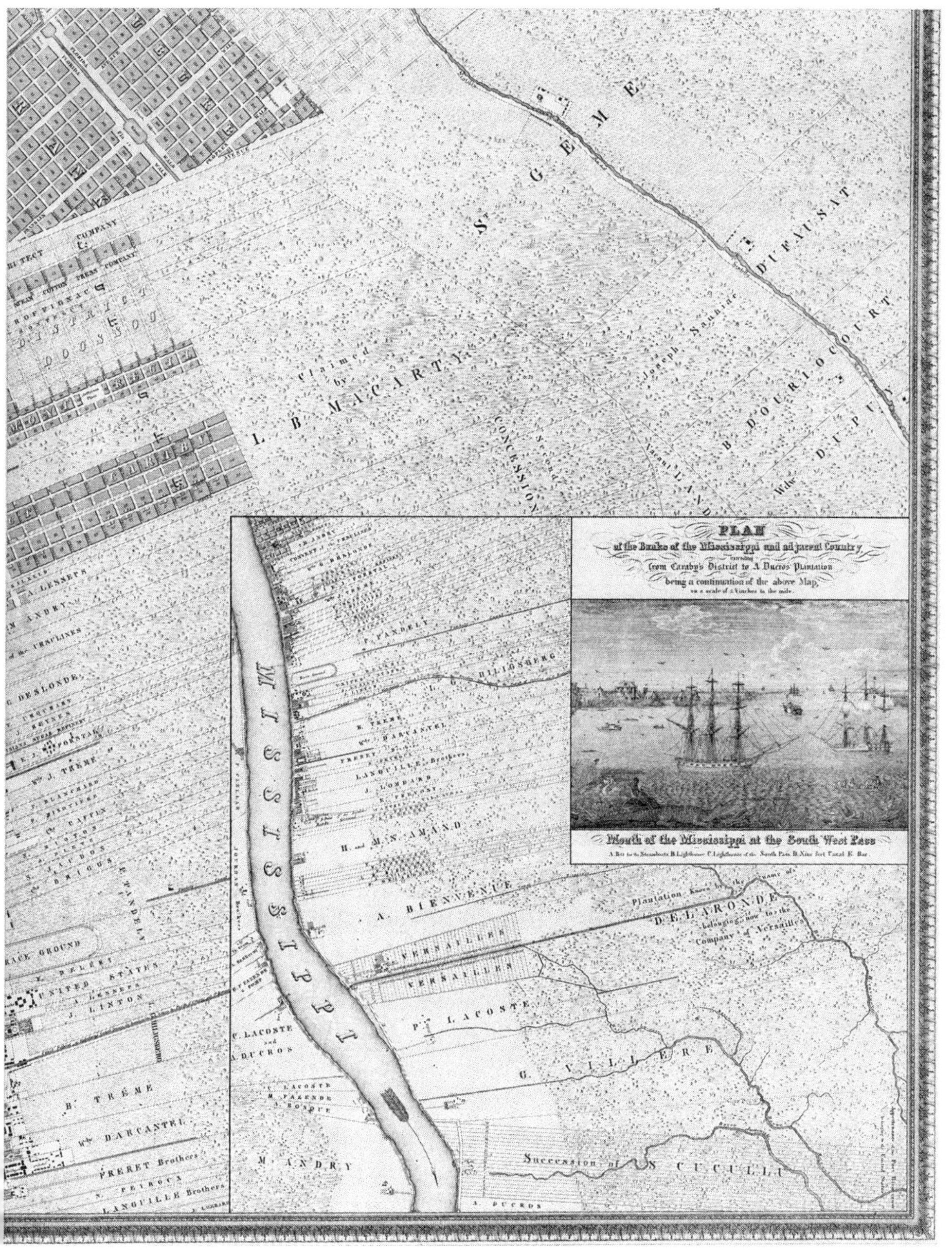

Detail of *Topographical Map of New Orleans,* showing the Sainte-Gême Gentilly property.

New Orleans in 1809. First, he was the godfather to Louis Leufroy's son Henri. Then he was one of the four witnesses at the recording of Louis Leufroy's last will and testament. We can only speculate, but we suspect that what brought the two men together was privateering and piracy. By the time Sainte-Gême arrived in New Orleans, privateering had been firmly established. Planters, merchants, and pirates had been supplying New Orleanians with a veritable department store of goods—and the slaves the colonial and American powers failed to supply. While there is no firm evidence that Louis Leufroy, or any of the Dreuxs, participated in illegal and sometimes violent commerce or active smuggling, the location of the plantation and its history strongly suggest it.

Sainte-Gême is another story altogether. In October 1814, eleven pirates faced indictment by the United States. Five were captured at Barataria. One of those was Henri de Sainte-Gême.[156] Sainte-Gême, along with a group of other privateers, was brought to trial by federal prosecutors, and all managed to avoid prosecution, though the prosecutors vowed to seek a retrial. Retrial might have been the intention of the prosecution, but the pirates arrested in 1814 were eventually pardoned in exchange for aiding the Americans in the Battle of New Orleans.[157] Sainte-Gême was no stranger to battle. While in Saint-Domingue with the French Army, he served as the commander of the Dragons à Pied and as captain of police. After leaving Saint-Domingue during the Haitian Revolution, he settled in Cuba, where he owned a plantation. In New Orleans after 1809, and after his trial for privateering, he served as major under Andrew Jackson during the Battle of New Orleans.[158]

When the Sainte-Gêmes handed Dorville the keys to the big house in the early spring of 1818, the Gentilly plantation had been in production for ninety-two years.[159] As Dorville's letters show, the big house was simple but in dire need of repair. Eventually it became so dilapidated that Dorville had it razed, building another, smaller house on its site. In an amusing note, Dorville mentioned to Sainte-Gême that he was living in the old chicken coop while the house was being built. The description of the materials used to build the newer plantation house are scattered throughout Dorville's letters.

The letters, along with the history of the Gentilly plantation, give us an op-

156. *United States v. Henri de Sainte-Gême,* case 0786. Indictment was handed down on October 19, 1814.

157. Davis, *Pirates Laffite,* 199; Gordon, "New Orleans and Bayou Saint John," 19–20.

158. Dessens, *From Saint-Domingue to New Orleans,* 72.

159. Louisiana became a state on April 30, 1812.

portunity to observe the *longue durée* of the plantation and its ties to New Orleans and the Atlantic World, especially the French Atlantic. Certainly, the Gentilly plantation was peculiar unto itself. After all, it evolved on the very edge of New Orleans, emerging from the mud cast off by the Mississippi River only two years after New Orleans was founded. From the beginning and throughout the nearly century and a half it operated, it was by its nature rural yet it was integrated into the life of the city. Interestingly, the plantation and its ties to New Orleans were a perfect example of what Bienville envisioned when he chose New Orleans for his settlement, a port town surrounded by an agricultural economy. New Orleans was the port town; Gentilly was the plantation.

What is more, it was not just integrated into New Orleans. Throughout its history, it operated as a part of the larger Atlantic World. Its foundation was African, French, and Canadian. Successive sovereign governments, from France, Spain, and the United States, imposed new populations, new legislation, new cultures, and new languages on the inhabitants. Even so, South Louisianians, Black and white, enslaved and free, continued to embrace the ways of the founding generation as only New Orleanians could.

Pierre, Mathurin, and Claudine Françoise Dreux were notable among the founding generation. Their history and the letters can be viewed as a lens into the formation of not just one plantation but of New Orleans itself as it took its place among the largest port cities in the world. The Dreuxs and their enslaved laborers impacted the formation of Louisiana's economy and culture in a personal way as they adapted to successive changes of governance. Each successive sovereignty changed the rules, affecting the legal, cultural, and economic norms of the populace, which was French and African, then Spanish and African, and finally American and African and Creole. The inhabitants of the Gentilly plantation, Black and white, enslaved and free, experienced and then incorporated the distinctiveness of each successive governance, taking what they wanted and tolerating the rest.

Indeed, the Dreuxs never abandoned the ways established by their founding generation. The first generation discussed here—Pierre, Mathurin, and Claudine Françoise Dreux, along with their enslaved Africans—exemplify an economic system, a culture, and a racial system that informed the identities of their descendants and the formation of New Orleans society. Their old ways and identities were accepted and adapted by their heirs, who built upon it, making it their own. The letters reproduced here are physical reminders of the way in which the plantation had an entangled history with that of the Atlantic World.

Gentilly le 18 juillet 1822

Je viens d'apprendre, mon cher monsieur Ste Gême, qu'il doit partir un Batiment demain pour le havre, je profite du court moment que j'ai pour vous confirmer L'envoie de traites que je vous ai fait le 21 de mai dernier, et vous dire le plaisir Que vous me feriez de m'en accuser la réception au plutot, si vous les avez reçu.

Plus d'occasion de Bordeaux ici, et d'ici à Bordeaux; d'après la tournure des choses il n'y en aura pas de longtemps, alors si vous m'écrivez je vous engage à faire Passer vos lettres au havre à quelque personne de votre connaissance qui à son tour me Les acheminera. Je ne saurais trop vous dire combien votre présence ici, serait Nécessaire pour vos intérets: je me rappele vous avoir entendu dire quelquefois, mon Cher monsieur Ste Gême, que l'oeil du maitre engraisse le cheval: personne plus Que moi n'est de cet avis. C'est ce qui peut me permettre de vous engager à faire, Pour quelque temps, le sacrifice des liens qui vous retiennent en france, et à vous Rendre à mes demandes, ou plutot à vos intérets.

Mdme Vve Dreux, Mr Dreux et sa dame m'ont chargé de mille amitiés pour Vous, madame votre épouse et mademoiselle Hermina. Mdme Desbois leur fille ne Tardera pas je crois à leur faire verser encore bien des larmes. Cette malheureuse jeune Personne est dans le même état qu'était sa soeur mdme Bermudez, et les médecins pour Elle ont déja épuisé leur savoir. Par mes lettres du 21 mai je vous ai mandé Que le pauvre Basile est poitrinaire, il ne va pas mieux quoiqu'il ne souffre qu'à Peine de la poitrine, mais il a les jambes les pieds et les bras tout enflés. Tous les autres Esclaves se portent bien, Clarisse et amarilie sont toutes deux grosses, et Avancées. Nous avons eu ces jours derniers un coup de temps très fort; j'avais 22 Arpents de beau maïs, prêt à être plié, qui a été abimé.

Je vous prie, mon cher monsieur Ste Gême, de vouloir bien offrir de ma Part à votre aimable et intéressante famille, les choses les plus honnêtes et les Plus respectueuses, et me croire, mon cher monsieur Ste Gême, votre sincère et dévoué serviteur

Auvignac Dorville

P.S. Depuis que je vous ai écrit je n'ai pas eu de nouvelles de Mr Boze.

Auvignac Dorville to Henri de Sainte-Gême, July 18, 1822. Sainte-Gême Family Papers, MSS 100, folder 61, Historic New Orleans Collection, Williams Research Center, New Orleans.

The Correspondence of Auvignac Dorville, 1818–1851

The fifty-four letters that follow, written by Auvignac Dorville from 1818 to 1851, reveal the unique history of the Gentilly plantation, located at the intersection of New Orleans, one of the busiest port cities of the nineteenth-century United States, and the Atlantic World. They are only part of the 218 letters Dorville wrote to the Sainte-Gêmes. He began writing in 1818, just after the Baron Henri de Sainte-Gême, his wife, and her two children moved from New Orleans to Bagen, a small village in southwestern France, where the Saint-Gême family property and chateau were located. After Henri's death, in 1842, Dorville addressed his letters to Henri's son, Anatole de Sainte-Gême. Dorville wrote regularly, although infrequently, until Marguerite de Sainte-Gême's death in 1793.[1] Despite the sale of the Gentilly plantation by the Sainte-Gême heirs in 1850, Dorville continued living there until 1855, when he moved to the city. When the plantation sale was finalized in 1851, Dorville stopped giving the Sainte-Gêmes precise information about the plantation, and he almost never mentioned the enslaved people who remained on it.[2] His subsequent letters were mostly dedicated to informing the Sainte-Gêmes about the property they continued to own in the city.

Since the focus of the book is solely on the plantation, among the Sainte-Gême family's many holdings in New Orleans, we have limited our selection

1. Mrs. Marguerite Delmas, October 22, 1874, Succession Records, 1846–1880, Louisiana District Court (Orleans Parish), Petition Papers, 36925.

2. There is only one further reference to the enslaved people living on the plantation. In his letter of May 4, 1855, Dorville reported the death of two of them, naming only one, Zaïre, who had belonged to the Sainte-Gêmes. Ste-Gême Family Papers, MSS 100, folder 347.

of letters to those written from 1818 to 1851, that is, when Dorville lived on the plantation and managed it, but more importantly, when he wrote extensively about it. The selection begins with Dorville's first letter, dated March 14, 1818, written just after he moved to the plantation and agreed to manage it. It ends with the letter of March 6, 1851, the last one in which he gives information about the plantation. In that year, John McDonogh's estate finalized the purchase of the plantation, a process McDonogh had begun before his death in October 1850.[3] According to the records, following the terms of McDonogh's last will and testament, the City of New Orleans leased the plantation to Dorville.[4]

As is apparent from the letters, Auvignac Dorville and Henri de Sainte-Gême were business associates. Dorville understood that his position was one of deference, which clearly showed in the closing comments of each of his letters. Throughout their relationship Dorville showed great respect to Sainte-Gême and always expressed his gratitude for the trust Sainte-Gême had placed in him, recollecting in his first letter to his employer that "before leaving the plantation, you [Sainte-Gême] honored me with you trust." Despite his subordinate position, Dorville expressed affection for Sainte-Gême, generally ending his letters with the mention that he was "devoted and affectionate," or "devoted and attached," or "humble and devoted." He wrote openly of his affection for Madame de Sainte-Gême, Marguerite Delmas Dreux, and her children, Hermina and Edgar, Sainte-Gême's stepchildren and the children of Louis Leufroy Dreux.[5]

Dorville and Sainte-Gême also shared many close friends, the closest being Pierre Lambert, with whom Dorville hunted. Lambert often stayed on the

3. John McDonogh (1779–1850) is a controversial figure in New Orleans history. He was, throughout his life, an extremely wealthy land speculator and slaveholder whose property inventory still listed ninety-five enslaved people upon his death. However, he was long remembered and celebrated in New Orleans for emancipating 118 enslaved people and sending them to Liberia as part of the American Colonization Society's program, as well as for the role he played in furthering the education of some enslaved people and funding the public school system of New Orleans. John McDonogh Inventory 38 (1850), probate report, Notarial Archives and Special Collections, Civil District Court for the Parish of New Orleans, Adolphe Mazureau archives, NONA.

4. In his will, McDonogh bequeathed half of his estate to the City of New Orleans (the other half to the City of Baltimore, his birth city). John McDonogh, last will and testament, 1850, State of Louisiana, Fifth District Court of New Orleans. In the digital collection *Making of America Books*, University of Michigan Library, https://quod.lib.umich.edu/m/moa/ABK9835.0001.001.

5. For instance, on July 14, 1821, Dorville asked Sainte-Gême to "offer [Madame, Sainte-Gême], as well as Mademoiselle Hermina, my most honorable and respectful thoughts . . . and send proof of my friendship to my comrade Edgar." He finished his letter by asking Sainte-Gême to send him some of Edgar's letters, if he received any.

plantation, where the two men liked to talk about their good time with Sainte-Gême, whom Lambert affectionately called "le bourgeois," constantly expressing his wish to see him return to Louisiana. Dorville's letters were also filled with news of other common acquaintances.[6]

However, the tone and content of the letters changed after Henri's death, when Dorville began writing to Henri's son, Anatole. Those letters are far less detailed, certainly less personal, and are generally much shorter and much more practical. They mostly opened with "Dear friend" or, less often, "Dear Monsieur, dear friend," which suggests a more equal situation, probably on account of Anatole's age, even if "Monsieur" still acknowledged an employee position. Those letters generally ended on a casual "I shake your hand" instead of the affection Dorville showed to Anatole's father. On several occasions, however, Dorville mentioned that Anatole de Sainte-Gême was his son's godfather, a testimony to the persisting close bonds between Dorville and the Sainte-Gême family despite the geographic distance and the fact that Anatole had been born after his parents had left Louisiana and had always lived in France. Although Dorville had never mentioned his family life in the extant letters to the Sainte-Gêmes, on February 16, 1846, he wrote, "My two poor little orphans are growing every day, more in malice than in anything else. Your godson asks me every day why his godfather 'pi oule vini encore,' which translates as does not want to come here again."[7] In his letter of March 27, 1855, he thanked Anatole for the interest expressed for his two sons, mentioned that they were still attending school but that he thought he would soon put the elder to work, adding, "Your godson has not forgotten his godfather." In his letter of January 5, 1863, Henry Anatole Dorville, who was named after the two generations of Sainte-Gêmes, wrote to his "dear godfather," wishing him a merry Christmas, promising him a present, asking for one from him, and sending him his love.[8]

Not all the correspondence from Dorville to the Sainte-Gêmes has survived. Dorville sometimes refers to letters he had written but that are not in the fam-

6. In his letter of April 20, 1818, Dorville wrote to Sainte-Gême, "To remember all the people who asked me not to be forgotten when I would write to you and your family, I should have walked around with a pencil and paper in my pocket all the time. Here are those I remember: the Dreux, Chevalier Morans, and Dutillet families; Mademoiselle Ferréole, Messieurs Lambert, Chevalier Hazeur, Destoup, Salles, my father, and my brothers."

7. There is no mention of his wife, the birth of his children, or the death of their mother in the letters contained in the Ste-Gême Family Papers. These short mentions strongly suggest that there were other forms of communication between Dorville and the Sainte-Gêmes.

8. Ste-Gême Family Papers, MSS 100, folders 346, 398.

ily papers. Perhaps those letters never reached France.[9] Or perhaps they were discarded, destroyed, or lost within the household. Occasionally, duplicates of Dorville's letters can be found in the Ste-Gême Family Papers. The duplicates are usually exact copies of the originals that were sent to France via another vessel, or entrusted to someone traveling to France on another vessel.[10]

Considering the enormity of Dorville's obligation to the Sainte-Gêmes, his letters were shorter than might be expected. For the most part, they were limited to one or two pages, although some are longer, especially in the years when they are infrequent. There may be several reasons why Dorville kept his letters short. First, although he was descended from an old Louisiana and somewhat prosperous plantation family, his writing skills were inadequate. He complains in one of his early letters that he does not fully grasp the skills of letter writing. His lack of literacy would be no surprise to historians of Louisiana, who know that educational opportunities for young men were limited in Louisiana. Besides his difficulty with writing, although it improved over the years, he also frequently voiced his concern about the expense of posting letters. Although the explanation might be more rhetorical than factual, in the missive he wrote to Henri de Sainte-Gême on July 21, 1819, he complained that he would write more often "if I had some happy topic to impart in my correspondence and if I had not thought that it would cost . . . more than it would be worth." Finally, he was also often pressed for time.[11]

Although it is obvious that he wrote more letters to the Sainte-Gêmes than are on deposit in the Sainte-Gême papers, Dorville's letters were posted sporadically. The number of the early letters translated in the present volume varies from six in 1823 to none between 1833 and 1835. Most years, especially after 1823, there are only one or two letters. Another reason Dorville sent so few letters, according to him, was that he was not always able to find a ship sailing from New Orleans to Le Havre or Bordeaux when he was ready to post a letter. In fact, it appears that he often wrote when he knew a ship was being prepared for

9. His letter of January 10, 1851, for instance, ends: "I hope my latest letter of December 16 reached you without trouble." There is no trace of any letter bearing this date in the Ste-Gême Family Papers. In September 1854, complaining about not receiving any letter, he mentioned the SS *Arctic*, which had capsized, as a possible explanation for this silence.

10. To quote a single example, in March 1851, Dorville wrote two strictly identical letters which are both archived in Ste-Gême Family Papers, MSS 100, folder 318. One mentions "Per Boston Steamer via England," the other "Per New York Steamer via England."

11. On January 26, 1819, he hastily wrote that it was "ten o'clock and the vessel is leaving for the open sea at noon, which makes me rush to finish this letter."

departure.[12] He sometimes expressed uncertainty at sending a letter via a ship with an unknown captain. Whenever possible, he placed his correspondence in the hands of an acquaintance leaving for France.[13]

Although the extant letters are infrequent, they often read as if there had been no interruption between them, Dorville regularly commenting on the information he had given in a previous letter, sometimes written months, even years, before. Despite their paucity, the letters offer a continuum of the development of the organization, revenue, and production of the plantation. They often include information about the enslaved people who provided the labor on the plantation. When he does focus on the Gentilly bondspeople, Dorville emphasizes his control over their bodies and the ways in which their production and reproduction enhanced or diminished the bottom line of the plantation. As is evident in his letters, childbirth, the reproduction of the slave force, and the health of his "people" was a repeating topic, though even then he only rarely demonstrates concern for the enslaved. Dorville was much more interested in reporting on the evolution, or lack thereof, of the economic circumstances of the plantation.

Note on the Translation

When translating the Dorville letters, we tried to stay as close as possible to the (oftentimes confusing) original. When necessary, we simply made the phrasing clearer, restoring, for example, the subject when the pronouns were too distant from the original name they stood for. Finally, we sometimes cut extremely meandering sentences to make them more legible, and we slightly altered the punctuation and capitalization to make them correspond to more modern usages. Even then, we decided to keep as many direct translations of the text as possible. Although the sentences are sometimes awkward, they allow the reader a more direct knowledge of exactly what he was communicating.

The vocabulary Dorville uses is often relatively limited. He repetitively uses

12. He wrote on May 22, 1821, that if he had "remained six months and a few days without giving [Sainte-Gême] news of Louisiana, it is the lack of transportation opportunity that deprived me of this pleasure." Then, on June 18, 1822, he wrote, "I just learned . . . that a ship is leaving tomorrow for Le Havre and I am seizing the brief moment I have to confirm that I sent you drafts on the 21st of May last."

13. In his letter to Sainte-Gême of April 22, 1824, Dorville wondered whether Sainte-Gême had received a letter that he had sent to Saint-Gaudens with Monsieur Dispain the younger.

words such as "beautiful" or "interesting," which we initially thought we should change to reflect his subject more accurately. We eventually decided to leave them as they were.

Finally, Dorville keeps using various currencies (dollars and cents, gourdes and escalins, piastres and picayunes), switching back and forth from one to the other, sometimes even mixing them. Although we initially thought that the reason for this was that several different currencies (French, Spanish, and American) were in use, we ended up understanding that he used the currencies interchangeably, thanks to the conversion in francs he keeps mentioning.

Oftentimes, Dorville referenced people or events that were obscure to us. In those cases, we worked to identify the person or event in a footnote, especially if they seemed central to the meaning of a letter. If not, we chose not to footnote them. Very often, as well, we were unable to footnote people that were indebted to Sainte-Gême in Cuba, for lack of sources and because what was interesting was their status and geographic location rather than their identity.

Another ongoing challenge was Dorville's penmanship. It was not the best. His spelling of names gave us the most trouble. In those cases, we searched through census records and other archives to try to identify the person, which was only partially fruitful. We had other problems with the clarity of some of the original French words or sentences. When that happened, very infrequently, we footnoted our translation options. Even Dorville recognized that his writing was sometimes nonsensical. He wrote on July 19, 1820, "Rereading a copy of my last letter I found out that there was a sentence that had no meaning."

We also chose to leave the French titles of Monsieur, Madame, and Mademoiselle instead of translating them. By leaving the appellations in French, we hope our readers will remember that Dorville's primary language throughout his life was French, although the presence of one sentence in Creole suggests that he may also have mastered that.

Finally, we chose to leave the French *nègre* and *négresse* for lack of proper translation options. A direct translation was not imaginable, and translating to "Black" or "slave" or "enslaved" would have singularly flattened the original phrasing.

We accept that any errors in the translations are entirely our responsibility.

[MSS 100, Folder 20] March 14, 1818, 11 at night

I apologize, Monsieur Sainte-Gême, and beg you to forgive me for not coming to town to bid you farewell. I am still suffering from fever and do not have the strength. Before leaving the plantation, you honored me with your trust. I hope one day to be entirely deserving of your esteem as well, even though, earlier this year, Monsieur Marigny's offers to me cast a slight cloud on the way you considered me.[1] I partly revealed to you the reasons for it, the main one being that I needed to flee from you and your family, to regain a long-lost rest. But our friendship was so strong that I opened my heart to you, resolving to wait for the blow that might come later and be more painful.

If fervent prayers to the Creator can take you safe and sound to your destination, I promise you to pray to Him every day so that He may grant you a pleasant voyage. If I am sometimes fortunate enough to be in your thoughts, do me the favor, when you reach Bordeaux, of giving me news from you and your amiable family. My heart can only be satisfied by sending your family the most honest and respectful wishes. Farewell, my dear Monsieur Sainte-Gême. I give you a warm embrace and will always be devoutly yours.

P.S. If you demand that I come to town, I will.[2]

Auvignac Dorville

1. Bernard Marigny de Mandeville was an affluent and influential New Orleans Creole. He was a large property owner and occupied various political positions (among them, serving as president of the Louisiana State Senate in 1822 and 1823). He is largely remembered for subdividing his property and selling it in lots, thus giving birth to the faubourg that still bears his name today. Unfortunately, we have no information about the proposal Marigny made to Dorville. We hypothesize that he offered Dorville a position, which would have prevented him from managing the Sainte-Gême plantation after the family's departure for France. For more on Marigny and the creation of the eponymous faubourg, see Ellis, *Faubourg Marigny of New Orleans,* 9–92.

2. This letter summarizes the relationship between Dorville and the Sainte-Gêmes. It reveals the trust placed by Sainte-Gême in Dorville, the acknowledgment of the hierarchical position, as Dorville is ready to obey any command by Sainte-Gême, but also the warmth of the relationship and Dorville's propensity to speak his mind.

[MSS 100, Folder 22] Gentilly, April 20, 1818

My Dear Monsieur Sainte-Gême,

I want to always instruct you about the various moves I make for your interests so that you may approve or disapprove. So, I inform you that, eighteen days after you left, I canceled the rental lease that you had signed with Monsieur Duhamel. I would need to write better than I do and to write at least four pages to delineate the difficulties I am having with him. Your agreement with him said that you left the house to him in good condition and that he had to give it back in the same condition at the end of the lease. It is now very bad, and to repair it would cost three to four hundred piastres.[1]

I think that all the troublemakers of Louisiana were waiting for your departure to come and get me at my retreat and to force me to go to the city at this moment in time that is so precious to the planters.[2]

A few days ago, Adeline Renaud went to court and had the négresse whom she says belongs to her seized. I immediately went to town and stopped her by promising an amicable arrangement to which she agreed and which I am taking care of now. I will give you the details once it is done.[3]

Monsieur Chabaud, who has power of attorney for Monsieur Dangen, who is executor of the will of the deceased Monsieur Juste Causse, and also has the power of attorney for Monsieur Delisle, tutor of the minor children, wishes to

1. The currency mentioned by Dorville was left in all the translations. It is sometimes piastres, sometimes gourdes, and sometimes dollars. Although we originally wondered whether several currencies might have been in use in the city, it became clear, upon reading the letters, that Dorville was using piastres, gourdes, and dollars interchangeably. Indeed, the amounts expressed in gourdes or piastres are consistent with those given in dollars (as is the case here), and whenever Dorville gives the correspondence in francs, it becomes obvious that all these currencies amount to about five francs.

2. April was indeed the main season for planting in Louisiana, especially for the market crops that Dorville was growing in Gentilly. There is no immediate contextual explanation for why Dorville uses the plural when mentioning the troublemakers. One of them was Adeline Renaud, whom Dorville mentions in the subsequent lines. As for the others, we do not know.

3. In an October 11, 1819, document for the indenture of Auguste Brouard with Barbarin F. and Son, the sponsor, Auguste's mother, is Adeline Renaud. She is described as a free woman of color. Her son is described as a young free man of color of twelve years of age, native to Saint-Domingue. New Orleans (La.) Office of the Mayor, Indentures, 1809–1843, available in the Louisiana Digital Library. If this is the Adeline Renaud mentioned by Dorville, it testifies to commercial connections, albeit sometimes conflictual, between the Saint-Domingue refugees across the color line. It is also a sign that free people of color did not hesitate to lodge legal complaints against white people. Dorville's letter of September 7, 1818, details his subsequent agreement with Adeline Renaud.

settle your part of this succession with you.[4] There is one person who is kind enough to lead me by the reins in this business. I hope I can be successful. This person is Monsieur Boze who has just arrived at the plantation. I gave him two letters that Chabaud had written to you so that he could understand the substance of the matter and then write to you at length and in detail. I asked him to tell you about some things I have done for you, hoping he would do this better than I could.[5]

Monsieur Lafonta[6] says he will launch a vessel in about 15 days, and I will seize this opportunity to send a barrel of sugar to you at his brother's address.[7] He is just back from visiting Monsieur Beauregard who asks me to tell you that the bad roads prevented him from fulfilling his promise to send it to you before you left.

I retrieved from the post office on the 14th instant five letters from France addressed to you and one addressed to Madame, your wife. I proceeded to open

4. The long conflict concerning the Causse succession is several times alluded to by Dorville and is detailed in Jean Boze's correspondence, the other main correspondence archived in the Ste-Gême Family Papers. Laurent had been given to Sainte-Gême in Cuba to guarantee a debt from Monsieur Juste Causse to Sainte-Gême. Laurent manifestly followed Sainte-Gême when he was expelled from Cuba and went to New Orleans. Even though Boze went to Cuba to try to retrieve the money residents in Cuba owed to Sainte-Gême, he was unable to settle this debt. Boze and Dorville spent years trying to resolve this matter, faced with the refusal of the Causse heirs to honor their debt. Dorville dunned Laurent until the debt remained unsettled. This episode reveals much about the persisting relationships between the Saint-Domingue refugees and their first asylums before their arrival in New Orleans—in the present case, Cuba. For more on this, see Dessens, *Creole City,* particularly chapter 4, "Crossroads," 140–148. Also see Dessens, "New Orleans between Atlantic and Caribbean," 153–172.

5. Jean Boze, the author of 158 letters to Henri de Sainte-Gême, archived in the Ste-Gême Family Papers, managed Sainte-Gême's business (save the plantation) from 1818 to the late 1830s, when old age sent him to live his last years on the Gentilly plantation. He had come to New Orleans from Cuba with Sainte-Gême, on the latter's vessel. While Dorville always managed the plantation, he also took on the management of the other financial aspects of Sainte-Gême's Louisiana property once Boze no longer could. Boze was also in charge of writing to Sainte-Gême, which he did with remarkable perseverance for twenty years, since his 158 letters cover some 1,200 pages penned between April 1818 and August 1839. When Boze was no longer able to write, Dorville took over, often unwillingly, which explains the relative increase in the volume of his letters after 1840. For more information on Boze and a detailed study of Boze's correspondence, see Dessens, *Creole City.*

6. Lafonta was a prominent New Orleans merchant and longtime friend of Sainte-Gême. Boze's and Dorville's letters mention the Lafontas recurrently. The families were eventually united by marriage in the late nineteenth century. The name of the last Sainte-Gême who occupied the Chateau de Bagen before its sale in 1989, Nancy La Fonta de Sainte-Gême, is testimony to this union.

7. This is one small example of the active circulation of people and products in the Atlantic World and of New Orleans's place within this network.

them, not out of curiosity, but with the wish to satisfy their requests. The persons who wrote to you were not expecting you to return to France that early; some of them (Messieurs, your uncle and your brother Ovide) can tell you in person how happy they are to see you in Europe with your American family. As for the others (Monsieur J^{es} Verdelin and Monsieur Salles Senior), they thank you for taking care of their sons.[8] The fifth is from Monsieur Latapie. It does not say much. As for the one addressed to Madame Sainte-Gême, it is from Madame Latapie and I gave it to Madame Dreux, her mother.[9]

To remember all the people who asked me not to be forgotten when I would write to you and your family, I should have walked around with a pencil and paper in my pocket all the time. Here are those I remember: the Dreux, Chevalier Morand,[10] and Dutillet families;[11] Mademoiselle Ferréole, Messieurs Lambert, Chevalier Hazeur, Destoup, Salles, my father, and my brothers.[12] Although I did not note them down, I have the impression that my memory is recalling so many others that all the names will fill in my page and will deprive me of the pleasure of begging you to express my respectful feelings to Madame, your spouse, and to Mademoiselle Hermina. A kiss for Henriette and for the little brother she must have by now. I still think of my comrade, Edgar.[13]

8. "Jes" probably stands for Jules.

9. Antonia Celeste Dreux was the daughter of François Dreux and Marie Hazeur, thus the sister-in-law of Marguerite Delmas Sainte-Gême. She married Jean-Baptiste Severino Latapie on February 1, 1813. AANO, Marriages, February 1, 1813.

10. The complete name was Chevalier de Morand. The Morand family was an old Louisiana family. The first Morand had purchased land from the India Company in 1731. The original Morand plantation was located on Bayou Road. For more on the family, see "Morand's Heirs *vs.* Mayor, etc. of New Orleans," March 1833, in Miller, *Louisiana Reports,* 226–243.

11. The Dutillets were related to Madame Sainte-Gême. Charles Dobévil Dutillet, who was Marguerite's nephew, had manifestly served under Sainte-Gême in the New Orleans militia. On January 28, 1826, he wrote to Sainte-Gême, calling him "my dear captain." In this letter, which gives news of Madame Dreux, he also says that Irma (one of Sainte-Gême's slaves, who was also Dorville's daughter, see note 14) is staying with him, that she has not grown much but enjoys good health. He shares that he has been appointed captain in the city guard. Ste-Gême Family Papers, MSS 100, folder 102.

12. The list is a mixture of Louisiana friends of Sainte-Gême (and Dorville), like Pierre Lambert; of new migrants from the vicinity of the Chateau de Bagen, recommended by Sainte-Gême when they reached Louisiana, like Destoup and Salles; of relatives of the Sainte-Gêmes, like Hazeur; and of Dorville's relatives. These names recur throughout the correspondence, which progressively unveils information on these people and their connection to Sainte-Gême.

13. Hermina and Edgar (originally called Henri Antoine) were Madame Sainte-Gême's children with Leufroy Dreux. Interestingly, Edgar, born on July 12, 1809, and baptized on June 19, 1810, was Sainte-Gême's godson, which attests to the connections that existed between Sainte-Gême

Although I do not have the honor of knowing your father, your mother, and your brothers, I would be happy if they accepted the assurance of the respect of the one who calls himself, my dear Monsieur Sainte-Gême, your very humble and devoted servant.

Auvignac Dorville

P.S. Nérisse is still sick. I hope she can be restored to health by my care. Irma is doing well. She grows fatter every day.[14]

Poor Monsieur Broutin died.[15]

Mademoiselle Ferréole is going to settle at Pointe Coupée and she will find there what she has been missing for a long time, that is good health.

If you write to me, acknowledge reception of my letters, please. This one is my first.[16]

---

and the Dreux family before he married Marguerite in April 1816, two years after Leufroy Dreux's death. For Edgar's baptismal record, see AANO, Baptisms, June 19, 1810. Henriette was the first of Marguerite's children with Sainte-Gême.

14. Irma was one of Sainte-Gême's Gentilly slaves. She was also, as we learn through a subsequent letter, Dorville's daughter. In his letter of August 31, 1819, he writes about "Irma, who I do not count in their [the slaves] number because she calls me papa." Dorville often refers to her, her religious instruction (letter of March 11, 1820), her training (letter of February 5, 1821), her apprenticeship (letter of May 9, 1827), her pregnancies, her delivery of a still-born baby (letter of February 28, 1832), and her loss of a second baby (letter of April 9, 1845). We also learn from the correspondence that Dorville purchased her from the Sainte-Gêmes for the sum of eight hundred dollars (letter of March 15, 1841), although we do not know if he manumitted her. For more on slave manumission, see, for instance, Gould, "Urban Slavery—Urban Freedom," 298–314; Gould, "'If I Can't Have My Rights,'" 179–201.

15. François-André Narcisse Broutin, born in Louisiana in 1759, died on April 6, 1818. Broutin was notary public in New Orleans and his name is connected with many of the notarial acts passed in the early nineteenth century. See Narcisse Broutin archives, NONA.

16. Dorville added the PS after folding it, as there are blank spaces corresponding to the folds of the letter. When he indicates that his letter is his first, he means that he is also sending a duplicate (sometimes even a triplicate) via another carrier to ensure reception of the letter.

[MSS 100, Folder 25] Gentilly, September 7, 1818

My Dear Monsieur Sainte-Gême,

I received the two letters you wrote me from Bordeaux. You may judge with your good heart the indescribable pleasure your first letter (which I received only eight days after the return of the schooner to New Orleans) gave to your friends. One of the passengers of this schooner said when he arrived here that he had seen you disembark dangerously ill, that you were even carried off the schooner by four men.[1] I put an end to the sadness that had spread in New Orleans because of the false rumors of your death, and I replaced it with the pleasure that the good news of your health gave to all those who are fond of you.

I told you in my letter of April 28th about Adeline Renaud's order for the seizure of the négresse who was subsequently put in jail but was bailed out by Monsieur Dupuys. Fearing, for many reasons, a court procedure, I proposed to Adeline, after consulting with Madame Dreux (whom I consult for everything I do) to initiate the necessary steps to insure she would obtain the nègre, provided that she would pay all the fees and she agreed.[2] I hoped I could terminate this business in this way, but Monsieur Dupuys betrayed me after I confided my plan to him. He seemed to agree with the plan. He promised me, as he had promised you, according to what he said, not to make any claim in this business as he had done concerning the business with Monsieur Coyron. And he even promised that he would give me the bank draft he had from Monsieur Brouard in case I needed it. Once that business was terminated, he forgot his promises and asked what was due him. Surprised at his request, I reminded him of his promise, but he refused to listen to me. All he agreed to was for me to give him a bank draft of 308 dollars payable in April of 1819. I will try to extend the term to give you time to write to him asking him to renounce his request and I hope he will have more consideration for you than for your representative.[3]

The nègre belongs to Adeline who made a perfectly legitimate sale of the négresse. This sale cost her 200 dollars in fees.[4]

1. This letter sheds light on how news was passed between both sides of the Atlantic.

2. Madame Dreux is Leufroy Dreux's mother, Marguerite Delmas-Dreux-de Sainte-Gême's mother-in-law.

3. Although this narration is rather obscure for any reader, it reveals the complex web of commercial relationships, particularly those concerning enslaved people.

4. The two hundred dollars corresponds to the fees incurred on the sale and not to the price paid for the purchase of the enslaved woman, which was undoubtedly higher, although Dorville does not mention it as it is not in Sainte-Gême's benefit.

The business about Laurent is unchanged.[5] In fact, I think he will remain for a long time with me. I am not unhappy about this because he is a really good subject.

Jean-Louis died of consumption after 2 months and 27 days of sickness. I am finished with reporting sad subjects to you. I can imagine your emotions while you are reading my letters.[6]

I rented out the house in town to good persons who pay well. And with the same conditions that you had leased it to Monsieur Duhamel, except that I was content with a private agreement before witnesses to avoid having to pay fees to a notary. I am also satisfied with the people who rent the house in the faubourg, which I rented out for 15 dollars a month, payable by trimester. I have not yet managed to sell the two soup tureens. I intend to sell them in a lottery. There will be 24 tickets of 25 dollars each, of which there will be two winners. I think it is the only way to get the price you have set. I am working on completing some of the debt recovery you entrusted to me. The crop is beautiful this year and I hope that, when the next one starts, there will be enough money left for Monsieur Dreux to afford what you asked him to acquire.[7] I heard through Monsieur Boze that you had received the barrel of sugar I sent you. Thinking that you would be far from Bordeaux when it arrived there, I addressed it to Monsieur Lafonta without being civil enough to write to you. Captain Davis is bringing to you ten bottles of natural wild cherry juice, a barrel of sweet potatoes, and one of fresh pecans from the plantation.[8] There is also a little package of laurel seeds. I addressed

5. Laurent is the enslaved person left with Sainte-Gême in Cuba to cover Causse's debt.

6. This type of remark is what would suggest that the Sainte-Gêmes's interest in Gentilly's enslaved people was not just commercial, although, as was discussed in the introduction to the plantation's history, the letters written in the 1850s tend to disprove this. It is of interest to the historiography of slavery in that it shows why early historians of slavery used this kind of wording to support the argument that slavery was a paternalistic institution.

7. Monsieur Dreux is Leufroy Dreux's brother, François Dreux, who inherited half of the Gentilly plantation at their father's death. The way in which the plantation was divided at the death of Mathurin Dreux and then reassembled by his grandsons is discussed in "Gentilly Plantation: A History," this volume.

8. Robert Davis was a ship captain who most often sailed between New Orleans and Bordeaux. A letter from him to Sainte-Gême, dated January 26, 1819, indicates that he knew Sainte-Gême very well, which explains why letters and products were most often entrusted to him. In the letter, he apologizes for not visiting Sainte-Gême, explaining that the crossing took fifty-four days and thus prevented him from spending time with Sainte-Gême. He gives news of his family, saying that his wife has just opened a shop at the corner of Bienville and Royale. Ste-Gême Family Papers, MSS 100, folder 29. There are several letters by him, in English, which were systematically translated into French, sometimes dated a few days after the original letter. Again, this shows the frequency

these to Monsieur Lafonta, asking him to get them to you. I also sent you a nice male wood duck, so that you will have the pair, since Captain Davis, who has purchased several, told me he wanted to give you a female. This brave man never stops praising you. Here are his expressions: he says you are worthy of being a prince and that he would like you to be president of our United States.

I am not sending you oranges because we have not had frost yet. I will remember to send them when the time comes. The letter I have enclosed comes from Rouen. I do not know its content, although I opened it to retrieve another letter addressed to Monsieur Bouffetin. I gave that letter to Monsieur Boze. The latter has done better than I have because he has written to you several times. Madame, your wife, will be, I hope, satisfied. I wrote a letter to her in which I gave accurate details on the slaves without forgetting my daughter Irma.

What follows is from Monsieur Lambert.[9] He regularly spends two or three days a week with me. I am writing while he is dictating.

"I received, my dear Monsieur Sainte Gême, the letter you were nice enough to write to me. I was very moved by it but even more so by Madame Ste Gême's silence. I think she has forgotten me, and I am tormented every day, thinking of her and you and your children. I often visit Auvignac, whom we call old Dorville. While I am there, we wage war against the ducks.

I admit that I am a good duck hunter thanks to you. However, I am not to be feared because Valery killed more than we did this year. He sends you his best. You know that he brags so much about the advantage he has on us that he thinks he could be ten points above you.

Together with my family, I pray you to kiss yours for us.

Farewell.

I wish you all kinds of happiness and I will always be your faithful friend and servant.

Pierre Lambert"

Now I am so much stronger that I can hunt feathery creatures as I sometimes hunt deer, although I do not often have the chance. We have, however,

---

of exchanges within the Atlantic and the web of personal relationships connecting people in France and Louisiana.

9. Pierre Lambert was a close friend of Sainte-Gême's and had become Dorville's friend. He spent much time on the plantation and was Dorville's favorite hunting partner (and Sainte-Gême's, when he was still living in Louisiana). Saint Domingue, AANO, Baptisms, February 2, 1816.

killed five or six deer since your departure. We would have killed more if we had not had the misfortune of losing two dogs, the famous Clairon and the good Marcian. The first was eaten by raccoons.[10] The second died of illness. I hope that when you come back you will find them replaced and that we will sometimes have the pleasure of hunting with you. Messieurs Hazeur and Fortier asked me to send you their friendship. My family also wishes me to send you their best. Please allow me to send to your father, mother, and brothers my perfect respect. I am, my dear Monsieur Sainte-Gême, your devoted servant,

Auvignac Dorville

P.S. I forgot to thank you for the good and fine scythes that you sent me and to send you my condolences for the loss of your poor dog Mirau which will also be replaced.

10. The original reads "bandit," which in French is also used to designate a raccoon, in reference to the fact that raccoons look as if they are wearing a mask. We opted for the latter translation, although raccoons generally feed on much smaller animals. Dorville may be misusing the word *manger,* meaning that the raccoons bit and killed the dog, not necessarily that they ate it entirely.

[MSS 100, Folder 26] Gentilly, November 13, 1818

My Dear Monsieur Sainte-Gême,

My first letter was already sealed and I had given it to Captain Davis when Adèle asked me to let you know that her intention was to sell her nègre Caprice because he gets into fist fights every day, and she fears that he might get killed. She wants 600 piastres and wants you to have first choice. I do not think you will agree to this business, but I have always fulfilled my mission and I want you to tell me what your thoughts are about this.

I forgot to tell you in my previous letter that I sold the dog, Cupidon, for 60 dollars and the horse, Alezan, for 110 dollars.[1]

Farewell my dear Monsieur Sainte-Gême
Auvignac Dorville

P.S. Promise me please, before opening the small letter that is included that has no address, that you will burn it or tear it up after reading it. If I had not expected this mark of friendship from you, I would not have sent it.[2]

1. The phrasing in this short letter reveals where the enslaved stood in Dorville's mental depiction of the organization of society.

2. As much as we would like to know what the letter contained, Sainte-Gême probably complied with Dorville's request. Historians have shown that letters were generally passed from hand to hand, or even read aloud to the whole family. Given the topics Dorville addresses in his letters, the Sainte-Gême family probably passed the letters to friends and kin who were either involved or simply interested in Louisiana. See, for instance, Gerber, "Epistolary Ethics," 12–13.

[MSS 100, Folder 30] Gentilly, January 26, 1819

I have received through Zaïre, on the 18th of December 1818, the letter that you, my dear Monsieur Sainte-Gême, wrote me dated the 6th of October of the same year.[1] I hope that Captain Davis will have remitted to you in person the letters that I addressed to you. It is true that for a time I have been silent, and here is the reason: the business of this négresse has so cruelly worried me that you must have noticed it through the embarrassed style of my first letter. I wanted this business to be over before I wrote to you. Finally, I wrote with an extreme repugnance, and I seized the occasion of the first ship to sail after your departure, which was that of Captain Davis, to send to you and Madame, your spouse, news from Louisiana.[2] You give me the hope that you will come for a short stay next year. How can I express the pleasure I feel? And what would I not give to be one year older.[3]

Monsieur Boze is waiting for the end of summer before leaving for Havana. He desired that I make it known to you that his chargé d'affaire advised him to do so, in the hope that his requests would be fulfilled little by little.[4] I find that he looks much older. I do not know if it is love that is the cause of it, but I strongly believe that he is not congenial enough to make up for his appearance. If only he was rich, the fair sex would say, like Boileau, gold gives an appearance of beauty even to ugliness.[5] I fulfilled the mission you asked of me concerning him.

1. Zaïre had accompanied the Sainte-Gêmes to France. A passport issued to Henri de Sainte-Gême on June 26, 1818, by the mayor of the city of Bordeaux allows the safe and free passage from Bordeaux to Saint-Gaudens of Sainte-Gême, his wife, three children, and a young *négresse.* Ste-Gême Family Papers, MSS 100, folder 616. She had returned to Louisiana, carrying a letter from Sainte-Gême. It was not unusual for Louisianians to travel to France with their slaves. Gould, "In Full Enjoyment," 107.

2. The letter referred to here is that of September 7.

3. From the subsequent letters, we know that Sainte-Gême never returned to Louisiana, despite Dorville's recurrent supplications.

4. Dorville writes "poque à poque," gallicizing the Spanish *poco a poco,* which means "little by little." There are interesting borrowings in the various languages spoken in Louisiana. Jean Boze was in charge of retrieving money owed to Sainte-Gême by residents of Cuba. Although there is no precision, the chargé d'affaires was most certainly in Cuba, a go-between helping Boze.

5. "L'or, même à la laideur, donne un teint de beauté / Mais tout devient affreux avec la pauvreté," wrote Nicolas Boileau, the famous French poet (1636–1711), in his *Satires* (1660–1711). What is interesting in this reference is that Dorville, a young Creole of rural Louisiana who had started managing the plantation at an early age, was sufficiently learned to be able to quote Boileau in such a casual way.

Zaïre is apprenticed as Madame, your spouse, desired.[6] After she gave me news from you, I asked her how she would describe what she had seen in France. She told me that everything was beautiful, that there were only the black walls of the high houses of Bordeaux that she had not liked, and that the government had not allowed them to be returned to their original white color.[7]

Madame Dreux, who has written to you, must have told you that she had decided to join Madame Latapie. When that day comes, it will be great for her because she often cries at the absence of her dear Celeste.

Although the latter told her about her accident, she still does not know that she has broken one of her teeth. Madame Beltremieux complains much that Madame Sainte-Gême has not written to her as she has promised. Maybe she will also make the trip with Monsieur Dubreuil. Clementine told me she had not received your letter. Maybe she has received it but, for fear of having to reply to it, she pretends not to have received it. I forgot in my previous letter to let you know that Mr. Johnson, our representative in Congress, had written to you, addressing his letter to New Orleans. He said: "After the first claim you made for the animals killed during the war, your last claim comes late but I will not forget you if there is a way to do something for you."[8] Monsieur Haigneil[9] is so difficult to deal with that it is impossible to do anything for him. He asked for 8000 dollars for his old hovel. Concerning this topic, Monsieur Dreux told me the intentions you now have. His family joined him in asking me to send you and yours their sincere friendship. Monsieur Lambert speaks of going with you to France when you are returning there after being here. He still has a passion for hunting. He told me: "When you write to the bourgeois, tell him that I still think of him and that I have killed 345 ducks since the beginning of the hunting season, two-thirds of which were French."[10] About politics, there is nothing

6. For more on the practice of the apprenticeship of the enslaved, see Lachance, "To train them to habits of industry and usefulness," 94–120.

7. This passage shows that Zaïre gave Dorville an account of her journey to France and that Dorville granted her narrative sufficient attention to reproduce it here.

8. Sainte-Gême apparently lodged a complaint for the loss of part of the Gentilly cattle during the war of 1812.

9. Sometimes spelled Hesgniel.

10. Lambert used the words "bourgeois" and "bourgeoise" to familiarly refer to the Sainte-Gêmes. In nineteenth-century French, "bourgeois" was used to designate the owner of a corsair ship, which most certainly explains Lambert's use, in reference to Sainte-Gême's past activities in the Antilles.

new, except that Pensacola, which had been taken by the Americans, has been returned to the Spanish.[11] There are still many foreigners coming to Louisiana. At the pace it is going, New Orleans may be, within ten years, one of the most commercially active cities in the world.[12]

I am relatively happy about all the nègres except Amazilie who got an abortion a few days ago.[13] I wanted to send you three barrels of oranges but, according to what several persons say, there are some really beautiful and very good ones coming from Portugal to Toulouse and they are not as expensive as the ones I would have sent you. I more than once thought of the sadness Madame, your spouse, must have felt when she had to be separated from Edgar, and also of that of Mademoiselle Hermina. I sincerely share it since I do not have the satisfaction of asking you to offer any pleasant thought to these persons that are so dear to you. It is ten o'clock and the vessel is leaving for the open sea at noon, which makes me rush to finish this letter. I am now forced to stop. I will not finish, however, without asking you to be the presenter of my respectful affection to your wife and your respectable family. Farewell. I am, my dear Monsieur Sainte-Gême, your devoted and obedient servant.

Auvignac Dorville

11. After the Louisiana Purchase of 1803, Spain controlled West Florida, which included Pensacola. In 1819, General Andrew Jackson captured Pensacola during the First Seminole War. It was soon retroceded to Spain and remained under the control of the Spanish until it was ceded to the United States through the Adams-Onís Treaty (February 22, 1819).

12. Dorville was not far from the truth. In 1840, twenty years after he wrote these lines, New Orleans, with its 102,193 inhabitants, had become the third most populated city in the United States, behind New York and Philadelphia, which represented an increase of 121.8 percent in twenty years. See Gibson, *Population of the 100 Largest Cities.*

13. This remark shows the attention paid to enslaved women's reproductive function. For more on this, see, for instance, Follett, *Sugar Masters,* 46–89; Ingersoll, *Mammon and Manon,* 80–83.

[MSS 100, Folder 32] Gentilly, April 17, 1819

My dear Monsieur Sainte-Gême,

Included is a letter from Monsieur Boze who believes that you will soon arrive in New Orleans. Many people think like him. Someone called Campardon, who has been here for a few months, has affirmed that you have told him that you would return soon. From Monsieur Boze's letter, you will see that he must leave before long for Santiago de Cuba.[1] You will soon receive 30 to 35 bales of beautiful cotton that will cost 24 cents. I will send the bales through Monsieur Lafonta. Even though its price has fallen in France, Monsieur Dreux preferred to send you the cotton instead of money, considering that pirates are still committing crimes in the Gulf of Mexico.[2] All safeguards will be taken, and I hope that you will profit from them. I honored Monsieur Dupuis's bank draft that I wrote to you about.[3] It is the only business that could prevent me from receiving your approbation, but you will come back, you will hear me, and you will judge me. Monsieur Lafonta wrote to tell me that he had Captain Davis deliver to you all the things I had sent, except for the wood ducks that died during the crossing. Commerce here is in a dire situation. Money is not circulating.[4] That is what prevented me from putting the tureens in the lottery. For the same reason,

1. In fact, Jean Boze did not leave until 1820. The letters he wrote to Sainte-Gême from Cuba detail his stay, his occupations, his efforts to recover the debts owed to Sainte-Gême by several inhabitant of the island, his successes and failures. They cover the period from 1820 to 1828. Ste-Gême Family Papers, MSS 100, folders 43–117.

2. François Dreux was the brother of Louis Leufroy, Marguerite de Sainte-Gême's deceased first husband. He was the executor of his brother's succession. Leufroy's will also indicated that should his wife remarry after his death, François should become the guardian of Edgar and Hermina. See Louis Leufroy Dreux's will in appendix 3.

3. Dupuis was a friend of Sainte-Gême who was, like Sainte-Gême, living in France but had property in New Orleans. From a letter he wrote to Sainte-Gême from Paris on September 6, 1825, we understand that he owned a sugar plantation. He mentions arriving from New Orleans, where the crop was good that year. He writes that his plantation overseer, Morin, died just when they finished rolling the cane. He gives news of Madame Dreux and of Dorville and says that he could not go and see the new plantation house that Dorville had built because of the bad condition of the roads. Ste-Gême Family Papers, MSS 100, folder 100.

4. By 1819, the United States was experiencing its first financial crisis. The end of the war between Great Britain and France had sent the economy into a downward spiral. Banks failed, which led to mortgage foreclosures. Many people lost their homes, farms, and plantations. Falling prices hit the manufacturing and agricultural sectors especially hard, which caused the currency shortage that Dorville is mentioning here. See Marler, *Merchants' Capital.*

half the planters have not sold their sugar and debt recoveries are difficult. You probably heard about the huge bankruptcy of Monsieur Dominique Bouquette and his demise, which can be called tragic because, without settling his accounts, he drowned in the Mississippi from which he was recovered 15 to 20 days later. This unfortunate bankruptcy ruined several persons including men with families such as Messieurs Mayronnes, Cousins, etc. The public says that it will amount to more than 400,000 dollars.

How are your dear united families, particularly the one from Louisiana? A four-year habit enables me to ask for this testimony of friendship from you. You know the interest that I have in everything that concerns you.

You wrote to me that you would come for a visit to Louisiana in one year. If it is difficult for you to start so soon on this voyage, you can obviate this inconvenience by sending me your orders that I will follow and fulfill exactly and with pleasure.[5] Your foreign business would suffer only a slight delay since you can act from Europe as you would in America. Moreover, you know the diligence and faithfulness of Monsieur Boze.

I just did a small repair to the gallery of the plantation house, but it does not make it much stronger. That is why I want you to let me know whether you want me to sell the blue earthenware table service that you left in my care, since I do not think it is safe in the attic bedroom.[6] If your reply is positive, give me its price because I have not found anything that is related to this service in the receipts. I had a beautiful hen house made. It lodges a nice family of chickens that I raised, and will be, I hope, paid for in one year.[7] If you come back, do not eat too much chicken during the crossing because you would become tired of it* and would not be able to enjoy the capons that I will fatten for you. Monsieur Lambert is still fond of you. You must remember that he sometimes had a real talent for foreseeing the future. Well, his talent is now questionable because all the conjectures he has made on your voyage, your return, and what you would do, have not yet come true. If I narrated these particularities, they would make you laugh good-heartedly. What I find the funniest is that he always makes

5. This letter is another testament to the dual relationship between Dorville and Sainte-Gême, halfway between familiarity and service.

6. The plantation house was clearly rudimentary and in dire condition, far from the mansions upon which the historiography generally focuses.

7. This type of occasional remark is extremely valuable because it gives firsthand information on what the plantation produced and the profitability of the various products.

fun of me for my cheese dish. If you have forgotten this stew, please give some thoughts to the one who made you think of it and believe him forever, my dear Monsieur Sainte-Gême, your humble and devoted servant.

Auvignac Dorville

* Please forgive me for this joke.

[MSS 100, Folder 33] Gentilly, April 23, 1819

Monsieur Sainte-Gême
St. Gaudens, Haute Garonne

You must have received, my dear Monsieur Sainte-Gême, via *le Joseph,* my letter dated the 19th of this month, which tells you to expect the arrival of cotton. At the same time I sent the cotton to you, I sent Monsieur Lafonta 30 bales of first-quality cotton. It costs 24 cents, and the entire amount comes to 2,419 dollars, without counting the insurance and a few other small fees. I have not yet paid the interest to Monsieur Dreux, but I will do so before long and I will also pay the commissions.

The enclosed letter is the duplicate of the letter from Monsieur Boze that was included in my previous letter, although he asked me to keep it with me so that I may give it to you when you arrive. I preferred to send it to you for safe-keeping. Please give my respectful homages to all those you have an interest in and believe me, my dear Monsieur Ste Gême, to be your devoted and respectful servant.

Auvignac Dorville

[MSS 100, Folder 39] Gentilly, July 21, 1819

It has been a long time, my dear Monsieur Sainte-Gême, since anyone here has had any news from you. I think that the great distance that separates you from the ports is what prevented you from sending news to your Louisiana relatives on the various vessels that left since your last letter of February 8th.[1] I would write you more often if I had some happy topic to impart in my correspondence and if I had not thought that it would cost you more than it would be worth. It is not the same from you to me and you know that I could never pay too much for the pleasure that a few lines from you would bring me. I told you in my last letter about Nérisse's disease, and also about that of Colas. The former's health has now returned. The latter has not had the same luck and he now has scrofula in his neck and his groin.[2] You know that this unfortunate disease is most of the time unforgiving. If good care and perseverance and remedies, however, can reestablish his health, I hope to see him cured. In the same letter I told you about Basile's walking away.[3] If I had delayed my letter by one day, I would not have told you about it because he surrendered the next day. I am satisfied with his service as of all the others. They all fare well including Irma who has grown a lot. I take once more the occasion of telling you that Amazilie is 5 or 6 months pregnant. I hope that she will remember the lesson I gave her for her previous miscarriage and that, this time, she will carry her child to term.[4] Please reassure your wife about the delivery of this négresse. I will act as she had already requested of me.[5]

1. The Chateau de Bagen, located at the foot of the Pyrenees, approximately halfway between the Mediterranean and the Atlantic Ocean, is about two hundred miles from the nearest Atlantic port, Bordeaux. It was an important distance at the time, which may explain the difficulty Sainte-Gême had in sending mail to the Americas. This was especially true because, as Dorville explains, Sainte-Gême tended to count on acquaintances to carry the mail. Although the factual explanation is easy to give, Dorville's phrasing might also be a strategy to complain about the lack of mail without sounding too critical.

2. Scrofula is an infection of the lymph nodes, often caused by tuberculosis or nontubercular mycobacteria. New Orleans and its surroundings were unhealthy in general, but it was especially unhealthy for slaves. Schafer, "New Orleans Slavery," 55.

3. "Walking away" was a term that implied that the enslaved had left the plantation, had not gone far, and planned to return after a few days or weeks. It was temporary relief from the rigors of labor. "Running away," on the contrary, implied flight to freedom.

4. We cannot but wonder what Dorville means by "lesson." There is hardly any mention of corporal punishment in the correspondence, but "lesson" could be a euphemism for flogging.

5. This is another example that Madame Sainte-Gême's concern was genuine, although her requests probably had more to do with increasing the enslaved population of Gentilly.

The Chevalier women are on their plantation, and they ask me to remind your gentle family of them. Clémentine has once again asserted that she has not received any letter from you. She is angry at you even though, in fact, she is very fond of you. She told me that she would not have refused your hand if you had offered it to her, so if you were misfortunate enough to become a widower, you could become her Titan. I hope you will forgive me for this joke and will not take the comparison in all its implications. I do not know if it would obtain your wife's grace, but it can only justify the good choice she made.

I have not had news from Monsieur Boze since his departure for Santiago de Cuba. When he left New Orleans, Captain Dubreuil had promised to write to me. He has not fulfilled his promise. I would certainly have warned him if I had known his address, which he was unable to give me. It would please me if you told me his fate if you know it and, if you have an occasion to see him, to remind him of the promise he made me. Monsieur Fortier has been very sick. It has much changed him.[6] I fear he will be unable to hunt with me. Monsieur Lambert sends his fondest memory to you and to Madame, your wife. Promise me to be the interpreter of my respectful feelings to all those you love. Farewell. I am still, with a sincere devotion, my dear Monsieur Sainte-Gême, your very sincere servant.

Auvignac Dorville

6. Considering his probable age and connection to Sainte-Gême, Monsieur Fortier was most certainly Michel Fortier, who had taken part in the Battle of New Orleans with Sainte-Gême and died in 1819. The Fortier family, whose first member had settled in Louisiana in the mid-eighteenth century, was always highly involved in the political life of the colony, and then of the state. Michel's son and grandson were sugar planters. His great-grandson was the famous professor Alcée Fortier. For more on the Fortier family, see, for instance, Arthur, Campbell, and de Kernion, *Old Families of Louisiana,* 44–48. Also see Le Glaunec, «'Grand Dieu quand serais-je Délivré de ces tracasseries,'" 95–113.

[MSS 100, Folder 40] Gentilly, August 31, 1819

I send you, included, my dear monsieur Sainte-Gême, a copy of my books in which you will see not only the state of the revenues of the plantation but of all your properties. As one cannot live without expenses, I have also included the state of the general expenses, as well as a copy of my bank book. In this last, you will see that Monsieur Dreux did not want to handle the funds that I collected and requested me to do it for him, which I did without telling you for fear of hurting you. You will see, from the balance of my books, that there is an error of 11.72 dollars. Although it is in profit, I would have preferred that this balance would have been correct. You owe me three hundred and some piastres which I will pay myself before long. The painful attempts I made to collect the debts that you have left for me to collect have been unsuccessful. Some of your debtors are absent and the others are of bad faith and destitute. I hope nevertheless to collect the debt of Monsieur Eline and that of Monsieur Tessier. I have still not been able to find a favorable moment to place the two tureens in the lottery. Business is still bad. Since we are speaking of business, allow me, my dear Monsieur Sainte-Gême, to express my opinion about yours and to recite to you the proverb that says that he who pays his debts grows rich. This is why I believe that it would be to your advantage to do so, and to satisfy the debt that you have to Madame Dreux. It costs, every year, interest that you can never hope to regain. If you consented to this proposition, I would tell you to remain in France until the debt is paid (this could be done by next April or March) or even until the second good season: then I would like to see you in Louisiana so that I could advise you to employ the funds available to you to the establishment of a steam mill, which, placed at La Vacherie, would be likely to yield a great revenue.[1]

I have spoken to you in my last letter, the one I sent to you this past 21st of July, of the condition of Colas. Monsieur Conund's skill could not save him. The poor devil died the 12th of this month.[2]

I pray for you to send my best memories to your interesting and amiable

1. La Vacherie was Sainte-Gême's second piece of property, also located in Gentilly but slightly farther from the city, on both sides of Bayou St. John, as listed in the 1814 Dreux inventory (see appendix 4).

2. Monsieur Conund was the doctor Dorville called to tend to the Gentilly slaves when their sickness was beyond Dorville's simple medical skills.

family. I was as touched as could be by the honor you afforded me and the friendship you extended to me by sending me news from them.

In my letter before last, dated the 29th of March, I gave you news of the slaves. Clarisse and her child are well, as are all the others. Irma, who I do not count in their number because she calls me papa, also enjoys good health.[3] I made a suggestion to you in this same letter, a suggestion that you made 14 days before, concerning the state of your revenues. I do not know if you have noticed how much we think alike.

Monsieur Destoup is well, but he is too lazy to write his parents.[4] I believe that he has not done it three times since he has been in New Orleans. Monsieur Salles is still at Attakapas.[5] I have been told that he was to marry before long. Monsieur Ribon left in order to join the Spanish insurgents.[6] I do not remember where exactly, but I believe that it is somewhere around Chile. If I was not suffering a lot now, I would write of many other things. Please remain assured of the devotion of the one who is, my dear Monsieur Sainte-Gême, your very humble servant.

Auvignac Dorville

3. Beckles, "Black Female Slaves," 111–125.

4. Antoine Destoup had come to Louisiana from Toulouse. A letter of May 25, 1824, from Destoup's brother, the Baron Destoup, addressed to Sainte-Gême, states that Baron Destoup had learned of his brother's death (at age thirty-six) in New Orleans on December 3, 1823. He prayed Sainte-Gême to ask Dorville to send copies of his brother's death certificate. Ste-Gême Family Papers, MSS 100, folder 85.

5. Monsieur Salles was a friend of Destoup's, also from the vicinity of Bagen. A letter of August 10, 1818, by Jean Boze mentions that Salles had apprenticed himself to an upriver merchant. Ste-Gême Family Papers, MSS 100, folder 23.

6. Beginning in 1809, the whole of Hispanic mainland America was shaken by the Latin American independence wars. Wars erupted against the Spanish monarchy across the Spanish colonies. In 1819, battles were raging in Chile, Greater Colombia, Mexico, and Peru. Boze's correspondence shows that a nonnegligible number of New Orleanians joined the Latin American rebellions, including the armies of Simon Bolivar in Greater Colombia. For more on the involvement of Louisianans in these movements, see Dessens, *Creole City,* 144–146. On Latin American independence wars, see Chasteen, *Americanos.*

[MSS 100, Folder 41] Gentilly, March 11, 1820

I would have written to you, my dear Monsieur Sainte-Gême, three or four months ago, if I had not been awaiting the departure of Captain Davis who was supposed to leave any day for Bordeaux. He is finally departing for Le Havre by the grace of God on the *Cora,* the boat that he is commanding now.[1] I am not unhappy about this delay because in the meantime I had the pleasure of receiving, on the 11th of January 1820, your letter of the 7th of October 1819. It made me decide not to send you the two barrels of your sweet potatoes and two of sugar, of premier quality, which I had already acquired.[2]

I ask that you tell me that you have received my last two letters, one of the 21st of July, the second containing the state of your revenues, dated the 31st of August, both of last year. I am satisfied with the production of the plantation. Here is an overview of it. I have made a thousand and some piastres selling milk. From timber and firewood etc. 898.50 dollars. I have delivered hay for 996 dollars. The oranges have already given me 566 piastres and 4 escalins and I hope that this revenue will exceed 700 gourdes.[3] I made a small profit with the harvest of rice, which I estimate to be from sixty to seventy straw barrels. I do not intend to put it on sale, since I have more work at the plantation than can be executed.[4] My harvest of corn has been abundant. I sold some for 45 dollars and I will still sell the surplus beyond the quantity necessary for use on the plantation. I also hope to sell some sheep; the little flock continues to grow.[5] There are other little things, which I make profit from, but I will not write about them because you might find them perhaps too minute. I would not give, my dear Monsieur Monsieur Sainte-Gême, all these details if I did not think they would bring you pleasure.

From time to time, Nérisse suffers from the illness that she had when you were still here. I believe that Monsieur Conund does not understand anything.

1. Delay between letters was often due to the scarcity of ships crossing the Atlantic and to the fact that it was safer to entrust someone with personally carrying the letters and ensuring the transportation of goods.

2. Dorville sent Sainte-Gême produce of the plantation, but this letter also shows that he did send goods that he acquired for Sainte-Gême.

3. This is a good example of the way in which Dorville refers to gourdes, piastres, and dollars interchangeably, even, as here, when referring to the same revenue (from the oranges).

4. Dorville's remark shows that the plantation could not be profitable due to insufficient manpower.

5. This letter is also a good example of information on the plantation's production and the revenue collected from the various goods produced.

If you could consult with a good doctor in your country, I could try any advice that you could give me from him. Here is the condition of this négresse: she sometimes has, at moments when she should feel at her best, some red and white discharges that last ten or twelve days. These discharges cause her to have strong headaches and stomach aches. Only tepid baths seem to make her better. I do not consider her seriously sick but in the long run her illness could become more serious.[6]

I told you of the pregnancy of Amazilie. She delivered after seven months, without accident or provocation. But her infant did not live. She is well, as are all the other slaves of whom I am relatively satisfied. Irma has grown a lot; she is fat, she enjoys good health, but she is not encumbered with intelligence. She is unable to conceive of anything. For more than a year I have tried to teach her to pray, and she still does not know how to make the sign of the cross.[7]

I am satisfied that you made some profits on the cotton you received; the intentions of Monsieur Dreux were good when he preferred to send you cotton rather than money.[8] Fortunately, you dealt with Monsieur J. B. Lafonta, about whom I will not forget your recommendations.

I have received with pleasure the school report from Sorèze by which I saw the progress made by Edgar in several fields of studies.[9] I also learned with much pleasure that the Black Ladies treat Mademoiselle Hermina as well as she deserves.[10] When she was in Louisiana, she already showed signs of the pleasure she would give her family. Madame Sainte-Gême must be very proud to have such children, and you, my dear Monsieur Sainte-Gême, must give them a great place in your heart. As for me, I remain in admiration of them.

Your fear that your letters might not reach us was well founded. The ship the *Highlander* and Monsieur Latapie were no longer at Bordeaux when they arrived. You saw, from the above, when I received them. Monsieur Latapie has

6. Nérisse was twenty in 1814, when Leufroy Dreux's inventory was made for his estate. She was then twenty-six. Dorville's comments prove the attention he paid to the health of the enslaved and the finely detailed knowledge he had about their condition.

7. Dorville paid obvious attention to his daughter's instruction, although his remark about her lack of intelligence is offensive.

8. Sending goods across the Atlantic was a way of avoiding losing on money transfers, and even, as is the case here, a way to make profit.

9. Sorèze is a small town in the department of Tarn in southwestern France, famous for its school. The abbey, originally founded in 754 by the Catholic Benedictine order, was known for its innovative teaching methods. It was designated a military school between 1776 and 1793 under Louis XIV. It closed in 1991 and is now a museum.

10. "Black Ladies" are nuns, which means that Hermina was then attending a Catholic school.

traveled to different posts in our country in order to collect what is due to him. He is now at New Orleans where he is ready to leave for France next month. Madame Dreux, his mother-in-law, should follow.[11] She is happy at the prospect of turning the head of some old marquis or baron in Europe, so that she could change countries and names at the same time. I will take advantage of this good opportunity to send you some money I have left. Monsieur Dreux, having married off his young daughters, warned me that he was in need of two thousand piastres. It is impossible to refuse it. I think that you will miss this sum. If, by the time Monsieur Latapie leaves, I can procure it, as well as other funds, I will have it delivered to you.

I tried to sell the two tureens at the lottery in vain. I have not lost hope of finding a more favorable moment than this one. One only hears talk of bankruptcies. The planters cannot sell their sugar and their cotton is without value. Zaïre will soon finish her apprenticeship. She will remain another year, but rented to the bourgeoise, Victoire Garcin, in order that she may perfect her skills. Dobévil had been imagining things when he thought she was pregnant at the time that he wrote to you. I have doubts about these things at this moment. If they are realized, I will let you know and will tell you about Dobévil. I think that he really wrote to you but that you did not receive his letters.

There should be a nice hanging here: sixteen pirates, who have been taken in the Gulf of Mexico by a small American boat, have been condemned to hang by the criminal court. To execute them, we are waiting for the president to sanction the court's judgment. They say that the chief of these brigands comes from a very good family in Bordeaux. He is 28 years old and bears the name of Lafarge.[12]

I have told you that the planters of Gentilly published a public notice, about 18 to 20 months ago, in imitation of those of Chapitoulas, banning hunting on their property. The public notice was presented to me, and I was reluctant to sign it because I then thought that I would be obliged to imitate them, which I ultimately did because, as I had remained neutral, too many hunters were com-

11. Dorville's letters, which often mention people traveling back and forth between New Orleans and France, suggest the frequency of Atlantic exchanges. For more on this, see Dessens, *Creole City*, 118–136. Also see Dessens, "New Orleans between Atlantic and Caribbean."

12. The Gulf of Mexico was, from the late eighteenth century to the mid-nineteenth century, a favorite space for corsairs and pirates. Henri de Sainte-Gême was known for his privateering activities in Cuba (1804–1810) and for his connections with the Lafitte brothers and their pirate community in Barataria. Dessens, *Creole City*, 13–14.

ing to the plantation. My notice made a lot of people protest but I do not care because I prefer tranquility to entertaining those who like gossip.

You have without a doubt learned of the death of Monsieur Hazeur, the planter.[13] The malady of which he had been afflicted for a long time went to his chest and took him to the grave. He left 2,000 dollars to Monsieur Chevalier as well as to Madame Dreux and the rest to Monsieur l'Ainé. Monsieur Fortier has also finished the course of his life.[14] He was generally missed.

Monsieur Lambert is still fond of you, he prayed me to let you know of it. My family was touched by the greetings of Madame, your spouse. They asked me to offer their respectful homages to her and their civilities to you. Monsieur Villanueva sends you all a thousand friendly thoughts. My aunt Bienvenu sends her civilities to Madame Sainte-Gême and Mademoiselle Hermina, and she sends her fondest recollections to you. I give a hundred kisses to charming little Henriette and to her little brother. Farewell, my dear Monsieur Sainte-Gême. Please, be my interpreter with your interesting and amiable family and transmit to them the respectful feelings with which I am still your devoted servant.

Auvignac Dorville

13. Louis François Xavier Hazeur, born March 25, 1748, interred October 20, 1819. AANO, Funerals, October 20, 1819. He was married to Marie Josèphe De Luce, native of Mobile.

14. Michel Fortier, age around sixty-nine, interred on September 20, 1819. AANO, Funerals, September 20, 1819.

[MSS 100, Folder 42] Gentilly, May 28, 1820

Madame Latapie informed us, my dear Monsieur Sainte-Gême, of the horrendous event that occurred in your family. Please receive my condolences. And remember, my dear Monsieur Sainte-Gême, that a good Christian knows how to resign himself to God's will.[1] This unfortunate accident makes me reluctant to tell you that your presence here would be absolutely necessary. If this is not too great a sacrifice for you, I urge you to come and spend if only one month in Louisiana, after which time you will return to the persons who make you love life, reassured about the future, leaving me informed about your interests. The first reason that makes me want to see you is that Messieurs Danger and Delisle, in charge of the late JB Causse succession, observe that Marianne was not the guardian of his children and thus had no right to commit a property belonging to this succession. I fear that Monsieur Chabaud, the signatory of these two men, may attempt, according to their will, to seize Laurent, maybe without compensation. The second reason is that your house in town is falling into ruin. Instead of having it repaired because it is not worth it, you should have another one built, one that would yield a higher profit. After carefully examining the problem with Monsieur Dreux, I lowered the rent by 60 piastres per trimester, on condition that the house would be given back to me immediately once I would know if you had agreed to finish the year at thirty piastres a month. I inform you, my dear Monsieur Sainte-Gême, that there are only two apartments in the whole building that are habitable, which is why the price has decreased, but that the people living there pay well.

On this occasion, I also send you, via Monsieur J. B. Lafonta, the sum of twelve hundred piastres, including a note of 253 dollars that I received as payment for the rent of the house in town. Madame Goyffon has paid to me the amount of the commission that will be due in France for the transaction. I was hoping to send you an additional 200 gourdes, but I could not recover them. I will before long obtain almost 400 more piastres that are owed to me. I have never found it so difficult to have money as this year. I owe Monsieur Dreux two thousand three hundred piastres including interest. He informed me of his wish to obtain the whole sum at once. So, I prayed him to continue to wait until next year and, for a total of 1,482 dollars, I will meet his request. I

1. There is no mention of who died in Bagen.

only drew sixty-four piastres of my salary for last year and will pay myself the rest before long.[2]

I wrote to you on the 14th of last March. I had just put my letter in the mailbag when I retrieved from the post office, on the same day, the one you had written on the 14th of September. I waited for the occasion of Madame Dreux's visit to reply to it in more detail.

I immediately forwarded to Monsieur Boze the letter you had addressed to him, and I told Monsieur Delmas of your worries about his silence.[3] He wrote asking me to forward to your wife the letter included here. Monsieur le Chevalier Hazeur, as prudent as ever, has also asked me to send in my envelope the letter he wrote to you. Monsieur Latapie was kind enough to agree to take a crate containing 6 bottles of bitter and a pack of wood herb seeds for Madame Sainte-Gême. The crate is unmarked as what it contains is contraband. He will attempt to cautiously pass it through. Madame Dreux promised me that she would give you some seeds of this small fiery pepper. Mademoiselle Dalila married Monsieur Desbois. Marriage did not make her better. She still has poor health. That young lady's family has entrusted me with sending your family and you a thousand marks of friendship. Madame Chevalier Morant is still really annoyed with you and Madame Sainte-Gême for not writing to her, but she and her two daughters asked me to remind you of them. Monsieur Garidel is as angry with you as is Madame Chevalier. He asked me: "How can Sainte-Gême, whom I have the pleasure to be fond of, have forgotten me? I do not write to him because my letter would contain only reproach."

Madame Sainte-Gême is asking for detailed news of all the slaves.[4] I will readily satisfy her request, starting with the oldest. Old Marie-Louise is peacefully living with César who is rejuvenated by her cooking.[5] Big and little Josephs,

2. The recurrent mentions of debt owed by Sainte-Gême to the Dreuxs shows that Dorville was struggling to collect debt and that the plantation did not yield sufficient profit to cover prior debt.

3. Valentin Delmas, the brother of Madame Marguerite Delmas Sainte-Gême, owned a plantation in Pascagoula, Mississippi. The Valentine Delmas House in Pascagoula, constructed in 1812, is no longer extant, but photographs of it can be found in the Historic American Buildings Survey, HABS MS-17, Library of Congress.

4. Although Dorville gives frequent news of enslaved individuals, it is rare to read such a detailed account of the Gentilly enslaved population. The account informs us about the occupations of the enslaved, including the renting out of some of them, generally women. There are mentions of this practice throughout the correspondence.

5. The original reads "La vieille Marie-Louise fait paisiblement chaudière avec César." "Faire chaudière" refers to a person in a port town who ran a house where mariners would get their food cooked. It is also used in old French to mean "live together."

the two Basiles, Hector, Bacchus, and Charles are all good as far as health is concerned and relatively good as far as work is concerned. I am still satisfied with Laurent. I would not like to see him leave the plantation. I made a carter and a ploughman of him. He digs, shovels, and pickaxes well. Catherine is still a little crazy. Nérisse is not doing much. She is sometimes good sometimes bad and, to be frank, she is a mean creature. Amazilie keeps getting pregnant. My doubts about Zaïre's pregnancy were confirmed. She is rented out in town for fifteen piastres a month. Clarisse is also rented for twelve piastres a month. Her child is with her, and he is in good health. Augustin and Honoré are the two greatest rascals I know. They are cowherds part of the day and domestics, gardeners, and egg and poultry sellers the rest of the day.[6] With all that, they often give me the devil. Irma is still in perfect health. Victore, who is now only known as the Spanish gentleman, is also doing well. I take good care to instruct and nourish these two children.[7]

The two tureens remain unsold.[8] I offered them to several planters, with a ten-month or one-year term, but my offers were useless. With no more luck, I tried twice to put them in a lottery. To relieve my conscience, I am pleased to inform you, my dear Monsieur Sainte-Gême, that I purchased a barrel of wine without putting the expense in the accounts. As I used the money from the bitter oranges for this purchase, I had no scruples using the money this way, especially now that I am informing you.

I could not obtain any positive news of Messieurs Ribax and Pageot. Two of the pirates whose arrest I told you about, the captain and the Scottish boatswain, who was also acting as doctor, were condemned to be hanged. The latter was pardoned. The others have had their sentences suspended for two months. I do not know what will happen to them.

6. This comment, and others throughout the correspondence, indicates that the enslaved went to the market to sell the plantation produce. Milk, eggs, poultry, fruit, and vegetables produced on the plantation fed the population of the city. Some of the enslaved thus had access to the city, which made their experience original, halfway between rural and urban slavery.

7. Sometimes referred to as Victor. When he is mentioned, he is associated with Irma, suggesting that he has a different status on the plantation, confirmed by the fact that Dorville takes special care to "instruct" these two children. We do not know whose son Victor was, but the reference to him as the "Spanish gentleman" suggests that he was racially mixed. He could have been Dorville's son, but Dorville does not acknowledge it, contrary to his clear mentions of Irma as his daughter.

8. The frequent references to Dorville's unsuccessful attempts to sell these two tureens are puzzling. He was probably trying to fulfil one of Sainte-Gême's specific requests; hence the importance he gives to these otherwise anecdotal goods.

These days, I must have your small house in town mended by having good blocks put under it. All the old ones are rotten, so the rear of the building touches the ground. I will also have a new fence built around the house in the faubourg. It is in great need of it. The rice I produced is still unsold. It is of such low value at the moment that I am saving it for next year. I hope to rid myself of it with a good profit since the river withdrew very rapidly this year and we are undergoing a drought that will prevent us from producing any for next year.

My family asked me to never forget to mention them when I write to you. Monsieur Lambert is still fond of you. He often comes to the plantation and gives me the pleasure of telling me about the people who no longer come to the plantation. I will not write in this letter everything I have to write to you because I would not have any space left to fulfill my greatest pleasure, that of saluting you. Please accept from me, my dear Monsieur Sainte-Gême, and share among your amiable family, everything respectable and honest that may be offered. Adieu and rest assured that I am always, my dear monsieur Sainte-Gême, your devoted servant.

Auvignac Dorville

[MSS 100, Folder 44] Gentilly, July 19, 1820

This time, my dear Monsieur Sainte-Gême, my letter will not be long because I doubt you will receive it, considering the long voyage it is destined for. Since the departure of *Le Jérôme* on board which Monsieur Latapie and Madame Dreux traveled, not a single vessel has left for Bordeaux, which prevented me from sending to Monsieur J. B. Lafonta the second bill of exchange after the first one, of which he must have acknowledged receipt to you. I am obliged to send it to him through Captain Davis who will land in England and, maybe, go from there to Le Havre if the commerce treaty is signed between the French and the Americans.[1]

Please render me the service of writing to me two or three words every time you receive one of my letters. I always fear they have not reached you. Monsieur Eline died without leaving enough to satisfy all of his creditors. I got 66 dollars for your credit note. The crop this year will not yield as much as last year's. All the slaves are faring well. Nérisse has been feeling much better for some time, and Monsieur Conund hopes to reestablish her health. Speaking of the latter I asked him for his bill. He refused to give it to me, telling me that he wanted to have the pleasure of settling it directly with you. Rereading a copy of my last letter I found out that there was a sentence that had no meaning. It is about what I told you concerning the rents of your house in town. I meant to say that the house was rented for 30 dollars a month but only conditionally and that it would be returned to me when I knew better your desire. Monsieur Lambert is not forgetting you. Monsieur Dreux and his family have entrusted me with a million testimonies of friendship to you and yours. Farewell my dear Monsieur Sainte-Gême. You know everything I can wish for you and your interesting family. I am always your attached and devoted servant.

Auvignac Dorville

P.S. The *Artus* just set her destination for Le Havre and I prefer to seize this occasion.

1. President Monroe's Fourth Annual Message to Congress (November 14, 1820) indicated that negotiations had started but that they had not yet come to a successful conclusion. For more on the United States' international relations during Monroe's term, see Sexton, *Monroe Doctrine.*

[MSS 100, Folder 48] Gentilly, February 5, 1821

My dear Monsieur Sainte-Gême,

It is after eleven months of anticipation that I received, on the 13th of January, your letter dated the 23rd of August 1820. I would have written you more often and mentioned sooner that you appear to forget your interests, had there been a courier.

Monsieur Boze has finally succeeded in obtaining the necessary documents for the claim of your maritime properties seized in 1809 and sold by the Spanish government in Cuba.[1] In order to reach this goal, he needed 200 dollars and has drawn it from me by a note payable to Monsieur Martel, resident of New Orleans. I cleared it as I could not reasonably refuse to accept it. He wrote me that he had sent the paperwork to you, duly certified, and that he was awaiting a new occasion to send you the duplicate of these first documents. He made it known to me as well that he had fulfilled the mission you had given him with Messieurs Danger and Delisle (the former being the tutor of the minor children in the Causse succession, the latter the testamentary executor of the said succession). He also told me that the Messieurs, after having carefully calculated the interests of this sum, had decided to send me the sum that is owed you in order to retrieve the nègre Laurent and that the note for this sum had already been prepared when the heirs opposed this decision. The older son threatened to come here to try to obtain in court the delivery of this nègre without paying anything. I responded to Monsieur Boze that I did not mind the threats of this unfair person and that I was ready and waiting if he dared to make this move and that, anyway, he was not the only one who could travel. I added that he should fear that I might go there myself, armed with good proof, to attack the equivocal probity of his mother and to make her submit to the punishments due to her crime since she is culpable of the offense of forgery. Upon reflection, I see nothing to fear from the impertinent threats of this heir, who is a minor. After all, if I am obliged to defend myself, I will put forward your rights down to the smallest.

1. When the nonnaturalized French citizens, a majority of whom were Saint-Domingue refugees, were expelled from Cuba, all their properties were sequestered by the Spanish authorities in Cuba. Ships Sainte-Gême used for his privateering activities, *Le Masséna* and *L'Impériale,* were among the goods sequestered. In the 1820s, Boze went on a long mission to Cuba to try to retrieve the sum received by the Cuban authorities in payment for Sainte-Gême's sequestered property as well as to collect money from a large number of Sainte-Gême's debtors. See Dessens, *Creole City,* 12–14.

In a little while I will end the business with Monsieur Dreux concerning the plantation. He will be good enough to give me a personal receipt, and furthermore, he will entirely discharge the mortgage he has on it. When I have paid him 1,482.50 dollars, I will do my utmost, by next April, to gain 2,000 gourdes that I will send you, after taking the necessary measures to lose none of it. In my letter of the 28th of May, I spoke to you of the repairs that I must make to the outbuildings at your house in the city. They have been more significant than I believed. They have amounted to 178.56 dollars. They would have been less if I had made them right after your departure. I do not regret having made this expense since it will increase the rent of the house.

I am now working to make a fence with my neighbor Hopkins, who is hardly reasonable.[2] I have had some heated arguments with him concerning his animals. Nevertheless, he does not hasten too much to protect me from them. After having completed what I must, I will take him to court to show him that I am not really a child.

Last year, I repaired the main road of the plantation. The property in front of the slave cabins has been carefully drained and elevated, which has contributed to the good health that they have enjoyed this past summer, and even until the present. Amazilie is finally the mother of a pretty little girl who was born on the 22nd of September last at eleven o'clock at night. As she was sick for a long time before delivering and because this is her first baby, I will spare her until the good weather returns.[3] Then I will rent her out. Instead of Amazilie, Zaïre is now selling the milk because this activity is too profitable to be neglected. I was deceived twice about Zaïre's pregnancy. I thought she was pregnant, but she was only late.[4] Clarisse is still rented out at 12 dollars a month on condition that the person who rents her maintains her child. In two or three months she will enrich you again with another little slave, which means that she will not bring in any rent for some time. Nérisse is well at present. I hope that will continue. Victor

2. The first-person possessive pronoun used here indicates that, as the keeper of the keys, Dorville considered Gentilly his home.

3. Dorville was clearly attentive to the slaves' health, to ensure both their productive and reproductive functions.

4. Again, it is clear that Dorville had an intimate knowledge of the lives of the enslaved and that he carefully monitored the enslaved women's ability to increase the enslaved population of the plantation, as is confirmed by the subsequent comment on Clarisse. The reproductive function was clearly more important than the rent he collected from her work. For the cycles of work and pregnancy, see Cody, "Cycles of Work and of Childbearing," 51–60.

is beginning to serve me at table.[5] He already knows a lot. As for my daughter Irma, she is with Madame Dobévil, who is showing her how to sew.[6] She will remain apprenticed for two years and maybe more, unless, my dear Monsieur Sainte-Gême, unforeseen circumstances bring you back to Louisiana with your family before that time.

I have been selling firewood up until now. I will soon begin working on the harvest of 1821. This year I estimate I will have 38 to 40 thousands of oranges. I have taken more care than usual to preserve them. And I have advertised in the public papers the offer to sell them, packed in barrels, so that they can be exported to the North. But I have not had any requests for them yet. If I succeed, I will not make less than two piastres and a picaillon per hundred, all fees paid.

I hope very sincerely, my dear Monsieur Sainte-Gême, that God may respond to your desires and give good health to Madame, your mother. It is on that condition that you may come to Louisiana. As I hope that your prayers will be answered, I will not send you the balance of my books this year because I hope that, before it ends, I will have the good fortune of doing it in your presence.

I fulfilled your requests and transmitted your friendly salutations. Monsieur le Chevalier Hazeur charged me with telling you the interest he has for you and your amiable family. Madame Beltremieux asked me to tell Madame Sainte-Gême that she was always in her heart. My family is grateful for your memories and offers you a thousand honorable thoughts. I have not had the pleasure of seeing Monsieur Delmas for a year.[7] However, I have had fairly frequent news of him. He is well as is his family.

I just received a letter from Madame Dreux, my old mamma; she tells me that you are supposed to go and see her with your family; that she must return to New Orleans in three years and that she hopes that her part of beast will

5. Dorville sometimes writes the name Victor, sometimes Victore, probably to play with the boy's nickname as the "Spanish gentleman."

6. Madame Dobévil is the wife of Charles Dobévil Dutillet, an infantry captain and native of Paris. AANO, Baptisms, March 15, 1817. Madame Dobévil, as she fancied herself, was by birth Eulalie Villanueva, a New Orleans resident. In a St. Louis Cathedral baptismal record dated April 5, 1818, Constance Dreux, descendant of Mathurin Dreux, is listed as the grandmother of Carlos Thomas Francisco, son of Charles and Eulalie. This letter gives much information about the life of the Gentilly enslaved. We learn about the various situations: some were selling goods at the market, others were rented out, and still others were apprenticed.

7. Madame Sainte-Gême's brother.

have less stench if she carries it with silver money rather than with poor copper coins.[8] She treats me very maternally, so I pay her back with gratitude.

Monsieur Lambert tells me: "Write to the bourgeois that if he thinks of me as I think of him, we have nothing to reproach one another." It is now my turn. Please be kind enough, my dear Monsieur Sainte-Gême, to pay your wife my respectful homage. I pray her to share them with her amiable children. Farewell. Please be always, my dear Monsieur Sainte-Gême, my messenger to the people you love, and believe in the sincere attachment of your devoted servant.

Auvignac Dorville

P.S. I forgot to tell you that my intention is to order, next winter, the wood necessary for the construction of a little house. The habit of occupying the one I now occupy often prevents me from seeing the danger of remaining here.[9] However, my dear Monsieur Sainte-Gême, I will not act until you have agreed.

Madame Lacoste is deceased.[10] She left life with all the resignation of a good Christian. I have not made this known to Madame Dreux to whom I write on this same occasion. Monsieur Dreux will fulfill this terrible duty.

Our mayor is now Monsieur Roufiniac and our governor is Monsieur Robertson, whom you surely know. Monsieur Destoup has promised me that he will write to his parents. Shortly after you departed here, Monsieur Salles went up to the Attakapas. He has ignored our prejudices and married a woman of color.[11] Since then, he has not come to the city.

My letter was written and, to date it, I was waiting for the moment when I put it in the postal bag. In this interval, I received through Monsieur Doussan, recommended by you, the one that you wrote. I will always be willing to please you. How can I manifest, my dear Monsieur Sainte-Gême, enough gratitude to you for the interesting details that you give me about your amiable children?

8. Madame Dreux was not in fact the mother of Auvignac Dorville. He uses the term "mamma" as one of affection. The original "part of beast" (*partie de bête*) evokes the reward (intestines and blood) given to the hounds after a hunt. In this case, the allusion is unclear, except that Madame Dreux manifestly expects to return to Louisiana richer than she was when she left.

9. Several times, Dorville mentions that the "château," as he sometimes calls the big house, is in such a bad condition that it is beyond repair and needs to be replaced by a new one, which he does later. See letter of November 9, 1824.

10. Madame Lacoste was Pélagie Dreux, born in 1776. She married Auguste Robin Lacoste on August 28, 1794. She was the daughter of François Louis Pierre Mathurin Dreux and Jeanne Marie Constance Delorme Hazeur. See AANO, Marriages, August 28, 1794.

11. This is an interesting comment, especially with the use of the possessive pronoun "our," from a man who twice married women of color.

May God grant you a long life as well as to Madame, your spouse, so that you may enjoy the happiness of seeing them grow, embellish, and always enjoy happiness.

I really believe that you are mocking me when you say that I live cheaply. I assure you that I live honorably and that I would live still better, that is to say that I would eat more, if my appetite had not deserted me long ago. It is still worse at this moment when a cold with complications makes me suffer much.

I owe you more thanks than you owe me. So, my dear Monsieur Sainte-Gême, if you continue to thank me, you will make me an insolvent debtor.

The poor Castaing de Luscan died last summer of an insignificant fever.[12] It is fear that killed him.

Monsieur Lambert is still fond of you. He is rejuvenating although he says that he has a foot in the grave. I saw him perfectly content 32 times last year and we have killed 32 deer. A beautiful pack of good hounds is waiting for you here. Good-bye my dear Monsieur Sainte-Gême.

12. Justin Castaing was born in Castres, in Tarn-et-Garonne. He migrated to New Orleans, recommended to Dorville by Sainte-Gême. AANO, Marriages, May 11, 1820; Baptisms, August 31, 1821.

[MSS 100, Folder 50] Gentilly, March 24, 1821

My Dear Monsieur Sainte-Gême,

Included is a note for 1,665 piastres or 8,325 francs, at a sixty-day term, drawn up, as you can see, by Monsieur Roumage, a merchant of New Orleans for Monsieur Courtois in Toulouse, a man, who I was assured is very well known in this city.[1] I have had this note at 5 francs 55, which makes a benefit of 165 dollars that you will make on the 1,500 dollars that I have accounted to Monsieur Roumage, with a payment of 1,300 dollars and a note of 200 dollars payable on the 15th of the month of next May. Ships going to France are so infrequent that the departure of the *Jerôme,* which I am benefiting from, has rushed me and prevented me from adding a few entries that would have augmented this little sum. I could have had some notes for Paris at 5 francs 60, but you would have been obliged to go to Toulouse and perhaps lose 1% on these notes, which made me prefer the one you will receive. I will send no more gourdes.[2] The insurance they require, the freight, and the commission rob any benefit that they could yield and even a part of the capital. I wrote on the 5th of last February, and I told you about many business matters. The plantation is entirely free of mortgage. Monsieur Dreux was satisfied with 1,352 dollars and 60 escalins.[3] There was an error of 100 dollars that was corrected. Monsieur Boze has not written me at all for a long time, which makes me hope that he has informed Messieurs Danger and Delisle of what I think about the business of the nègre Laurent and that the Messieurs have talked the Causse heirs into reason.

Despite all the care that I put in preserving the oranges, I have lost at least one third, and I have made only 511.20 dollars. I still have some to sell. The orange trees will not produce at all this year. A severe cold that we experienced damaged them. I do not know which direction I should choose in order to balance this year's revenue with those of the previous years since our country has changed much in the past two years. Nothing is selling here. Everything is given away. Life is costly. The flour of the best quality is at 2–4 dollars; a great part of the sugar is not consumed; cotton is without value; the beautiful firewood at 4 dollars and 5 dollars a cord; hay for the north at ¾ a pound. However, if the

1. Another example of Dorville's tendency to use several different currencies interchangeably, as the exchange rate to the franc shows clearly that what he calls "piastres" is in fact dollars.

2. An old form of French money, which Dorville uses interchangeably with dollars and piastres. It is still in use in Haiti today.

3. He uses "escalins" interchangeably with "cents."

weather blesses me, I will produce a lot of the latter. The inhabitants of the north will perhaps become tired of losing money on their merchandise. The thing on which I count the most is the milk. I made sure my cows would have a lot of little calves next winter.

I have reclaimed from Monsieur Dupuis 100 piastres for his part of the 200 that Monsieur Boze sent me to obtain the documents that he sent to you. Monsieur Dupuis alleged he had had roughly a third of these claims that you know well, and only wanted to remit to me 66.75 dollars, demanding a receipt from me, although I had shown him all the letters from Monsieur Boze.

The slaves are still doing well. Amazilie's little girl is doing very well. Clarisse is going to be a wet nurse soon.[4] Irma is beginning to sew.

Otherwise, my dear Monsieur Sainte-Gême, please seize the first occasion to give me news that you have received the note and to tell me if you are satisfied with the manner in which I forward you your funds.

Monsieur Lambert is still fond of you. He wants you, Madame, your spouse, and her interesting children to remember him. Adieu, my dear Monsieur Sainte-Gême. Please extend the thousands of my most honorable and respectful thoughts to your spouse and to your entire amiable family. I am still your affectionate and devoted servant.

Auvignac Dorville

4. This is another indication that Dorville took advantage of all situations to make money through the enslaved women of the plantation.

[MSS 100, Folder 52] Gentilly, 22 May 1821

I just received, my dear Monsieur de Sainte-Gême, on the 14th instant, your letter of the 10th of February last in which you acknowledged receipt of the letter I sent you on the 19th of July 1820.[1] If I remained six months and a few days without giving you news of Louisiana, it is the lack of transportation opportunity that deprived me of this pleasure. I must admit, however, that there were one or two ships bound for Le Havre, but I never knew about them. Since then, I wrote you, on the 5th of February 1821, a long letter in which I redeemed myself for the lost time. And one more on the 24th of March of which I sent you a duplicate on the 15th of April last. In these letters, I told you about various business matters and in this one, I could expand on the business matters, but I am reserving this pleasure for the next accounting when I will seize the opportunity to send you a summary of the state of your earnings and expenses in Louisiana. You would receive a report as detailed as the one I sent you on the 31st of August 1819 if I did not fear that the package might be too voluminous. If you want it so, however, I am always ready to please you.

Your mother's health is not good, and she requires your presence. I can only approve the decision you have made to devote all your care to her. The waters of the fountain of Bagen, as you tell me, my dear Monsieur Sainte-Gême, rival those of the Mississippi. I even think they surpass them after hearing of the favorable effect they had on your wife. Before I move forward, please allow me to congratulate her, begging her to accept my respectful homages and to agree to share them with Mademoiselle Hermina. I do not forget my old comrade Edgar, to whom I send a thousand marks of friendship. I send sincere kisses to the charming little Henriette and her three little brothers. To come back to the fountain of Bagen, I think its waters only produce boys. If you received the letters I mentioned above, you must know about the mistake I had made about Zaïre's pregnancy. Clarisse gave birth to a little boy who survived only eleven days. He was taken away by lockjaw after three days of suffering. Amazilie is rented out. Clarisse will be before long. All the slaves are faring well, except for Nérisse who suffers, from time to time, bouts of her illness, although they are less frequent than before. A woman who is an expert in those diseases has

1. This sentence gives measure of the delay in the delivery of the letters (six months for Sainte-Gême to acknowledge receipt of Dorville's letter and three months for Sainte-Gême's letter to reach Dorville) and explains the irregularity of the exchanges.

been treating her for a few days and she promised me that, in three months, she would have perfectly recovered.[2]

In the package from Monsieur Boze, which you told me was in the hands of Monsieur Lafonta, you must have seen that the business about Laurent is not over yet. I wrote to you about it. Monsieur Boze has not given me any news in a long time, and I do not know how to account for this silence. I will write to him whenever there is an opportunity of transport to St Yago and I will tell him about Messieurs Danger and Delisle.[3] Monsieur Boze probably knows what these Messieurs think and what they definitively wish.

My family was extremely touched by your memories and asked me to send you their greetings, as well as the most honest and respectful thoughts to Madam, your wife, and to Mademoiselle Hermina. Monsieur Lambert is still fond of you. He is starting to realize that he is no longer 25.

Adieu. Until the next occasion. Meanwhile, please be, my dear Monsieur Sainte-Gême, the presenter of my respectful sentiments to your amiable families and believe in my sincerest attachment.

From your devoted servant
Auvignac Dorville

P.S. Monsieur Dreux has caused much worry to his family, and he has been very sick. He is convalescent at the moment. Madame Chevalier Morant was about to lose her sight, but she is doing slightly better at the moment. Clémentine is still unmarried despite the richness of her character and the charms she possesses.[4]

2. Dorville apparently resorted to a healer after Dr. Conund failed to cure Nérisse. Although we do not have details on the woman mentioned here, it shows how medical knowledge was shared between doctors and nonprofessionals.

3. "St Yago" is the spelling he always uses for Santiago de Cuba. It was the current spelling among Francophones at the time and Jean Boze uses the same throughout his correspondence to Sainte-Gême.

4. Clémentine was Chevalier Morant's daughter.

[MSS 100, Folder 53] Gentilly, July 14, 1821

I wrote to you, my dear Monsieur Sainte-Gême, on the 23rd of May last, and I promised to send you an overview of your revenues and expenses here; not to bother you with a detailed account that would be too long, I tell you that I have made, since the month of August 1819 and until now, 8,400 dollars and some piastres, which have been used on different things as you are going to see.

The capital and the interest paid to Monsieur Dreux	3,652 dollars
What I sent you on two different occasions	2,700 dollars
Monsieur Boze's note of which I have spoken to you about	123 dollars
Monsieur Dupuis remitted 66.75 dollars to me for his part	
	6,475 dollars
The repairs that I made on the outbuildings in the city	178.50 dollars
Which gives a total of dollars	6,653.50

without counting the part of my salary, my food; the taxes for the city, the parish, and the state; the apothecary, the blacksmith, the wheelwright; and many other small expenses that appear to be nothing until they are all taken together.

You will undoubtedly find, my dear Monsieur Sainte-Gême, that I have earned very little during the past two years but that is a consequence of the small proceeds the planters obtain from their work, since I may have worked more, in proportion, these past two years than from the 19th of March 1818 to the 17th of August 1819.

Monsieur Boze wrote me on the 15th of April last. He did not speak of the business of the nègre Laurent, but he told me that he would remain in St Yago de Cuba until you have acknowledged receipt of the packages that he sent you. After that, he will then return to New Orleans, at least if his presence there is no longer required for your interests. I wrote him on the 15th of May that you had received his dispatches and I urged him to see Messieurs Danger and Delisle and to tell them that I was disposed to amicably terminate the matter with them, and that the nègre would be at their disposal as soon as they would give me the 800 and some piastres that the Causse succession owes you; I will probably receive some news from him before long and I will give you some in turn.

Monsieur Lafon, property owner on Chef Menteur, died.[1] His land has been divided and sold to several individuals who want to establish themselves there and who will indubitably demand that I provide them with a pathway, which I will not do with any speed because it will cover nearly a league in a place that is not easy and because I have so few workers. My neighbor, Mr. Hopkins, has finally decided to have his fence built. It will divide our two properties. He is working on it at the present.

As soon as I have earned a thousand gourdes, I will send them to you, gradually, as you want me to, but it will not be soon. You know, my dear Monsieur Sainte-Gême, that the planters customarily earn the biggest part of their revenues at the beginning of the year.

Mademoiselle Hermina must be, at present, back with your family. I am sure that the debt in caresses of the pretty little Henriette and her little brothers must have been well augmented since her return, and that Madame, your spouse, must also have felt how sweet it is to be reunited with one's children after having been separated from them for such a long time. Please offer her, as well as Mademoiselle Hermina, my most honorable and respectful thoughts, my dear Monsieur Sainte-Gême, and send proof of my friendship to my comrade Edgar. If he sometimes writes to you and if my request is not too indiscreet, it will give me pleasure if you send me some of his letters.

The slaves are all still faring well.

Monsieur le Chevalier Hazeur, Monsieur Villanueva, Monsieur Dreux, Monsieur Lambert, and my family ask me to recall them to you. As for me, I am, my dear Monsieur Sainte-Gême, your devoted servant.

Auvignac Dorville

P.S. There are a lot of grosbeaks this year; the deer have not diminished in number although we remove some from time to time. We have killed some since the beginning of the year, which enrages Valery who is still at New Orleans.

1. Bartélémy Lafon was a notable engineer, architect, and surveyor, and it has been suggested that he was also a privateer and pirate associated with Jean Lafitte. He was born in Villepinte, France. He was interred on September 29, 1820. AANO, Interments.

[MSS 100, Folder 56] Gentilly, February 4, 1822

My dear monsieur Sainte-Gême,

I acknowledge receipt of your letter of the 21st of May, which I received five months and a few days after you dated it. I have no doubt that your letters are strongly neglected in Bordeaux by the persons in charge of sending them to me. Indeed, is it possible, my dear Monsieur Sainte-Gême, that you did not take advantage of several ships that departed from Bordeaux and arrived here recently, to let me know whether you received my letter of the 24th of March 1821, its duplicate copy, and the drafts I sent to you? Since then, I wrote to you in vain on the 23rd of May and on the 14th of July, expecting you to reassure me about the drafts I am mentioning. The *Jérôme,* which is bringing Madame Dreux back here, has been expected for a long time. We are worried at her delay, but she will arrive soon, I hope, and I will be happy to kiss my good mamma. She will give me news from you.

I intended to summarize Monsieur Boze's correspondence to me. But one of the triplicate copies that I just received and have included in this letter, will let you know what stage he has managed to reach and where he stands now concerning that thief Don Pepe Lara. And also, what Messieurs Danger and Delisle have caused us to hope concerning Laurent.[1]

You are asking me if it would be expensive to have a house built in brick and my answer is yes. But it would be less costly for you than for anyone else considering that most of the wood would be produced at the plantation. As for the bricks and metal hinges that you may send, I think they would be less expensive if you purchased them here, especially the latter.

I have already felled the wood necessary to build a small house for myself. To spare money, I will do everything I can myself. Last year, the house suffered several tremors. From June to September, we had really unusual weather: almost constant rain and episodes of wind that made the tide rise six times to such a point that no planter had ever known before. It spoiled our crops slightly and damaged our pastures. A harsh winter, on top of that, caused a great number of our animals to suffer and perish. Thanks to some eighty carts of hay, I augmented the feed for the livestock on the plantation. I deem myself fortunate

1. For details on the business conducted by Boze in Cuba, see the letters he sent to Saint-Gême between 1820 and 1828. Ste-Gême Family Papers, MSS 100, folders 43–117.

for having lost, until now, only nine cows, including 6 old ones, 3 oxen, and 12 or 15 calves.[2]

I can tell you that our city is shaping up nicely. Streets are being paved, and beautiful lampposts, built on the model of those of Paris, have been hung in the center and light it up well. It is now compulsory to install *banquettes* in the Faubourg Marigny.[3] I was the first one to comply with the order passed. This area has been gaining favor ever since the fort was demolished and the barracks sold.

As I had foreseen and wrote to you about earlier, the buyers of the Chef Menteur land asked me to open the pathway from La Vacherie. I partly opened it from one end to the other and will work a little on it every year. I hope they will be satisfied.

As for Destoup, his character is so changed that I no longer recognize him. He told me he had written to his uncle but some grudge he seems to hold against this relative may well have made him slightly alter the truth concerning what he told me. I would not be surprised to see him return home. He is homesick.

I gave Monsieur Cadet Mouton the message you entrusted me with concerning his godson. Some endorsements recently occasioned a loss of sixteen to seventeen thousand gourdes for him, which made him respond not too positively to what I asked on your behalf. If he finally decides to give something, I will send it to you next month, together with the modest revenues of last year. Poor Castaing died in Mouton's home and the latter had to pay for his burial. The unfortunate has left so little that I do not know if the succession will suffice to pay for the death certificate his relatives are asking for.

Two or three days ago, I left Monsieur le Chevalier Hazeur in the disposition of writing to you. He told me: "In case I cannot do it, to ensure Monsieur Sainte-Gême, my niece, and her children, of my most sincere attachment."

Around the 20th of July last, a sunstroke I had on my head almost left the plantation without a guardian. I remained sick almost two months. In the meantime, your interests also suffered from it as I could not take care of my work. All the slaves are faring well, no one even suffers from the slightest cold. Since

2. Louisiana agriculture depended on the extreme weather conditions encountered. The location of the plantation and relatively small production it yielded made it still more sensitive to climatic incidents. See, for instance, Dessens, *Creole City*, 31–34.

3. At this time in New Orleans, sidewalks were called *banquettes*. New Orleans was then undergoing significant urban improvement. See Dessens, *Creole City*, 79–86.

she took the treatment from the woman that I told you about, Nérisse has not complained about her ordinary disease. I think she is cured.

Monsieur Delmas has not come here in a long time. I have had news from time to time and he was faring well. Monsieur Lambert is still fond of you. He recalls himself to your memory and to that of Madame, your spouse. My family has asked me not to forget to send you their respects.

I am extremely touched by what you send me from your amiable families. Please give them the respectful homages of the one who still is your attached and devoted servant.

Auvignac Dorville

P.S. A ship that arrived here from Bordeaux has announced to us that the *Jérôme* had left 24 hours before her, but we still have not heard from the *Jérôme.*

[MSS 100, Folder 59] Gentilly, May 21, 1822

My dear Monsieur Sainte-Gême,

Difficulties that would be too long to write about prevented me from sending you the included sum of 10,200 francs in one note, which Mr Vincent Nohlte is holding in Paris. I obtained these notes at 5 fr 10 cts thanks to Desbois, Monsieur Dreux's son-in-law.

From 14 July 1821 to 16 May 1822	
Benefits	3,439.25 dollars
Expenses	1,463.93 dollars
Balance	1,975.32 dollars

NB: As I cannot have notes for less than 2,000 dollars, I borrowed 50 dollars for a few days while, in my balance, there is an error of 25.22 dollars that I could not correct.

Madame, your spouse, will be sad to learn that poor Basile has been suffering from consumption. Monsieur Conund told me, as did Monsieur Chabert, a doctor with an excellent reputation here, that only nature's efforts could save him because this disease comes from an old vice. It is in his blood and could not be completely eradicated when he was treated, which happened 2 or 3 times. However, he has been much better for 15 or 20 days. He is taking syrup for syphilis, as well as milk and plants. I really wish to see him cured. His absence would leave a void on the plantation.[1] From one moment to the next, I expect that Laurent will be taken by Messieurs Danger and Delisle. Monsieur Boze writes to me often and he tells me that they will comply with your request without delay, once the Causse minor children have cleared the debts they contracted to acquire slaves. In his letter, which I forwarded to you, you must have seen that Monsieur Boze requested José Lara's notes be sent to him. I did as he wished, and he acknowledged receipt, telling me that Monsieur Jean-Jacques Bonnes, wishing to prove to you that he is still your friend, has agreed to be the intermediary in this business with José Lara, to make him acknowledge the justice of your claim and to please you whenever he can.

1. This sentence shows how difficult it is to interpret the concern the Sainte-Gêmes and Dorville expressed for the enslaved. Madame Sainte-Gême will be "sad" to learn about Basile's disease, but Dorville adds that his death would leave a void on the plantation, which may either mean that his manpower would be missed or that he was an important figure among the enslaved.

He also wrote to me about his claims against Monsieur Dallest. As nothing has been decided yet, I am waiting for him to give me good news to be able to communicate them to you in turn. According to your wishes, I told him about the letter you were supposed to write to him concerning your settlement with José Lara.

My good mamma finally arrived on the 21st of February. She gave me the letter you had entrusted her with. I will tell you about her later. Through your letter, I learnt about the wish of Madame, your spouse, to have the plantation house entirely repaired. I am sorry to tell you that this is utterly impossible. It is in such a state of rot that, even with a lot of money, we could make only bad repairs. I hope that I will have the pleasure, my dear Monsieur Sainte-Gême, to show you in the spring that my opinion is not exaggerated. Expecting this happy moment, I will try to build the small house I told you about, to accommodate you. But for that, I need your permission. Until now, I have only had the timber felled.

As I write to you above, my good mamma arrived here on the 21st of February after a long and painful crossing. From Madame Latapie, to whom she wrote from Guadeloupe, you must have learned about the storm she weathered in the Bay of Biscay.[2] She is faring well and has kept her usual amiability in depicting for me the happy days she spent with you. She told me: "Just imagine, my friend, a picture of the perfect unity of this amiable family, well beyond everything that can be said. Monsieur Sainte-Gême is called Poulou. Everyone there resembles him. Marguerite, Hermina, Edgar, Henriette and her little brothers are all my children." In short, I would never finish my letter if I told you everything that proves her attachment to you. All this made me wish I could witness this for a moment but, as it is impossible, I ask you, my dear Monsieur Sainte-Gême, to please tell all these amiable persons the pleasure all the honorable things you told me about them gave me and to attest to them my sincere and respectful devotion. Madame Dreux told me the tragic events you experienced. What can we do against Providence? It placed us on earth only for a moment. Happy are those who depart with a pure conscience and unhappy those who have regrets!

Long before I received your letter, Monsieur Dupuis had left for France. I strongly doubt he will take the trouble of visiting you, although he told me he intended to. This man is a villain who probably does not like me much because I wrote him a not too gentle letter that he might show you, if he visits you after

2. This demonstrates Louisiana's connection with the other territories of the Americas, especially the Caribbean. For more on this, see Dessens, *Creole City,* 140–148.

all. I have not yet had the pleasure of seeing Monsieur Villanueva. As soon as I do, I will pass your message on to him.

Enclosed is the death certificate of poor Castaing. Monsieur Jumonville, for whom he worked, owed him, and still owes his family, some fifteen or sixteen gourdes that I have been unable to retrieve.[3] If you can make the advance of this sum to these unfortunate persons, I will ask for this sum and will spend it as you wish.

Following your recommendation concerning the young man named Capdeville, I went to see him. He sometimes comes to the plantation and is hoping to be employed in a cotton press, but it will not be until next year. In the meantime, he is well and is managing a refreshment stall, which gives him enough to live on.

In your letter of the 21st of May, you told me that someone wanted you to make a debt recovery of 500 dollars from Monsieur Durive. I obtained information and was told that he had nothing. I spoke twice to Monsieur Cadet Mouton about his godson without being able to obtain a positive answer. I told him I was writing to you, but he still has not told me anything.

Monsieur Garidel has not been in good health for two years. He has changed so much that you would not recognize him. He spent some time on the other side of the lake and I learned that he was feeling slightly improved.[4]

My father and my brothers have entrusted me with offering you a thousand honest thoughts. I think that Monsieur Lambert has visited a fountain of youth. He looks rejuvenated to me. He often tells me: "I would have much pleasure in seeing the bourgeois again. When he returns, we can entertain him now that we have made some good discoveries and that we have good dogs. And it is never too late to flush when he is with us." He asked me to tell you that he is still fond of you.

If we were closer neighbors, you would not have had to take pains to replace the four dogs you lost. I have one of the most beautiful packs in the country. You would have pleased me by choosing those that suited you. I hope you will give

3. Again, this suggests how interconnected New Orleans and France were through the French-speaking community of Louisiana. The next paragraph, about Capdeville, as well as the pain Dorville takes in assisting migrants from France recommended by Sainte-Gême, confirms this and informs us about the migratory circuits to Louisiana.

4. Juan Ambrosio Garidel was a native of Assion, Canton de Vans, department of Ardèche in France. At the time of his death, he was a resident of the city of New Orleans. AANO, Funerals, February 25, 1823. It was common for New Orleanians to spend some time out of the city for health reasons.

me the pleasure of believing that I remain, my dear Monsieur Sainte-Gême, your sincere and attached servant.

Auvignac Dorville[5]

P.S. All the slaves are faring well, except for Basile, as I already told you. My poultry is superb, with many ducks, a few turkeys, about fifty geese, and more than two hundred hens, two thirds of which are white.

I did not want to have this document legalized by the French consul because this one, added to the other, would have cost 4 dollars which are thus spared to the unfortunate who want it.[6]

5. This letter has a duplicate copy. Both are almost exactly the same except for two line breaks and the addition of "déjà" in the PS.

6. This is written on a loose piece of paper included in the letter and most certainly concerns Castaing's death certificate.

[MSS 100, Folder 61] Gentilly, July 18, 1822

I just learned, my dear Monsieur Sainte-Gême, that a ship is leaving tomorrow for Le Havre, and I am seizing the brief moment I have to confirm that I sent you drafts on the 21st of May last and to tell you the pleasure you would give me if you acknowledged receipt of them as soon as possible if you have received them.

There is no vessel from Bordeaux to here or from here to Bordeaux and there is not likely to be any for a long time.[1] So, if you write to me, I advise you to send your letters to persons you may know in Le Havre who will then bring them to me. I must tell you how necessary your presence here would be for your interests. I remember hearing you say sometimes, my dear Monsieur Sainte-Gême, that the eye of the master fattens the horse.[2] No one agrees more with this than me. For this reason, I allow myself to advise you to sacrifice, for some time, the connections that keep you in France and to yield to my requests, or rather to your interests.

Madame widow Dreux, Monsieur Dreux and his wife asked me to send a thousand marks of friendship to you, to Madame, your wife, and to Mademoiselle Hermina. Soon Madame Desbois, the daughter of Monsieur and Madame Dreux, will probably cause them to shed many tears. This unfortunate young lady is in the same condition as her sister, Madame Bermudez, was, and the doctors have already worn out all their knowledge.[3] In my letter of the 21st of May, I told you that poor Basile is consumptive. He is not doing better although he does not suffer much from his chest. But his legs, feet, and arms are swollen. All the other slaves are faring well. Clarisse and Amazilie are both pregnant and far into their pregnancies. These past days, we had an episode of very severe weather. I had 23 acres of beautiful corn ready to harvest and it has been damaged.

Please, my dear monsieur Sainte-Gême, give your amiable and interesting families my most honest and respectful thoughts and believe me to be, my dear Monsieur Sainte-Gême, your sincere and devoted servant.

Auvignac Dorville

P.S. Since I last wrote to you, I have not heard from Monsieur Boze.

1. The summer and early fall were seasons when exchanges between New Orleans and France were at best scarce, due to the yellow fever epidemics and storms that plagued the city. Ships resumed service once the hurricane season had ended.

2. This expression means that profits arise from the attention of the master and suggests that Sainte-Gême's plantation would benefit from his presence.

3. Desiree Dreux Bermudez, married to Toussaint Bermudez, was Marguerite Delmas Sainte-Gême's niece. AANO, Interments, August 27, 1822.

[MSS 100, Folder 62] Gentilly, October 4, 1822

You have perhaps received, my dear Monsieur Sainte-Gême, my three letters written on the 21st of May and the 18th of July, before I received the two you sent on the 22nd of March and the 8th of July. They reached me five or six days ago. The last was remitted to me by Monsieur Sémiac, the young man who you recommended to me. He arrived safely and fled from the city where the disease that mostly affects foreigners causes them to pay with their lives the tribute to this country.[1] This young man is with me on the plantation and will only leave when this ugly sickness that is terrible this year will have ceased its ravages, which we expect with the arrival of frost.

I refer to my two letters from the 22nd of March in which I included a note for 10,200 francs as well as two death certificates for Castaing that I sent you at the same time.

Monsieur Boze, with whom I correspond frequently, recommends to me, each time that he writes to me, to not forget to tell you what he is doing, and to remind you of the patience and obstinacy that he is exercising in his pursuit of your debtors. Well, I will tell you that, with the aid of Monsieur Jean-Jacques Bonne, he has succeeded in negotiating a new firm settlement with Monsieur José Lara. This does not change the total sum this rascal owes you but only postpones his payments as first arranged. His payments will be as follows, according to four notes that I have in my hands: the 1st of 800 dollars payable during the month of June 1823, the 2nd for 800 dollars during the month of August 1824, the 3rd of 500 dollars during the month of March 1825, and the 4th of 633.90 dollars during the month of August 1825. Without counting two notes of 200 dollars each that Monsieur Boze has had made to his order and payable last August, which gives 3,133.90 dollars. He writes me that these amounts will be credited to your account as soon as they are paid. Poor old Boze has to defend himself against Monsieur Dallest who is angry at him for legally pursuing the debt of 3,546 dollars he owes to you. Monsieur Dallest, in turn, personally attacked Monsieur Boze to be reimbursed for the amount of 3,500 dollars for room and board. He tells me that he has no fear on this subject, that in this country one cannot be put in prison for debts, and that the claims of Monsieur Dallest are as imaginary as they are extraordinary and arbitrary. Despite the continuous

1. Dorville is here referring to yellow fever, which plagued the city in the summer and affected many of the newcomers not yet acclimated. See Trask, *Fearful Ravages.*

annoyances to which he has submitted Monsieur Robin Despaigne, he still has been unable to obtain the 48 dollars that you loaned to this Monsieur who continually promises to repay it at the next harvest. On the 8th of June last, he sent to Monsieur Dumas, your debtor by some 380 dollars, an order from the mayor to go to the tribunal and acknowledge his signature and pay, or to renew his bond that is 14 years old by setting a new date and interest rate. I have sent him, at his request, the paperwork that is necessary to the effect of claiming what Messieurs Bonafond and Thomas Macary owe you. The original paperwork of the first has been taken from him. It is his current account that I sent him. He wanted me to write two letters about Laurent, one to Messieurs Danger and Delisle and one to his little masters, hoping to convince them to keep their promise more promptly. For a long time, I have refused to do these things, for fear that these Messieurs would suspect something, and thus justly accuse me of using cunning in this business with them. His requests have been repeated so often that I have yielded, recommending him to take good care in the way in which he would forward these letters. This business does not worry me. In whatever manner that it turns, we will always have what we must have. Concerning the claim that Monsieur Boze has against Monsieur Macary, he writes me that he had the kindness to warn you that this debtor made journeys from Nantes and Bordeaux to St Yago de Cuba, as you had an interest in these loads and supercargoes, and that you never responded to him about this matter. He complains much for not having received any letter from you in a very long time, of your indifference to being paid by your debtors, and mostly of your laziness in writing, observing that it harms your interests. Do not be angry at me, my dear Monsieur Sainte-Gême, for the freedom with which I write to you. I would not write this way if you had not given me permission to be honest with you.

I have fulfilled with Madame Dreux the amiable mission that you have charged me with by giving her the letters from Madame Latapie meant for her. What I told her on your part occasioned a charming gaiety. Also, she tells me: "Does it not mean, my son, that I am worth something, if so many deserving people remember me in France? You have seen when I arrived how I was caressed. Judges and priests have come to give me compliments on my return." The conversation about your household lasted a long time and my good mamma entrusted me to send a thousand kisses for you all, without forgetting the compliments for your priest, surgeon, and neighbors &c.

Monsieur and Madame Dreux have charged me with recalling them to your good memories. They are still crying for the loss of their daughter Dalila. This young person has been dead for nearly a month.[2]

The French bricks cost here 156% of their value in France. Everything calculated, they would cost more than if you bought them here, and they will cost even less if they are made at the plantation. As for the metal hinges, I doubt that those that you could send could benefit you more than those that I could buy here where they are abundant on the market. But one indispensable thing that you must buy in France is some roof tiles. Buy more rather than less in order to not lack any. If any remain after the building has been constructed, we can sell them. Selling some is easy and relatively advantageous in New Orleans.[3] On the subject of building, I must tell you that the corner that was occupied by Monsieur Labarrure and for which Monsieur Hégniel once wanted 8,000 dollars was offered to me last winter for 3,000 dollars.

The LaHeuse succession is insolvent. This is why I will not charge Monsieur Dispan with your claim against it. Monsieur Cuvillier, the attorney that you know well, who traveled to Pointe Coupée soon after your departure, took care of this claim, but he did not pursue it, seeing that there was no money.

I am speaking again, my dear Monsieur Sainte-Gême, of the notes that I have sent to you, and I ask you to acknowledge that you have received them. If you have received my letters, I hope things are mended with me because they have proved to you that I have taken as much advantage as I could to speak with you on the rare occasions that have occurred. I make amends today, and I have hope of doing so often, now that the treaty of commerce has been concluded between America and France for the next two years.[4] In my earlier letters, I forgot to tell you that I again lost a lot of animals, at the beginning of spring, when grass started growing. The venom came on the plantation in the wake of winter. I am now cutting hay, and I estimate that I will sell nearly 200 carts of it. Oranges are in relatively good quantity this year, but they are not as beautiful as usual.

2. Petronille Dalila Dreux died of liver disease on August 22, 1822, and was buried August 27, 1822. AANO, Funerals, August 27, 1822.

3. Several of Dorville's letters have shown that goods were transported from Louisiana to France. Interestingly, this note indicates that the Atlantic commercial connections went both ways across the ocean.

4. This commercial trade agreement controlling the customs duties on products exchanged between the United States and France was signed on June 24, 1822, and ratified by France on November 6 of that same year.

I will soon be occupied with finding lodging in the city for Amazilie and Clarisse so that they can deliver there.[5] All the slaves are well except Basile who is decidedly consumptive and in a state of suffering that does not give him a moment of relief. I flattered myself into believing that I would see him recover, but at the present, with chagrin, I expect from moment to moment that he will pass. . . .

I made inquiries to obtain Dominique Lareye's death certificate. On my way to mailing this letter, I will include it and let you know how much it costs.

Monsieur Lambert asked me to tell you that he hopes at the present to have the pleasure of your embrace and of having you kill a few deer before going to the realm of moles.[6] He asks me to remind all of you of him.

It is time for me, my dear Monsieur Sainte-Gême, to take my turn and ask you to send on my part a thousand honorable and respectful thoughts to your amiable family. I have been extremely sensitive to your agreeable memories. So, I do not know how to express my gratitude. But always receive the reassurance of the sincere attachment with which I am, my dear Monsieur de Sainte-Gême, your devoted servant.

Auvignac Dorville

October 5th

P.S. Please remember, when you journey to join us, my dear Monsieur Ste-Gême, to bring me two dozen scythes reinforced with sticks like the first ones you sent me. They should not be as long as they would be too long. Two feet of length is what is good for this country.

I will also make a request that I beg you to satisfy if I am not going beyond what discretion permits. French-bred retrievers or setters are rare here and I would like to have one. So, if you encounter one to your taste, I would be in your debt if you purchased it on my behalf for up to 150 francs. I would pay it off when I have the pleasure to embrace you.[7]

5. Dorville's care to make sure the two enslaved women deliver their babies in the best conditions possible is, again, indication of the importance of the natural growth of the enslaved population of the plantation.

6. "Going to the realm of moles" means to be interred.

7. Dorville's requests (scythes and dogs) may seem anecdotal, but they attest to the importance of transatlantic exchanges, when two decades had passed since the transfer of Louisiana to the United States.

Monsieur Sémiac, who seems to be a good hunter and be knowledgeable about dogs, told me that it is possible to obtain what we want by asking Monsieur Lassus in Monréjo.[8] If it is not too difficult, please bring two instead of one because there is much to earn here, especially with dogs as strong as Cupidon. I am saving two retrievers for you, which are beautiful, and that is the least of their merit.

Please find enclosed Dominique Larey's death certificate. I will send you the other one on the first occasion. I spare the unfortunate parents the 20 francs it would have cost to have these documents legalized by the French Consul.

8. This is a misspelling of Montréjeau, a small town close to Saint-Gaudens. The de Lassus family still lives in Montréjeau, at the Chateau de Valmirande.

[MSS 100, Folder 63] Gentilly, October 20, 1822

I wrote to you on the 4th instant, my dear Monsieur Sainte-Gême, and my letter is in the mailbag and the ship is still here. I have time to let you know that Monsieur and Madame Dreux suffered another terrible loss 5 days ago. Poor Dreux is no longer. A pernicious fever took him away after nine days of sickness. Despite her courage, Madame Dreux is extremely affected. I consider with apprehension where such constant and repeated sorrows three times within five weeks can lead her. For the son of her daughter Emérite, to whom she was like a mother, also died, at the same time as Madame Desbois (her daughter Dalila). Everyone regrets the loss of the poor young people. With his education, his intelligence, his faultless behavior, he would have honored his country someday. I loved him like a brother, and I weep for him too. I was his friend, and I was not the only one. All the best people in town and in the vicinity showed his parents how strongly they sympathized with them in their sorrow by forming a decent and long procession to pay their last tributes to him. This yellow fever we have here, a plague and the terror for all foreigners, is terrible this year. We have never seen as many people die as in the past month and a half. It wreaks havoc in almost the whole state, in Bayou Sara, Pointe Coupée, Baton Rouge, etc. I make sure that Monsieur Sémiac stays with me, so that he will not be indisposed by the fever, hopefully. Of the two bakers who came over here with him, one—the one called Binos—died the day before last. The other has been really sick, but he is now out of danger. I ask you, as always, my dear Monsieur Sainte-Gême, to pass my respectful thoughts to your amiable family and to still believe me your sincere and attached servant.

Auvignac Dorville

P.S. I forgot to tell you in my previous letter that the death certificate for the family of Dominique Larey cost 1.50 dollars. I will send you a second one by the next ship.

10th of November 1822: You will receive the present letter via Monsieur Sémiac's brother.

I think the ship is finally departing today.

[MSS 100, Folder 66] Gentilly, January 16, 1823

Monsieur Davis, my dear Monsieur Sainte-Gême, had already left Le Havre when your letter arrived there but he received it and delivered it to me. Only then did I learn that you had received the notes you acknowledge receipt of. I have not received the letter in which you had mentioned them before.

I will try to tell you, in as few words as possible, about Monsieur Boze's correspondence although I must acknowledge that he is a thousand times more accurate than I am. I already told you about the settlement he made with José Lara and the way in which he finally ended the matter with this rascal.

In a letter dated September 15th, 1822, Monsieur Boze writes that, on the 11th instant, he settled with Monsieur Dumas, who owes 380 dollars.[1] Finding him unable to fulfill his commitment at the moment, he at least made him renew his 14-year-old bond, under the guaranty of Monsieur Robin Despaigne who employs him as an associate on his coffee plantation. Monsieur Boze says nothing about a date. He also made Monsieur Robin Despaigne replace his bond with another one dated December 1st. He writes that it was only on the 11th instant that he managed to settle with Sr Vincent Dallest, although the documents he sent me are dated September 7th; they were not endorsed until December 15th. He adds that it was because of various disputes that required smoothing out, that he avoided a trial that would have been extremely long, costly, and difficult to fight due to the judicial maneuvers of a shrewd debtor, who is both protected and of a first-class bad faith. Monsieur Boze writes that what made him agree to the compromise of receiving the bonds at the terms stipulated above and with the guaranty of a planter who is collecting 200 thousands of coffee, is to ensure their payment on the due date.[2] And Monsieur Boze adds: "Believe me, Monsieur, my dear friend, it was not without much difficulty and annoyance that I succeeded in obtaining such conditions. This strict settlement made me fall out with a friend of 50 years, but honor commanded me to sacrifice friendship to the trust I promised to uphold when I agreed to obtain the payment of your debts."

1. Boze's letter is not included in the Ste-Gême Family Papers because he addressed the letter to Dorville, who summarized it instead of transferring it. News on the debt settlements is given to Sainte-Gême in several letters written in 1822 and 1823. Ste-Gême Family Papers, MSS 100, folders 58, 65.

2. Dorville does not specify any measurement unit for the coffee. We may assume his count is in pounds of coffee beans.

Five bonds signed by Sr Vincent Dallest and endorsed by Augustin Laterrera y Oliva are in the same spirit and payable as follows:

The 1st dated September 10th is payable in	March 1823	300 dollars (to the order of Boze)
The 2nd	Sept 1823	246 dollars (to the order of Boze)
The 3rd	April 1825	200 dollars (to the order of Boze)
The 4th	April 1825	1300 dollars (to the order of Monsieur Sainte-Gême)
The 5th	in April 1826	1,500 dollars (to the order of Monsieur Sainte-Gême)
In accordance with his two notes		3,546 dollars
Agreed upon in 1807 and 1809		3,000 dollars
		546 dollars

I have the last two bonds in my hands.

Monsieur Boze informs me that he managed to reach a settlement with your debtors. He had to pay significant fees to those he employed in this unfortunate business with José Lara and Vincent Dallest. He also had to pay the commissions that had been promised to Don Miguel Ulloa in a notarized act, although he substituted his own power of attorney to ensure the success of this negotiation. The act did not include a revocation clause, due to a fault of the French notary. Because of the conditions of the act, Monsieur Boze was obliged to cover all the fees of the proceedings, whatever the result, gain as well as loss, and to respect Ulloa's advice without being able to depart from it or to claim any compensation in case of loss.

He reserves the right to present you with the costs, the truth of which will be proven by receipts when he sends his general account to you. And he hopes that, having acted to the best of your interests and having found himself in critical positions with these two debtors, you will not resent him if you are not fully satisfied with the manner in which he settled. He informs me that, by March, he intends to resolve to either stay in St Yago de Cuba or return here. In the first case, he will ask for a new power of attorney from you, which will revoke the one you gave him through an act passed on June 26th of 1820 by Monsieur Jean Joseph Gaudens Adéma, an inhabitant of your *département*.[3] According to

3. A *département* is a French territorial administrative unit. There are about one hundred départements in France.

a clause included in the previous notarial act, it will also revoke the substitution of Don Miguel Ulloa from St Yago de Cuba. This clause was very unpleasant to Monsieur Boze and he wishes to remain free to make these two debtors pay, now that they no longer have any reason to object to settlement, and he wishes to remain the only one accountable for the payments he will receive.

Monsieur Boze explained to me that the reason he was forced to allow the substitution of Don Miguel Ulloa for his power of attorney to oblige Monsieur Dallest to pay one way or another, was to avoid an imaginary claim from this debtor. The latter claims that Monsieur Boze owes him a 15-year-old boarding debt amounting to 3,000 dollars that he intended to compensate for by placing a claim against the bonds in your name.[4] Concerning Ulloa's demands, Boze said he was ashamed to see his own claims ignored despite the false witnesses Ulloa had gathered against him.

He asked me to tell you, when you are with me, that Don Juan Cavallo, who has a debt of 1200 dollars with you, has been, for about three months, in the Belain convent and that they host him at their hospital, feed him, and take care of his maintenance, so as not to see this unfortunate Creole starve to death. So, this debt has to be counted, as many others, among the losses. In a 3rd letter dated September 15th, he sent me an accounting of your debtors who still owe you a total of 4,418.92 dollars, telling me that it is not taking a risk to count them among the losses. As for the others, included in the general account of October 20th, some have paid, and others have renewed their bonds that had reached their terms, and Monsieur Boze has deducted these from the sum he must collect for you, unless payment is made.

General account of the debts whose titles have been lost in the Commercial House of Hardy & Company in Jamaica

Dead	Videau	Dollars	400
	Fontvielle		18
	Pedro Laclaux		200
	Emanuel de Soza		340
	Caminero Sr		32

4. Boze explains this in one of his letters to Sainte-Gême. When he lived in Cuba, before being expelled and settling in New Orleans, he lived at his friend Monsieur Dallest's. But Dallest, not wanting to pay his debt to Sainte-Gême, decided to ask Boze to pay a rent for the stay he had made at Dallest's fifteen years before, setting the amount of this rent close to that of his debt to Sainte-Gême and thus hoping to avoid paying, as Boze had power of attorney for Sainte-Gême. Ste-Gême Family Papers, MSS 100, folders 54–55, 58.

	Longchamp		50
	JM Caminero		650
	The same		60
	Jean Cavallero		1,300
			3,500

Account of the debtors who are dead, have no means, or are presently insolvent

Dead	Bellegarde	Dollars	500
Dead	The same		100
	Toirac		200
Dead	Lestage		40
	Brossard		500
	The same		88.92
			1,428.92
			4,478.92[5]

I still have room here to remind you of Monsieur Lambert who sends you a thousand marks of friendship. The Chevalier Morant ladies entrusted me with the same mission. You will find herewith a death certificate for Dominique Larey. It is the second one I have sent you. They cost 1.50 dollars.

Until now, I have mentioned business and I am not done. My dear Monsieur Sainte-Gême, I need now to tell you about mine since I started with Monsieur Boze's. The corner house of your property in town is still for sale. I proposed it for 2,500 dollars, 1,500 dollars next March and 1,000 dollars in March 1824. If someone agrees to my proposal, you will not receive a large amount since the crop is meager this year if we manage to collect it at all. And I will be happy to write to you if I do not have the pleasure of embracing you as you have made me hope. Clarisse and Amazilie have both given birth, on December 1st last, to girls but it is clear that, despite all precautions, Clarisse will be unable to save one of her children from lockjaw. Her last child only lived 4 days. He was the size of a finger. As for Amazilie, she is now with two fat and healthy daughters. May God keep them and all the others in good health as long as possible, but especially till the moment when I must return them to you one day, so that I may not experience the sadness of having to write to you that this one is sick and that one is dead.[6] I lost old César, on November 16th last of indigestion that

5. There is a mistake in the calculation. The total amount should read $4,928.92.

6. This letter also shows that among the reasons why Dorville took great care of the enslaved was that he felt responsibility for the trust Sainte-Gême had placed in him.

complicated a diarrhea that nothing could stop. His old age and lack of strength did not make him very useful on the plantation, but he was an old servant and was always there.[7] Poor Basile is still fighting his disease. I gave him a remedy from Doctor Le Roy and it provoked a very advantageous change. I am short of this remedy but there is much in the river and as soon as possible I will continue this treatment, in the hope of announcing to you one day that I saved him.[8]

We had an icy frost in November and since it had not been preceded by others it damaged all the oranges. I hoped to make 600 to 700 gourds with them this year, but I am not sure I will even make 200.

In case some of your compatriots wish to try their fortune here, I advise you, my dear Monsieur Sainte-Gême, to dissuade them. Our country is worthless and disease spares no one. Monsieur Sémiac wanted to open a bakery and he did not succeed. He intends to go to St Yago de Cuba in search of what is no longer found here. I am afraid he might be inconsistent and not succeed. I hope I am wrong.

I still have many little things to tell you but there is no room left except to pray you, my dear Monsieur Sainte-Gême, to let me pay to your amiable and interesting family the respectful homages of your very devoted servant.

Auvignac Dorville

7. From the inventory taken in 1814 after Louis Leufroy Dreux's death, we know that César was sixty at the time (see appendix 4). He was thus eighty when he died. To pursue the discussion on the motives for Dorville's care for the enslaved, this note indicates that his concern was sometimes driven by motives other than productivity.

8. Dorville does not explain what he can find in the river that would serve as a remedy, but he is probably referring to a certain type of algae, river plant, or fish. Remedies were often derived from folk medicine, a field in which people of African descent excelled, even if the prescription in this case comes from a doctor.

[MSS 100, Folder 68] Gentilly, April 22, 1823

I am still expecting you, my dear Monsieur Sainte-Gême, but rumor says here that there is trouble in France, which could have prevented you from carrying out your plan of coming here.[1] Since this seems to be the case, I am sending you herewith a package from Monsieur Boze. I have had it for some time.

Monsieur Chabaud received a letter from his cousin, Monsieur Delisle, in which he authorizes him to settle with me the business about the nègre Laurent. Money is so rare that Monsieur Chabaud pushed the settlement of his debt back one month and the month has been over for 8 days without a settlement. I think, however, that we will soon settle this old business that Monsieur Boze has, to some extent, helped move forward by often refreshing Monsieur Delisle's memory so that he may complete this settlement.

We will not eat Louisiana oranges for a long time. The cold has been, this winter, so unusual for our country that it has killed all our orange trees, all without exception. It left an empty space on the plantation, and I estimate the loss at about seven thousand piastres a year. I have not lost courage and I made a nursery with which I might, in a few years, replace the old orange grove as well as the one I had planted after your departure, which was splendid and would have started to produce this year.

There is something I could not resolve myself to let you know until now. Poor Monsieur Dreux is completely ruined. His sons-in-law left him destitute with the debts he endorsed for them. Monsieur Cadet Mouton will also be reduced to very little because of endorsements. In short, you cannot fathom the state of financial embarrassment in which business is in our poor country and I do not think this will end any time soon.

I will not send you the modest revenues of the past year until next month, once I have lost any hope of seeing you this year.

I am still treating Basile with Doctor Le Roy's prescription. He is feeling markedly better. With perseverance and God's help, I may be fortunate enough to see him restored to health.

Good Madame Dreux asked me to recall her to your good memories and to tell you that she still loves you with all her heart. Her son's ruin and the loss of

1. In 1823, France was at war with Spain. A French member of Parliament was excluded from the chamber in early March for his antiwar positions. His arrest on March 4 triggered riots in Paris. On April 7, the French army started marching into Spain. The April 22 letter probably refers to the war rather than to the troubles that occurred in Paris in March.

her children have affected her much and I do not think her happy. The Chevalier Morant ladies also asked me to send you a thousand marks of friendship.

You know, my dear Monsieur Sainte-Gême, that I am not good with words when it is time for me to send compliments to your amiable family but if you were kind enough to do it for me, I am sure it would be well done. In this expectation, I am still, my dear Monsieur Sainte-Gême, your devoted and attached servant.

Auvignac Dorville

[MSS 100, Folder 71] Gentilly, May 26, 1823

My dear Monsieur de Sainte-Gême,

Please find enclosed 620 dollars in one note of 3,224 francs. The exchange is 5fr20. It is impossible to have more at the moment. It was provided to me by Monsieur Clamageran who has the reputation of being one of the most trusted men to transmit funds to France.

Your advice concerning Messieurs Commagère was wise. They just had a 200,000-piastre bankruptcy. I almost lost 2,341 francs on Monsieur Latapie's behalf. Fortunately, their brother-in-law in Le Havre had committed himself to paying this sum in case I had not received it. They managed to hide their problems to the last. Last March, my uncle Bienvenu sold them, without any guaranty, 11,600 dollars' worth of sugar, all of which is lost to him now. My poor uncle Volant also came very close to this precipice when his whole crop was bought at the same time. But he was lucky enough to transmit his funds through Monsieur Norbert Fortier, one of these men's father-in-law. People do not speak honorably of their conduct. I would never finish if I started speaking about it.

The last time I sent you the account of our revenues and expenses was in February 1821. Since then and until now, the profit amounted to

Including some money that I then had	dollars 2257.62
And the general expenses	dollars 1214.62
Balance	dollars 1043.00

Including 620 dollars for the note, 400 dollars for my 1821 remuneration, and a few gourdes I keep in case of necessity.

In my last letter, I forgot to tell you that I collected from the Bank of the State of Louisiana all the notes I received on behalf of the ladies Courtade and M. Dastugue &c. But I told you I would collect the 5% commission granted to me at each due date. Considering that they only obtained half of what they hoped to earn, I will only take a 3% commission. Please, Monsieur de Sainte-Gême, let these people know. It did not cost me much.

Monsieur Delmas was in town these past days. He saw our old friend Lambert and asked him if I was not in town. If I had been, he would have visited me to obtain Madame Sainte-Gême's address to write to her. His business must have prevented him from fulfilling this good intention because I still have not had the pleasure of seeing him. M. Lambert asked me to recall him to you and

Madame your wife. I add the most flattering, the most pleasant things to my respectful homage that I pray you to receive, my dear Monsieur de Sainte-Gême, and to transmit to your amiable gathered families.

I am still sincerely, my dear Monsieur de Sainte-Gême, your devoted servant.

Auvignac Dorville

[MSS 100, Folder 75] Gentilly, September 25, 1823

The sweet hope that I had of seeing you, Monsieur Sainte-Gême, prevented me from writing you even though I promised you to do so in my letter of April 22nd. But you have not come. In the meantime, I have been busy with collecting the modest harvest of this past year. I had hoped to collect everything and then send you the net profit, but so far, despite many efforts, I could not realize it all. I still have 152 dollars to recover. A justice of the peace is in charge of pursuing it. Without going further, I present you the state of your revenues from May 1822 until September 1823.

Collection:	2465.18 dollars
Debts:	1636.93 dollars
Balance:	828.25 dollars
Without counting what I hope to collect	152.00 dollars
That will make you a total of	980.25 dollars

Which I keep and wish to use, without having asked your consent, to acquire two nègres. There is going to be an auction of seized creole nègres next month who will be sold on long term credit.[1] With the cash, I could perhaps have three and the rest will reproduce little by little. You are too reasonable, Monsieur Sainte-Gême, not to understand that the capital that you have entrusted to me is declining by the day. Especially in the present circumstances in which you find yourself, when there are not enough hands to give it value. The nègres have decreased in price, those of the plantation are aging, and we now have to work a lot for a small return. Laurent is still with me, although Monsieur Chabaud has been charged by his cousin Monsieur Delisle, as I made known in my letter of last April, of terminating this affair with me. I was informed by Monsieur Boze that Monsieur Chabaud was paid by someone the sum needed to clear this subject from my hands, without having executed the power that his cousin had given him in order to finish this old affair. Monsieur Delisle has been instructed on this fact and I await what he will arrange with Monsieur Chabaud in order to know what to think.

I informed you, on January 16 last, that Monsieur Boze has obtained from Monsieur Vincent Dallest the sum of 2,800 dollars and that he has made me

1. In the last decades before the Civil War, New Orleans became the main slave market in the United States. For more on this, see W. Johnson, *Soul by Soul.*

take two notes to your order, signed by the debtor and endorsed by Señor Augustin Laterrera y Oliva. Monsieur Dallest being dead, Monsieur Boze wrote me to return the notes to him so that he could take suitable measures to assure them. He has received them and tells me there is nothing to fear since the guarantee of the endorser is solid.

As for the obligations of Jose Lara, Monsieur Boze, to be prudent, did not want to be in charge of collecting them. So, he asked me to have one of your friends do it. As I could not do this business here and as I did not know anyone in the island of Cuba except Monsieur Pierre Rivery Jr., a man you also know, I sent him a power of attorney in good standing accompanied by the first note to your order of 800 dollars, which had to be paid in full before last June. Wishing that Monsieur Boze might have his own thoughts about it, I addressed the package without sealing it, so that Boze could send it to Rivery's address, if he thought it was a good idea.

Monsieur Boze still has not acknowledged receipt of these documents I sent him on the 21st of May. Enclosed is one of his letters in which you will see what he wants you to send him as soon as possible and you will also find the state of most of the debts that you have entrusted him with.

About the power of attorney I gave to Monsieur Rivery, I have to let you know, my dear Monsieur Sainte-Gême, that I loathed doing it because I encroached on the powers you left me which do not specify that I have the right to substitute and the law says that, if I do it, it will be at my own risk and expense. But I acted for the best of your interest and I hope that it will not cause you unhappiness.

The famous prince who owes you a thousand and a few piasters withdrew to France a few years ago. He is in Paris. You know that he seemed not to possess anything in New Orleans, but he must not have left without money. That is why I encourage you to obtain information about this person and about his finances. And if there is any way of obtaining anything, I will send you the necessary documents to oblige him to pay.

After much suffering, poor Bazile left this world on the 12th of the past month of June. The proverb which says that misfortune never comes one at a time has proven true for me. Eleven days later, I lost old Marie Louise.[2] She had

2. There were two enslaved men named Bazile in the 1814 inventory taken after Louis Leufroy Dreux's death: a Creole slave, age thirty-five, and a slave from Saint-Domingue, age twenty-four to twenty-five (see appendix 4). We do not know which one died. Marie-Louise was not on the plantation at Louis Leufroy Dreux's death as her name is not in the 1814 inventory.

a fever for five or six days. I had her purged and thought I would see her back on her feet again, but fate decided otherwise. An old humor she had in her legs went up to her chest and suffocated her.

Madame Widow Dreux, her son, and his family prayed me to remind them to your memory. It is always with renewed pleasure that Madame Dreux speaks of you and your amiable family with those who love you. It is easy for any of these persons to send you proof of their friendship in writing. Although the quill is not equal to real life, I pray you, my dear Monsieur Sainte-Gême, to give my respectful homages to Madame, your spouse, and to Mademoiselle Hermina, to give my civilities to Messieurs, your brothers, my friendly thoughts to my comrade Edgar and to the young family, and, before everything else, a kiss to charming little Henriette who is not yet old enough to deny me this right. I still am, my dear Monsieur Sainte-Gême, your sincere and attached servant.

Auvignac Dorville

P.S. I was forgetting Monsieur Lambert who does not forget you. He asked me to give you a thousand marks of friendships from him. I do not know if you have been informed of Monsieur Garidel's death. The sorrow caused by his unsuccessful business has significantly contributed to lead him to his grave.

I like to believe that you have written to me and that your letters have not reached me. The last one I received was the one Monsieur Davis gave me last January. I count on your kindness to send the enclosed letter to his address.

[MSS 100, Folder 76] New Orleans, September 26, 1823

My dear Monsieur Sainte-Gême,

You probably remember that I informed you, some time ago, that foreigners no longer find an occupation here and that Monsieur Sémiac intended to go to the isle of Cuba where hardworking foreigners can still do something. Fear that there might be some trouble delayed his journey and he is supposed to leave next month never to return. You know this country and the absolute necessity of having some means to start a small fortune. On this matter, Monsieur Sémiac would like you to speak to his brother-in-law, the doctor, since you are more likely than any to successfully intercede on his behalf. A sum necessary to purchase two nègres would be enough to help him move forward. Do as best you can and believe me to be always, my dear Monsieur Sainte-Gême, your attached servant.

Auvignac Dorville

[MSS 100, Folder 77] Gentilly, October 27, 1823

It is with the greatest concern, my dear Monsieur Sainte-Gême, that I shared your sorrows and that I mingled my tears with those you shed at the loss of dear Edgar. Absence had not diminished the sincere friendship I had for this young comrade who paid me back with his friendship. When he was still here, he often left his mother in town and came to join me and keep me company. I will feel this loss for a long time. And, as I watched with pleasure this poor young man progress in age and instruction, I always thought he would be the one coming to replace me, in three or four years, to take the reins of his property. But fate does not always favor weak mortals in their hopes, which often give way to painful sorrows. Madame, your spouse, has unfortunately experienced this and I know her too well to remain a stranger to all she has suffered.

I once wrote to you about Monsieur Hesgniel's house.[1] I was acting through a third party who could not complete anything. This property has belonged for a long time to an inhabitant of the Attakapas whom Monsieur Olivier Abat represents here. You know that the latter is as hard a nut to crack as is Monsieur Hesgniel. He did not want to agree to the price of 2,500 dollars, thinking I would still be paying too much for this piece of land, the house being totally worthless.

I hope you received via Monsieur Dispan, Junior a letter I wrote to you on the 25th of December last. He promised me to hand it to you in person. If you have received it, you must have seen, my dear Monsieur Sainte-Gême, how I intended to use last year's meager revenues. After calculating everything, I used them to purchase two handsome nègres, both age 20. I paid 1,000 gourdes in cash.[2] Until now, I have been extremely satisfied, and I think I made a good acquisition. I also told you what Monsieur Boze had obtained from your debtors. And also, that, following his advice to recover the amount of the notes from José Lara, I had forwarded to Monsieur Pierre Rivery the first 800 dollars note from this man, together with a substitution of my power of attorney, something I did despite the risk and expenses I incurred. All these documents, enclosed in a single package to Monsieur Boze's address, did not reach him despite the precautions I took. A short time after I notified him that I had sent the package, he replied that he had not received anything and reproached me for granting

1. Elsewhere spelt Haigneil.

2. This means that each of the purchased men was sold for five hundred dollars. This is the value estimated for Joseph and the two Baziles in the 1814 inventory, which suggests that the price of the enslaved workers had not increased in the twenty years since Louis Leufroy Dreux's death.

my trust to someone else, thinking that he was the only one who deserved it. I observed to him that I had acted only according to his advice, that he had indeed asked me if the power of attorney you left me could be used to revoke the one you gave him, as well as its substitution for Don Miguel Ulloa passed by Monsieur Jean Joseph Gaudens Adéma. Saddened and worried about the package not reaching him, I consulted with a lawyer and a notary to know whether I could transfer to Boze the power of attorney I received from you, considering that we are both working for you. They replied positively. Without losing time, I sent Boze a second substitution, so that he may recover this lost note of 800 dollars assigned to you. Boze will suffer from the delay but not from difficulties because he was careful enough to have it recorded, as he did with the others, with a good judicial office in St Yago de Cuba.

I also let you know that Monsieur Chabaud had received from his cousin Monsieur Delisle, the sum necessary to retrieve Laurent from me, but that he betrayed his cousin's trust by keeping the money that he used I do not know for what. Monsieur Delisle has entrusted Monsieur Boze with proposing several solutions to me, but none could satisfy me since prudence commands me to deliver this nègre with one hand and receive the money with the other. I thus wrote to Monsieur Boze that I did not want and would not accept any other guaranty than the sum of 839 dollars that the Causse succession owes you. If I succeed in terminating this business to my satisfaction, I will demand from the person with whom I will terminate it a notarized discharge to forestall unforeseen complications.

In case you have not received the letter which I am mentioning, I need to tell you that poor Basile died on June 12th, after much suffering. Eleven days later, I had the sorrow of seeing this loss followed by that of old Marie-Louise. She had been having a fever for five or six days. I had carefully purged her and thought I would see her up and about soon, but it was otherwise. Apparently, a tumor she had had for a long time in her legs suddenly went up to her chest and suffocated her. I told you in the same letter that the famous prince who owes you a thousand and a few piastres withdrew to France two or three years ago. He is in Paris. You know that he seemed not to have anything in New Orleans, but he probably did not leave without money. That is why I encourage you, my dear Monsieur Sainte-Gême, to seek information about him and his resources and, if there is any means to recover anything from him, I will send you the documents necessary to coerce him into paying.

I still nourished in my heart the hope of seeing you in Louisiana when you were an American citizen, but I have lost this hope now that you have disposed of this title and that you are knight of the order of St Louis.[3] I still think, however, that your presence here, for one or two months, would be necessary for your interests.

All the Creoles who left France to come here arrived safe and sound.[4] Madame Latapie was delighted by her crossing, which was a happy one, and of her captain who, although American, treated his passengers in the French way and showed her many marks of attention.[5] She has lost much of her portliness and her health is not perfect. The tears she has reasons to shed every day because of the loss of so many persons she loved and no longer found here could prevent her from recovering quickly. Fortunately, her business obliges her to take some exercise, which distracts her a little. I think you will have the pleasure of seeing her again next spring. Everything you asked me to do for her, for my good mamma, for Monsieur Dreux and his family, I do with much pleasure because my heart inclines me to. But if my heart did not incline me to do so, I would obey your orders anyway.

In truth, if you had not told me that you had been knighted with the order of St Louis, I would almost have guessed it from your letters. Your style is now that of man of the court. I hear that you often make compliments and that you make them well. As for me, unable to make compliments, I am condemned to loving you as you deserve in all respects without being able to say it otherwise and I remain heavily indebted to you. This saddens me, you know, my dear Monsieur Sainte-Gême, because I dislike being in debt.

I had written to the Messieurs Hazeur to comply with your request. I just received the reply of Monsieur le Chevalier. I have no choice but to cite what he replied to me concerning this matter: "My brother and I are very grateful for Monsieur Sainte-Gême's good memories. When you write to him, do not forget to thank him for us, and to let him know that, having a strong interest in everything that involves him and his respectable family, we cannot but learn with much pleasure and much interest that he has been awarded the St Louis Cross."

My family was extremely sensitive to your thoughts and has entrusted me with responding to them in the most honest terms.

There was word that Monsieur Noël Destréhan was going to be appointed

3. Louis XIV created the Order of Saint Louis in 1693 in order to honor his military officers.

4. The phrasing here confirms the frequency of the Atlantic voyages to New Orleans.

5. The cutting remark reveals the subtle hostility between the Francophone community and the Anglo-Americans. See Tregle, *Louisiana in the Age of Jackson.*

governor, but he died last summer, which changed everything.[6] Monsieur Bernard Marigny is in the running for this position.[7] I think, and you probably suspect it, that, whether he is appointed or not, this appointment will cost him more than one grand dinner and more than one carriage rent. He is used to gratifying those people who he thinks might not vote for him.

Business has not improved. As the sugar crop is looking relatively good this year, however, there is hope that it will encourage the banks to make some more money available and that there will be more in circulation here.[8] All the slaves are faring well. Amazilie is going in the right direction. She is pregnant again, and her two little daughters are quietly growing. Clarisse is also pregnant. She should avoid having children, since she is unable to keep them alive, but we will see what happens with this one, the third since you left.

It is time for me, my dear Monsieur Sainte-Gême, to ask you to convey my homages and respectful sentiments to your amiable and interesting family, and to tell you that I still am, my dear Monsieur Sainte-Gême, your devoted and attached servant.

Auvignac Dorville

P.S. Monsieur Lambert has not forgotten the *bourgeois* and his *bourgeoise.* He is still fond of them, and it is with renewed pleasure that he often mentions them to me. As usual, he spends almost as much time with me on the plantation as in town. We are still at war with deer. These past few days, I killed four myself. I am the luckiest of our little party which includes Monsieur Lambert, sometimes his nephew, Martin, who is our hunting whip, and Soniat, the youngest, who lost his arm hunting with us, the same accident as Lacoste. We lost the most famous of our hunting companions, poor Livaudais. This honest comrade died last summer of a deposit in his liver. He left behind a wife and five children. Soniat has four good dogs, and I have four that are perfectly suitable. Last year, I lost the flower of my pack.

6. Jean Noël Destréhan, born in Louisiana, was the owner of a wealthy plantation in St. Charles Parish, mainly involved in indigo cultivation until the late eighteenth century. In 1792, he purchased the present-day Destrehan plantation and started growing sugar. By 1803, the plantation had become one of the largest sugar plantations in Louisiana and Destrehan was starting a political career. He died on October 4, 1823, one month after the death of his sons Etienne and Guy. For more on the Destrehan family, see Cizeck, Lawrence, and Sexton, *Destrehan.*

7. Bernard Marigny ran for governor of Louisiana in 1824 and 1828 but was defeated both times, by Henry Johnson in 1824 and by Pierre Derbigny in 1828.

8. Whitten, "Tariff and Profit," 226–233.

[MSS 100, Folder 82] Gentilly, April 22, 1824

I have waited, my dear Monsieur Sainte-Gême, for Madame Latapie's departure to talk with you about your business affairs and to tell you that I have received all your letters dated from Paris. Yet, without a doubt, you were still there when I sent you a letter by Monsieur Dispan, the younger, the 25th of September last, which will have arrived at Saint-Gaudens. If you have received it, as I hope, you have seen that Monsieur Boze impatiently waits for you to send him some new powers that revoke those that were passed by the act of Monsieur Jean Joseph Gaudens Adéma and that also revoke his substitution in favor of Don Miguel Ulloa, so that he alone could be charged with the recovery of the obligations of José Lara as well as those of the Dallest succession. By these powers, he wants you to authorize him to pursue Monsieur Saint-Macary, who is at Nantes, according to the information that he obtained. . . . As you are in France, I think that you more than he can expedite the termination of this business. If you are not too busy to send him this power of attorney, do me the favor of attending to it at the earliest and send it to me if you cannot send it to him directly, my dear monsieur Sainte-Gême.

As I told you on the 27th of October last, I used the modest revenues from the year before last on two beautiful nègres, both aged twenty, who cost one thousand gourdes outright. As for last year's revenues, they do not amount to much, which made me tremble the past two years whenever I drew my salary. I remit to you the included bill of exchange for 3650 francs. I would have sent more if I had been able to finish the recovery of some debts and if it had not been necessary for me to have some funds to rehabilitate the faubourg house, which is in great need. Moreover, I will be obliged to make some small payments on one I am having built, considering the impossibility of repairing the old chateau where staying puts you in great danger. My intention, in the beginning, is to make a small cabin for myself. But thinking of the future that one cannot foresee and being certain that a house on a plantation always gives it more value, I prefer to make one house of four rooms that I hope, once finished, will not cost more than three hundred piastres.[1] I count on being lodged there before the beginning of hurricane season.

1. This detail shows the value of enslaved workers as the house will cost less than one of the two slaves purchased by Dorville. Dorville intended to limit the costs by producing the wood and the bricks on the plantation, but it also runs counter to the impression often given in the historiography of the grandeur of the plantation houses and attests to the diversity of situations in the plantation world of Louisiana.

If I did not have hope of making more revenue than I have made for the past two years now that my feeble forces have been augmented with more hands, I would tell you to come back my dear monsieur Sainte-Gême, so that we might determine what is in your best interest, so that when I put my head on the pillow I can rest comfortably.

Madame Latapie, who honored me by coming to dine at the plantation, could tell you that business here is still bad. It is said that it will get better, that a mortgage bank is going to establish itself here for which the state is going to borrow a quarter of a million gourdes. It has also been said that its terms will be 9% interest for five years. However, the way I see it, it will not be a relief for a great number of inhabitants whose fortunes are hanging by a hair. Their revenue, in general, and their capital are calculated with an interest of more than 6%. The public is not yet well instructed on the manner in which this establishment will be based. If it could be useful to my country, I will hasten to let you know.

I have learned from Monsieur Dupuis that you left Paris at the beginning of January, after having terminated, to your satisfaction, the business that had taken you there. He got this news from his brother-in-law; I fulfilled the commission you entrusted me with concerning his amiable spouse.

I forgot to tell you that I had a note at 5 francs 30. The bearer is solid, you will not have any difficulty. I also always forget to tell you that the house in the city is in such a state of disrepair that I cannot get more than 20 piastres a month. It is a pity that we are not thinking seriously of replacing it with a new one and even by two when time gives you the means to do so. When I have finished recovering some more small debts, I will send you a statement of your revenues and expenses for last year.

Madame Latapie, as I have already stated, came to bid her farewell to Gentilly. I verbally entrusted her with forwarding you what my heart feels for you and your amiable family. I join here my respectful feelings that I pray you, my dear Monsieur Sainte-Gême, to express to them, as well as a kiss for the younger family.

The Messieurs Sémiac learned with pleasure that their brother is living at the house of Monsieur Prudent Casamajor in Cuba where, according to what Monsieur Boze told me, he gets the salary of a novice . . . I asked that you bring me a pointer when you come. Back then I did not have any but now I have two. So, my dear Monsieur Sainte-Gême, I ask you at present not to take the pains of honoring this request if you have not already done so.

All the slaves are well. Clarisse was delivered of a big baby boy that she has kept. He will soon be two months old. Amazilie, as I have already written, is well on the way. She has two pretty little girls and she is pregnant again.

I have been much aggrieved in the recent past. I have lost my father and sister-in-law in the space of five months. The poor Monsieur Cadet Mouton is no longer. Grief shortened the life of this brave man. After having possessed a brilliant fortune, he died insolvent.

I renew, my dear Monsieur Sainte-Gême, my prayer to have you forward to Madame, your spouse, Mademoiselle Hermina, and your whole family, the respectful homages of the one who still is, my dear Monsieur Sainte-Gême, your devoted and attached servant.

Auvignac Dorville

P.S. A thousand marks of friendship from the whole Dreux family and from Monsieur Lambert who is still fond of you. My brothers prayed me to offer you their civilities and to recall them to your memory.

Someone here asked me as a favor, when I would write to you, to ask you to give me or to himself, some news of Monsieur Asnac. You do not need me to tell you who this person is since it is Marie Joseph.

You have learned without a doubt of the death of Monsieur Villanueva. I saw him a few days before he died. He told me to tell you as well as Madame, your spouse, that he would carry to his tomb memories of you that he had always cherished. He suffered for a long time and with firm and constant resignation.

[MSS 100, Folder 92] Gentilly, November 9, 1824

Monsieur Sainte-Gême, the American[1]
Saint-Gaudens, Haute Garonne

I seize the opportunity, my dear Monsieur Sainte-Gême, of a departure for Le Havre in four or five days, to send you herewith a package from Monsieur Boze that I received some time ago.

Madame Latapie wrote me from Paris a letter dated July 1st. She announces to me that she happily arrived in France and tells me that Monsieur Saint-Avid gave her news of your household and that everyone was in good health. I hope that God permitted this to persist and will permit it to persist for a long time. She also writes to me that, upon arrival, she immediately sent you one of my letters, which should already have reached you. She was sad that you did not reply to her because she could have let me know if my letter had reached you.[2] In this letter, I told you about a small house I was about to build on the plantation. Before I started, Monsieur Dreux, Monsieur Lambert, and a few others of my friends were indulgent enough to come to the plantation to give me their opinion on the location, which would be the most convenient. We agreed that the house would be hidden if it did not take the place of the old castle. Once the workers had started, the opinion was that a four-room house would be too insignificant. Yielding to the wish to make something beautiful for you and thinking that it would especially please Madame Sainte-Gême, I had another story added with a gallery in the front and the rear. The house has eight nice rooms, extremely convenient, six of which have a fireplace, and it is raised by four more feet than the old castle of which only rotten debris remains, since I used everything that was in good condition. As for the material, I had everything, or almost everything, made on the plantation. After using planks and bricks from the old wall and the former brick factory, I spent only 180 dollars to purchase more for the chimneys and pillars. I bought a few barrels of lime and, as the price was six escalins a barrel, I resolved to make the rest myself. I needed almost 300 barrels. I purchased oyster shells at three picayune a barrel, and since two burnt barrels yield three barrels of lime, I had my supply for a low price. I must confess to you that my life had never been as tormented as since

1. Although Sainte-Gême had renounced his U.S. citizenship, Dorville insists on the latter's connection with the Americas.

2. This paragraph reveals much about how news circulated in the Atlantic World. On correspondences, see Decker, *Epistolary Practices*; Gerber, "Epistolary Ethics," 3–23; Pearson, *Atlantic Families*.

the workers started. I had then rightfully counted 5 picayune a crate and, until now, I had to provide almost 700 dollars that has already been spent. I cannot tell you how much this house will cost me, and, for that, it needs to be finished. At the moment, we are roofing it, and it is maybe only in fifteen or twenty days that I will be able to leave the old poultry pen to occupy a room in it while waiting for the rest to be completed.

The town house was uninhabitable as long as it was raining. The tenants had warned me that they were going to leave, but owing to the arrangements I made with them, the house now has a new roof and its gallery has been raised. The kitchen, the servants' quarters, etc. have also been repaired, and since the tenants agreed to put their shoulder to the wheel, I hope it will only cost me about four months of rent. This past spring, I had the courtyard of the house of the faubourg filled in. The house requires some repairs I will take care of during the next nice season.

In the letter Madame Latapie forwarded to you, I told you, my dear Monsieur Sainte-Gême, that Clarisse had given birth. Her child seemed to enjoy good health and lived three to four months. Disease took the child away in two days. Doctor Conund, who came to bring his assistance, told me that all the symptoms of the disease led him to believe that the baby's liver was rotten. Some time ago, I thought that Amazilie was pregnant, but she was only fat. She is faring well, as are all the others.

I do not write more, this time, my dear Monsieur Sainte-Gême, because, although nights are long, and I take this opportunity to talk with you, they are often short for me. I will not finish, however, without fulfilling the friendly commissions I was charged with, for you and your amiable family, by Monsieur Dreux, his son, and his whole family. Monsieur Lambert, who proved me, on more than one occasion, that he is truly your friend, always asks me not to forget to mention him to the bourgeois and the bourgeoise. I would be ungrateful if I did not carry out this mission. Adieu, my dear Monsieur Sainte-Gême. Please accept, and share with your interesting and respectable family, the sentiments and respects of the one who still is, my dear Monsieur Sainte-Gême, your devoted and attached servant.

Auvignac Dorville

P.S. Please transmit my apologies to Madame Latapie. I do not have enough time to write to her before the ship leaves. I have 439.90 dollars that are hers. As soon as I can find exchange bills, I will have them transferred to her and will tell her more about the business she left with me. You will oblige me extremely, my dear Monsieur de Sainte-Gême, if you write to her about this matter and send my respectful homage to her and Mademoiselle Constance, and my civilities to Monsieur Latapie. I express to you beforehand my sincere gratitude for the trouble my request will cause to you.

You will please me if you inform me as early as possible that this letter reached you.

[MSS 100, Folder 94] Gentilly, February 8, 1825

Some time ago, but long after it arrived here, I received, my dear Monsieur Sainte-Gême, your letter of the 27th of June 1824 in an envelope addressed to Monsieur Destoup, the son. The latter wrote to me and should have put his letter in the bag, so that I could receive it through the mail. Instead, he gave it to someone, which often brings about extremely belated delivery and the loss of many a letter. I took care to obtain the documents he is asking for, as well as those you asked for in your letter of the 2nd of September last, which I received a few days after the first two. Despite the repeated requests I have made at the Court of Probate or at the office of the Will Register, since the 15th of December last, I was able to obtain them only the day before last, because the court has had too much to do. The court does not work for nothing, however, because the copy and the duplicate that I will send you of the inventory of the goods of the late Monsieur Leufroy Dreux cost me fifteen piastres. I had these documents certified by the French Consul, as well as your marriage certificate.[1] All of this is enclosed in the present letter: my letters sent to Monsieur Destoup via the same vessel have been taken through the same formalities. He will have to remit to you 23 dollars, or 125 francs, which is the cost of these documents: first, the first copy of the will of his deceased brother, 10 dollars; second, the duplicate copy of the same document, 5 dollars; third, the duplicate copy of the death certificate, 2 dollars; and fourth, the legalization of these four documents by the French Consul, 6 dollars.

I received yesterday a letter from Monsieur Boze. He is still writing about your business. What singularly grieved me is that he has not received the power of attorney you say you sent him via Monsieur Lafonta. I am all the more worried because he has found reasons to regret giving his trust to his substitute for your power of attorney (Don Miguel Ulloa). He now has to find indirect ways that give him little hope of being able to settle his matters with Augustin Laterrera y Oliva and José Lara. They show the worst bad faith towards the old man who tells me that, if he has not received by next month the power of attorney he is still eagerly expecting, he intends to return to Louisiana to live out his remaining days quietly amongst friends and on your plantation. He tells me[2]

1. The inventory is contained in the Ste-Gême Family Papers, MSS 100, folder 626. The marriage certificate is not.

2. The letter is incomplete.

[MSS 100, Folder 99] Gentilly, July 14, 1825

My dear Monsieur Sainte-Gême,

I must inform you of poor Monsieur Dreux's death.[1] I closed his eyes the day before last at a quarter past five o'clock in the morning. The repeated sorrows this respectable family man has felt have undermined him little by little and eventually led him to his grave. He was obliged by his lack of means to sell the small Gentilly property he still possessed. He had been going there every day for many years, which provided him exercise that was so necessary to his health, but, after the sale, he no longer went there. From that moment on, about fifty days ago, he could not surmount the sadness that overwhelmed him. It increased to the point that he had to remain at home, and it was with almost no bodily pain, so to speak, and with all his consciousness that he passed away. You must imagine what situation the unfortunate Madame Dreux finds herself in despite her strength of character. She could serve as a model to paint the saddest painting imaginable.

Having been by her side the last days that preceded this tragic event, and with my head still full of it, I do not evoke, my dear Monsieur Sainte-Gême, our last letters, so as to write to you in more detail.

I have been promising you for a long time a statement of your revenues and expenses. According to what I sent you last year, which concerned the year before, you could gauge the low income yourself. Those for last year, and until the present, have again been very small, as most of my slaves' time was spent building the house. These gains have nevertheless amounted to 2,000 and a few piastres that served to pay for the usual expenses, as well as those for the material for the house and the workers. I have not yet finished paying the whole. I owe 197.50 dollars. I have some money left but the taxes will take part of it. Despite all, I see with satisfaction the term approach when I can entirely liquidate my debts. Then I will think of myself. My salary for last year is still unpaid. I am now painting the house with the help of Laurent and once everything is finished, it will have cost me more or less 2,000 dollars. In a few days, I will know exactly how much to the last cent.

1. François Didier Mathurin Dreux, born December 5, 1768, married Marie Françoise Emelia Olivier de Vezin Dreux in 1795 and died on July 12, 1825. He was Leufroy Dreux's brother, and thus Madame Sainte-Gême's brother-in-law. AANO, Baptisms, 1768; Interments, 1825.

As the duty of an honest man is to be frank, I have always wanted to be frank with you, my dear Monsieur Sainte-Gême. Despite all that it costs me, I will thus tell you that, if I did not intend to bid you adieu in a few years from now, I would never have thought of adding value to your plantation with a house estimated at 5,500 to 6,000 dollars. A cabin would have been enough for me. Please, be just with me and do not believe that I will leave you for any new commitments. When I no longer work for you, my dear Monsieur Sainte-Gême, my ambition will be limited to withdrawing to a small plantation at Metairie and to living there quietly with the two brothers I have left. I will send you notice eighteen months to two years in advance. Although that time is not too close, I like to think that, when it comes, if I have deserved a few ounces of your esteem, you will always keep them for me, just as you, my dear Monsieur Sainte-Gême, allow me to say, will always retain one of the greatest places in my heart, as long as I live.

Madame Dreux, the mother, sends a thousand marks of friendship to your whole household. For some time, her health has been faltering. I think she has sorrows I am not allowed to try to penetrate, but one of the deepest, and which is visible by all eyes, is her condition almost bordering on destitution.

I must tell you that Clarisse is once again, and has been for two or three months, the mother of a beautiful little girl who displays signs of a relatively good health. But I will count on her only when she has reached one year. All the other slaves are faring well. Laurent is still with me, as you will have seen before.

Our good old friend Monsieur Lambert was telling me some time ago: "Do you know it would not be extraordinary for me to go and see the bourgeois in France? We have wanted to shake hands with him for so long that we could lose hope. He will never come back here." He always remembers to ask me to recall him to you when I write.

I now have to fulfill with you, my dear Monsieur Sainte-Gême, and Madame, your spouse, and Mademoiselle Hermina, what the most respectful friendship commands. So please transmit my humble sentiments to your amiable family and to your brothers and give a kiss to the younger members of the family. Adieu. I am always, my dear Monsieur Sainte-Gême, your devoted servant.

Auvignac Dorville

[MSS 100, Folder 103] Gentilly, February 7, 1826

My dear Monsieur Sainte-Gême, I have not had the pleasure of receiving a letter from you in a long time. You could rightfully address the same reproach to me. I agree that I would deserve it. The last letter I received from you, however, is dated the 8th of February 1825. It reached me on the 22nd of May, and the one you should have received from me is dated the 14th of July 1825. I do not need to tell you of the obvious pleasure receiving news from you gives me, especially when you include news of your amiable family.

Included is a note for 4441.41 francs. This corresponds to the 838 dollars of the settlement of the Causse succession for Laurent.[1] I terminated this old business in front of a notary on the 15th of August last. I kept the sum, hoping the exchange rate between francs and dollars would offer more benefits this season. But I produced only one percent more than I would have had in August.

The last accounting of your revenues and expenses that I sent was dated from the 25th of September 1823. At that time, I had 828 dollars, as I told you. Including this sum and that of the settlement of the Causse succession,

the revenues since that time have amounted to	6731.35 dollars
and the general expenses to	5488.75 dollars

If I only send you the 838 dollars I received for Laurent, it is because I considered this a sacred deposit. I keep the rest and I accumulate little by little to pay my 1824 and 1825 salaries, which I still have not received.

I can now tell you how much the Gentilly chateau cost me: 2,062.16 dollars. It is elegant; it is sheltered so that it can stand the test of hurricanes and animals cannot get close to it. It is surrounded by a square fence the front of which is slatted. I hope to embellish it with flowers and peach trees of the best species.

The house in the faubourg has been covered with a new roof and a few other repairs have been made to it. It all amounted to about 100 dollars. Of your town properties, I had the whole courtyard and garden of one of them filled in last summer. As the *banquettes* and the neighboring plots had been raised, water had stagnated and become infected. The neighbors were complaining, the police

1. Dorville does not give any detail on Laurent's whereabouts, but since he mentions the settlement, Laurent had probably left the plantation, leaving Dorville without one of his most efficient workers.

captains kept bothering me, and the mayor was sending me orders to have it done immediately. After managing to obtain permission to make the repairs after the river went down, I wanted to have the city carters do it for me. But the two hundred piastres they demanded horrified me so that I had it done by the nègres, the animals, and the carts of the plantation. It cost me time, very precious time. I had all the tiles from the garden brought to the plantation. I will use them for my galleries.

A few days ago, I received a letter, or rather I should say a bulky volume from Monsieur Boze. If I had enough space, I could perhaps tell you about all of it. I will only let you know, my dear Monsieur Sainte-Gême, that the poor old man was assaulted on the 30th of October last between 4 and 5 o'clock in the morning.[2] He was on his way to the Hotel de la Marine to have his cup of coffee as usual. After being brought down to the ground by twelve wounds, he was about to succumb under the blows of the assassins, when a white man with a nègre who was carrying bread to the market, made them flee. According to what he tells me, he believes that these scoundrels were hired by José Lara, whom he does not name clearly but whom he suggests through various means. Finally, he informs me that he is convalescent and will come to join me next April, by which time he hopes to have completed his business for you.

Last February, as you asked, I sent you duplicates of the documents relative to the late Monsieur Leufroy Dreux's business and to your marriage certificate. And I sent Monsieur Destoup an accurate state of the business of his deceased brother Antoine Destoup. I told you then what the amount was that you needed to ask from this family for the fees connected with these documents. I think my packages must have reached you because, at the same time and via the same vessel, I wrote to Monsieur Latapie who acknowledged receipt of my letters. I also wrote to you on the 14th of July to let you know of the death of poor Monsieur Dreux.

On the 15th of December 1825, I settled my debt with Doctor Conund for the care of your slaves from the 29th of July 1818 until today. His fees amounted to 30.00 piastres. I thought I owed him much more.

If Monsieur Boze wrote to you recently, he must have told you about the death of Monsieur Sémiac, the doctor, a short time after his arrival in Cuba. This unfortunate man set foot in a foreign country with little means. Following your

2. The assault is narrated in Boze's letter to Sainte-Gême of October 30, 1825. Ste-Gême Family Papers, MSS 100, folder 101.

suggestion, he went to Monsieur Boze to borrow $800.00. Monsieur Boze did not have the money, so he asked me for the money from the settlement of the Causse succession. He knew I was about to close the succession. So, he sent me the letter you had written to him and the notes drawn by the defunct Causse to Monsieur Isard from Saint-Gaudens who will endorse them for you.

Sending back all these documents to Boze, I replied to him that I could not accept his proposal and still less use a deposit entrusted to me. I thought that my reply would not please him. On the contrary, he was content and told me that, since Monsieur Gérard Sémiac had not left anything to his brother Victor in his will, my agreement to his notes would have placed him in a difficult situation.

Our country is still miserable. We hear about nothing else but bankruptcies and frauds which have never been heard of before among our Creoles. You know Barthelemy Grima, officer of the Louisiana Legion. After making counterfeited notes for a total of eighty or a hundred piastres by forging the signature of various private individuals, this unfortunate wretch was exposed. But he was sufficiently clever to retreat early enough to avoid the punishment that he was about to receive. We still profess ignorance as to where he went.

Lately, I have had the pleasure of having Monsieur Delmas twice at the plantation. When you left this country, his hair was turning gray. It is now almost white. He strongly prayed me not to forget to mention him to you, Madame, your spouse, and Mademoiselle Hermina. Mesdames Dreux, the mother and the daughter-in-law, have entrusted me with the mission of sending a thousand marks of friendship to you and your amiable family. The younger Madame Dreux is still extremely concerned by the business of her unfortunate husband, which has not yet been terminated. She was telling me, a few days ago, that she did not know if she would have a cent left.

The two Manent brothers arrived here safely. During their crossing, they put forward the recommendation you had given them, especially the elder. They bragged that they were supposed to get a considerable sum from me. Yet, they were probably aware of what you recommended to me concerning them. They were indiscreet enough to open your letter before they sealed it again and addressed it to themselves. The younger played a little trick on the keeper of the inn where they were staying. I think they both are at Pointe Coupée. The elder tried to start a correspondence with me. I did not honor him with a reply.

Madame Chevalier Morant's wishes have been fulfilled. Clémentine is married. She married a young man who, people say, is well brought up and has a very good education. He is a European from Normandy.[3]

Chickenpox has been wreaking havoc here for five or six months. It is a real plague. It has started retreating, however.

My work has progressed well. May God help me this year. I hope I will move forward. I am still thinking of making improvements to the plantation. This year I will finish a beautiful stable so that my animals might be sheltered and, next February, I will plant an orange grove.

All the slaves are faring well. Clarisse's young daughter is huge and still gives signs of good health. I suspect that Amazilie is pregnant. Her two little daughters are charming. I have nothing else interesting to tell you on this topic, except that Catherine is also pregnant, of course by her husband Sans-Soucis. He is a young nègre of eighty or a hundred years! This miraculous progeny should soon be born.

A joke I dared when writing to Madame Latapie is the cause of the one that she made to you when she told you I was going to France. It is true that I made the journey from Gentilly to Valence d'Agen in less than ten minutes.[4] If she was serious with you, I do not know, in truth, how she grounded what she told you. It is not, my dear Monsieur Sainte-Gême, that I have not sometimes deluded my imagination with the sweet dream of seeing the Penates of my ancestors and still more with the dream of being able to express directly to you and your amiable joint families, how filled I am with the good memories I have of you. But the thing is impossible, and since my quill is too weak to express it as I wish, I resort to you, my dear Monsieur de Sainte-Gême. I pray you to fulfill all that my heart commands for so many people who are good enough to think about me, and I proclaim myself, my dear Monsieur de Sainte-Gême, your devoted servant.

Auvignac Dorville

3. His use of "European" indicates that the person he is referring to is not a native New Orleanian. See Lachance, "Foreign French," 101–130.

4. Dorville's family originated in Valence d'Agen, a city between Toulouse and Bordeaux in southwestern France.

P.S. One word about our old friend Monsieur Lambert, as usual. He often spends three and four days a week with me. We always speak of the bourgeois and the bourgeoise. He prayed me to remind him to you.

Within about forty days, I lost two aunts, Madame Bienvenu and Madame Volant. The first one died in December and my aunt Volant early this month . . .

[MSS 100, Folder 112] Gentilly, May 9, 1827

Monsieur Sainte-Gême
Saint-Gaudens, Haute Garonne

My dear Monsieur Sainte-Gême,

On March 24th last, I wrote to you, at relative length, about your business matters. However, I reserve the pleasure of writing again as soon as I have finished collecting some of the debts owed you. As soon as I collect the debts, I will send you some money. When the letter you wrote me on January 16th reached me, which was not till April 21st, I immediately took care of what you asked, about which I will inform you in the greatest detail. But before moving forward, I need to tell you some distressing news. On April 7th, fifteen minutes after 9 o'clock at night, I lost poor Amazilie as a consequence of her burns.[1] The loss was all the more difficult for several reasons that make me regret even more what happened. First, I was not on the plantation when the accident occurred. Second, I can count only three good subjects on the plantation, and she was one of them. Third, she was in the habit of providing good service and now she has left two motherless children. Now, fifteen days later, I am experiencing the saying that when it rains it pours. Bacchus fought with one of my neighbor Hopkins's nègres who stabbed him twice with a knife. The first blow was one inch above his right nipple; the other was on his left arm. Fortunately, the one at the chest veered away from vital organs or else he would have died on the spot. His condition required the assistance of two doctors that Monsieur Hopkins will pay for. He is almost healed. I hope he can resume his work before long. All in all, I will come out of it with a loss of twenty days.[2] I would be happier if I did not have to write of such things, but my duty forces me to inform you of them.

For a long time, Martin had intended to purchase his wife and his two children.[3] Had he trusted me, I would most certainly have worked on obtaining from you what he wished, thinking that you would not have refused to manu-

1. There is no precise information on what happened to Amazilie but the accident was probably related to cooking. Such accidents were frequent on sugar plantations, though Gentilly had not yet started producing sugar.

2. The juxtaposition of these sentences shows that Dorville's concern is more with the loss of production than with Bacchus's health.

3. Martin had been freed in 1816. In his last will and testament, dated October 6, 1813, recorded by Michel d'Armas, Leufroy Dreux had specified that his testamentary executor must free his *nègre* Martin, about forty-two years old, two years after his death, as reward for his good and faithful service. See appendix 3.

mit a faithful négresse whom I never had to complain about except for her two miscarriages.[4] Martin has the same intention for his two daughters and begged me with folded hands to intercede for him to you so that you will sell them to him. The elder's name is Marie-Antoinette and she was born on September 23rd of 1820; the younger is Madeleine and she was born on December 1st of 1822. I give you these details, my dear Monsieur de Sainte-Gême, so that, if you grant him the favor that he requests from you, you may send me the power of attorney required to close the sale. If this is not the case, you will oblige me by letting me know what your thoughts are on this matter. It will be easy for you to be apprised of the value of these two children from the inventory I sent you last month. The mother was estimated, with them, at $1,200; the mother at 700, the daughters at 500.

I now broach the topic of the four heirs of late Monsieur Raymond Devèze who gave me their power of attorney. How could these people give me this power without fulfilling the formalities required by law? It was not legalized by an American consul. The court of probate refused to accept it and I was on the verge of sending it back to you when I learned from one of the employees of this court that it was already known in town that I had received it and that an individual I do not know wanted to petition the court with a decision request, so that one of these heirs' share, I think it is Monsieur Peychec's, be given to him to settle debts. There was no possible hesitation and I had to accept a sacrifice and entrust a lawyer (Monsieur Apé) to undertake the necessary moves to have this power of attorney acknowledged as valid and to be authorized by the court to receive what is owed to these heirs. Thanks to the investigation of my lawyer, I managed to have my wishes fulfilled. Their forgetting the formality required by law cost me 75 dollars and 75 dollars more that I gave to Monsieur Apé. The receipt is included in the enclosed documents. Monsieur Apé promises his services until final payment of the notes I received for the heirs. When you have carefully read these documents, I pray you, my dear Monsieur Sainte-Gême, to forward them to the persons I represent here and to let them know that I will consider myself relieved of the fees owed to the notary and the French Consul, since what they hoped to obtain is reduced almost by half because Monsieur Devèze bequeathed much more than what the sale of his goods produced. On the 29th of August next, I will obtain the payment of the first of the Devèze

4. It is clear that Martin's wife was Amazilie and that, after her untimely death, he was now trying to purchase his daughters.

notes and then, from the total sum of these notes, I will take the commission that is granted to me gradually at each term.

This Devèze succession has occasioned an ongoing trial for the bequest of 10,000 dollars he made to someone named Mayer, but it seems clear that this bequest will be null and void. Half of the 10,000 dollars, added to some other debts that the court hopes to collect, will amount to about 15,000 dollars, which will have to be distributed among all the heirs. I will take pains to let you know what happens. Monsieur Devèze's donations amount to 868,200 francs, but the net total of his succession only amounts to 481,093.30 francs after the fees have been paid. I do not deem it necessary to tell Monsieur Courtade, the son-in-law, the Courtade ladies, Marie-Anne Courtade, or Monsieur Peycheau, that they have funds to receive in Bordeaux from this succession. The Court of Probate from here sent the general summary of this matter to them.

It is true that I forwarded you, some time ago, a package from Monsieur Boze and that I did not take the opportunity to send a letter to you by the same vessel. I had received Monsieur Boze's package at the plantation via Monsieur Martel, and, following Monsieur Boze's advice, I went to town as soon as possible and took it with me. A boat was leaving, and I seized this opportunity without having time to add a few words. Writing is not something I do easily. Two or three lines would have authorized you, my dear Monsieur Sainte-Gême, to reproach me for being too laconic, a reproach I hope not to deserve for my last letter and the present one.

If Monsieur Boze comes to join me, please be sure that I will receive him as his age commands.[5]

In my previous letter, I bore testimony to the pleasure I had to receive the news you sent me of your interesting family, and I renew it in the present letter. Also, in the previous letter, I told you of the assault of poor Capdeville.[6] As for Messieurs Salle and Manent, the former is still in the Attakapas, while the latter is at Pointe Coupée or at Baton Rouge. I already told you frankly what I thought about them.

Irma is still at the plantation, and I am angered to have to tell Madame, your

5. Boze was born on September 26, 1753. Dessens, *Creole City,* 232, n2. He was thus almost seventy-four years old when Dorville wrote this letter.

6. There is no mention of Capdeville in the previous extant letter. Either Dorville thought he had written about this assault or there is a missing letter that never reached its destination or was lost in the Sainte-Gême household.

spouse, that she is as bad a subject as can be. Poor Madame Dobévil was too weak with her. I had entrusted her to this now deceased lady so that she would not get lost on the plantation and so that she would learn to sew.[7] Often, man repents for things he does with the best intentions. It is what happened to me. Madame Dreux, the daughter-in-law, will be kind enough to take care of her and I hope that, with good example and harsh punishments, she can keep her and make her learn to sew, wash, and iron.

I will try, once again, to put the two tureens at the lottery. If I do not succeed, I will entrust someone with this task and will pay that person a commission. I tried to sell them to several planters, with eight and ten-month terms, but the sum of 600 dollars that I ask for them, according to your instructions, always frightens them away.[8]

I forwarded in part your friendly messages. I always do it with exactitude, naturally, when the messages are for Madame Dreux, the mother. Even before you asked me to, I took pains, from time to time, to send her a few goods from the plantation, as I was certain you would approve.

Monsieur Lambert is still the same. Although he usually no longer drinks wine, after having stopped five or six years ago, he yields to the temptation to join those who, glass in hand, keep wishing you happiness. I hope you do us justice to believe that it is not during meals that we most often think of you. When will you, my dear Monsieur Sainte-Gême, fulfill the hope you have been giving us for so long to return once more to see the country where you are loved and respected by so many people? If it is within one or two years, the wine you offered me will have time to lose some of its strength and, instead of one bottle, we could drink two to your health.

Not many of those we are acquainted with got married recently. My brother Dorville, who was a widower, remarried in August last to Mademoiselle Célestine Chalon. She is one of my cousins. Aimée Volant just married or was espoused by the eldest son of Monsieur Deschapellier, the Breton, who was also a widower; and one of the Messieurs Bienvenu, the youngest lawyer, married one the Guichard damsels.

7. The suggestion that she would have gotten lost on the plantation is intriguing. We may wonder if he was shielding her from the influence of the other slaves, if he was protecting her chastity, or if he feared that being his daughter might endanger her in some way.

8. Considering prices elsewhere mentioned in the letters (for enslaved persons, for building material, for the produce of the plantation), we may only wonder what these apparently unsellable tureens were. This suggests that they might have been made of silver or another precious material.

My aunt Labarre has endured another terrible loss last year. Valcin, her last son, died, leaving a widow and a child. He was married to Mademoiselle Virginie Conrote.

My brothers, appreciative of your good memories, have entrusted me with expressing you their gratitude and they pray you to accept their civilities.

It is time for me, my dear Monsieur Sainte-Gême, to take advantage of the space left to send a thousand honest and respectful thoughts to you and your amiable families and to tell you that I am still, my dear Monsieur Sainte-Gême, your devoted and attached servant.

Auvignac Dorville

P.S. After almost two months of rest, we went deer hunting last Sunday and we killed one. It appears that we will have many grosbeaks this year.

[MSS 100, Folder 114] Gentilly, September 24, 1827

My dear Monsieur Sainte-Gême,

Please find enclosed a draft of 3937.20 francs, so that you may forward it to the four persons in whose name it was signed. Since the 3rd of this month, I have had at my disposal the 800 dollars which were owed to them from the first payment of the drafts I received on their behalf. Once my commission had been paid, there were 772 dollars left, which I used to purchase the enclosed draft from Monsieur Clamageran. I had it at 5.10 francs but payable on demand. At the moment, in this place, the exchange rate with France only yields a benefit of 3 % payable on demand at 60 days. This is why I forwarded the sum as soon as possible instead of waiting for the exchange to offer more in three or four months.

After waiting for a very long time, I received a letter from Monsieur Boze. It came only 15 or 20 days ago. He was obliged to request an execution of the justice decision against José Lara. He informs me he hopes to come and join me as soon as he sees the end of this business.

On the 15th of July last, I wrote to you via Monsieur Dastugue and I told you about a drought we have been experiencing for a long time. It is still prevailing, and I have to use tubs and pirogues to water my animals. I had wells dug in the middle of the bayou; they give me enough water for that. I took advantage of this drought to have a canal dug about eight arpents into the cypress grove of the lake. It is in the middle of the plantation, almost in the direction of the pecan trees. The canal will be advantageous because it will allow me to get wood out easily. Although the material for the stable has been brought to the plantation, I will not have the satisfaction of seeing my animals sheltered next winter.

Zaïre's accident slightly disfigured her.[1] It cost me three or four visits to the doctor in one month. On the 30th of the month, at one o'clock in the morning, Clarisse increased your wealth with a beautiful girl; she gave birth as happily as possible.[2] All the other slaves are faring well.

For two or three weeks, poor Madame Dreux has been having bile disorders, which make her suffer much. This inconvenience happens to her often and, considering her age, it will end up becoming pernicious for her. Madame Dreux, her daughter-in-law, joins her in sending you, Madame Sainte-Gême,

1. There is no mention of Zaïre's accident in the extant letters.

2. Another instance of the focus on the importance of the slaves' reproductive function, especially on a plantation with a limited enslaved workforce.

and Mademoiselle Hermina a thousand pleasant thoughts. After these ladies, it is my turn, and I take the liberty, my dear Monsieur Sainte-Gême, to pray you to be kind enough to transmit to Madame Sainte-Gême and Mesdemoiselles Hermina and Henriette everything that can be taken from this well of the most respectful friendship. I would be happy if your brothers accepted my most distinguished civilities.

It is with the sincerest attachment that I keep calling myself, my dear Monsieur Sainte-Gême, your very humble servant.

Auvignac Dorville

P.S. Monsieur Lambert is still with me. He is still fond of the bourgeois and his bourgeoise. He asked me to recall him to your memory. Not a drop of water in the ponds, and as a consequence no teal. Yet, many of them have already arrived. Although we miss this pleasure, we avenge ourselves on the deer. The past three Sundays, we killed four.

[MSS 100, Folder 118] Gentilly, May 3, 1828

My dear Monsieur Sainte-Gême,

The last letter I had the pleasure of receiving from you is the one you wrote from Toulouse on August 21st last. Since you gave me the permission to take care of Martin's request, I hoped I would soon receive the document necessary to fulfill his deepest wish, which he often mentions to me. You encouraged me to spend the sum he would give me to purchase a nègre. Hoping, as I told you earlier, to have this sum soon, I followed your advice and acquired a 28-year-old nègre who is the best looking on the plantation. He competes, as a good subject, with my Henry, one of the first I purchased, but he surpasses him in intelligence. I paid 600 dollars outright and now that I know him, I would not let him go for a thousand.

I informed you of my intention to unite with my neighbors to make sugar.[1] The Soniat gentlemen divided their plantation, and they intend to sell it. Several reasons prevented me from associating with Monsieur Hopkins, although he expressed his strong desire to do so. Thus, I remain alone, resolved to work without my neighbors. The hardship this kind of venture will cost me the first year will not change my mind. If God helps me, I will make sugar next year. My sugar factory will be all in wood. I already had the parts necessary to make beams for my tanks and cisterns brought to the plantation. The cylinders for the mechanical part have already been reserved, which will, I think, oblige me to place one of the two tureens with the Labranche brother who is providing me with the cylinders. I hope I will have something in return. I have six and a half acres of sugar cane which are as beautiful as can be hoped and with which I can plant at least thirty acres.[2] As I need a good stable, I will have one built this year, to avoid having to do everything at the same time.

As you can see, my dear Monsieur Sainte-Gême, I will need to spend a few piastres, because I need to employ half of my handful of laborers to establish my sugar factory while the other half maintains the crop. The result of this is that I am not planning to send you a single cent this year. I am far from asking you to

1. As becomes evident in the subsequent letters, sugar making required significant investment, which explains why it would have been more economical for small planters to join forces to start producing sugar. Whitten, "Tariff and Profit," 226–233. As is evidenced in Follett, *Sugar Masters*, sugar had become profitable in Louisiana by this time and it was natural for planters to engage in sugar making.

2. Original gives seven arpents and three-quarters, and forty arpents, respectively.

come to my assistance because I would have no merit if I have the satisfaction to succeed as I hope. I need courage and action. I will do my utmost to have both and if, one day, the main capital you originally left in my hands, with insufficient workforce to exploit it, ends up producing a reasonable interest, my heart will be filled with as much contentment as possible.

Mademoiselle Hermina must have let you know that she honored me with a letter when you were in Toulouse. Should I write to you seriously or jokingly about this? Let me please do both.

I am certain she must have thought several times that, although I may have once been somewhat honest and proper, respecting the duties owed to her sex, I may have lost all this and become so rude as to be unable to beg her to forgive me. Her letter remains without reply. Although I replied to her letter twice, I was so dissatisfied with my efforts that I tore my replies into pieces. I thought I recognized in my writing something that resembled my behavior to her when I last saw her, which was so unfavorable that the ten years that have passed since then have not been enough to erase it from her memory. Her letter is perfectly written, but I can read in it the constraint she experienced while penning it. I have always complied with Mademoiselle Hermina's wishes, and I would consider myself happy if I could prove to her, in an irrevocable way, that I am, and will always be, disposed to fulfill her simplest desires as if they were sacred duties. And that this man, who will soon walk towards his thirty-seventh year, may perhaps help himself and say, if he really was mean once, "today an old lion, I am soft and accommodating," to use the words of a great author.[3]

If you find that my banter is inappropriate, please do me the favor, my dear Monsieur Sainte-Gême, not to communicate it to Mademoiselle Hermina. I reserve the honor to decidedly reply, before long, to her letter, and I will let her know that the young man she had recommended to me had already left to join his brothers when her letter reached me. If this had not been the case, I would have acted with him as with a brother.

Monsieur Boze has finally arrived in Louisiana. After sojourning for some time in New Orleans, he has decided to settle with Monsieur Pierre Martel, who is now a resident of Gentilly, mid-way between the plantation and the city. You must have received news from him because I know he writes to you.

Our old friend Monsieur Lambert sent you, last year, in July, via someone

3. "Aujourd'hui vieux lion je suis doux et traitable," Nicolas Boileau, *Épître V.*

called Monsieur Dastugue, a beautiful finely crafted coconut rug.[4] He wants to know if you received it safely. He was telling me yesterday, almost in anger: "I think that the bourgeois is forgetting us, he never sends us any news." He prayed me to recall him to you, to Madame Sainte-Gême, and to Mademoiselle Hermina.

I am really saddened by the proposal you make concerning the late Capdeville. You must know me, my dear Monsieur Sainte-Gême. Such a trifle as what this unfortunate man owed me is so little that I would consider myself privileged if no one owed me more than this. I thought he might have something at his father's, which is the reason why I took the liberty to make the request I made with you.

You are almost reproaching yourself with giving one more citizen to France, but I congratulate you for it. You have everything necessary to make your family happy. Considering the fertility of the Louisiana land, as you say, I would not be surprised if the effort you consider as the last was not followed by a few others. But if not, you will easily agree with me that four is a much more beautiful number than three.[5]

I must tell you that Monsieur Poirier from Bordeaux, one of late Monsieur Devèze's main heirs, sent here one of his nephews, who brought a power of attorney from Monsieur Pierre Courtade revoking the one he made to me, and that Monsieur Poirier released me according to the law and paid me a commission.

The Dreux ladies are faring well. They prayed me to offer a thousand friendly thoughts to you, as well as to Madame Sainte-Gême and Mademoiselle Hermina.

Please offer my very humble homages to Madame, your spouse, and Mademoiselle Hermina, and my respectful civilities to your brothers. I do not forget the young family. I think that Mademoiselle Henriette is still at her boarding school.

Receive the insurance of the sincere devotion of the one who is always, my dear Monsieur Sainte-Gême, your attached servant.

Auvignac Dorville

4. In French, *coco ouvragé*. There is no context enabling us to determine what the object was, but the most probable reference is to a rug, since "coco" in French may designate a coconut but also the fiber that surrounds the coconut and is used to make rugs. We chose the latter option, although we may also imagine that the object could be a sculpted coconut.

5. We know from the act of sale of the plantation, in 1850, that four of Sainte-Gême's children were cited among the heirs: Anatole, Armand, Céleste, and Henriette. See power of attorney in appendix 5.

[MSS 100, Folder 127] Gentilly, October 8, 1828

My dear Monsieur Sainte-Gême,

Tomorrow, a ship is leaving for Le Havre, and I take this opportunity to send you a draft. It represents the second expired term of the three Devèze heirs who gave me power of attorney. As I told you on May 3rd, Monsieur Pierre Courtade released me from representing him. The sum, once my commission was paid, was 723.75 dollars at 5.17 francs to the dollar, which amounted to 3745.40 francs, the amount of the draft I had from Monsieur Clamageran payable in Paris and at 60 days on demand. I could not have any document payable in Bordeaux as I did last year.

Please, do not, my dear Monsieur Sainte-Gême, accuse me of being too brief. I really do not have time today to have the pleasure of writing as I usually do.

My old mamma is doing well. She prayed me to offer a thousand friendly thoughts to you and to the whole family. Our old friend Monsieur Lambert has been suffering for four or five months from a disease that has made his sturdy disposition decline. You still fill much space in his heart.

Please, receive from me, for you and your amiable family, the respectful homage of the one who remains, my dear Monsieur Sainte-Gême, your devoted and attached servant,

Auvignac Dorville

P.S. All the slaves are faring well after being ill from an epidemic that came through here. It did not cause any death but caused much pain to those who suffered from it and left a large part of them unable to use their limbs for a very long time.[1]

On the 3rd instant:

It was on the 14th of this month that, after waiting for more than a year, if I may say so, I had the satisfaction of receiving one of your letters. It is the one of April 6th last in which you informed me of Mademoiselle Hermina's wedding. May she be as happy as she deserves. It is the wish I make for her, and which comes from a sincere heart. And may you, my dear Monsieur Sainte-Gême, be

1. Although there is no precise information on what this epidemic might be, it could be one of the fevers transmitted by mosquitoes, such as chikungunya. See Downs, *Maladies of Empires.*

as happy for the fatherly and generous way in which you acted with this amiable person. You are very far from exaggerating her depiction with all the praises you make of her. Your modesty will not, I hope, be offended by my frankness. The great distance between us allows me to speak to you with an open heart.

I never intended to spring a surprise on you when I wrote that I intended to make sugar. I remain resolved. I like to think that the next year, if God keeps me in good health, will see my project implemented. I wrote about it in a letter I sent to you on May 3rd last. It was not the only one you must have received from me about it because, without speaking reproachfully, this will be my fifth. So, you see, my dear Monsieur Sainte-Gême, that if I do not prove in writing that I think of you, I hope I can prove it to you some day in another way.

Following your order, I informed Martin that I was disposed to close the deal with him and that you wanted 600 dollars for his two children. He replied to me that it was more than what he offered. I finally told him I would deduct 50 piastres and I am waiting.

I will never pray you and recommend you enough, my dear Monsieur Sainte-Gême, to give to all your amiable family, without forgetting the amiable Madame d'Ustou, the most respectable compliments and the most distinguished civilities from the one who repeats once more that he still is, my dear Monsieur Sainte-Gême, your very humble and devoted servant.[2]

Auvignac Dorville

2. Madame d'Ustou is Hermina Dreux, d'Ustou being the name of her husband, one of Sainte-Gême's relatives.

[MSS 100, Folder 137] Gentilly, January 18, 1829

My dear Monsieur Sainte-Gême,

It was on November 2nd that I received your letter of September 1st in which you told me of the tragedy that happened to the unfortunate Madame d'Ustou, to you, and to your whole family.[1] I understand and share your sorrows. I unfortunately know, from experience, the grief caused by a loss such as the one you have lived through. And I am today going to make you shed more tears by telling you about the death of our good mamma, Madame Dreux, on the 27th of last month, after two months of suffering. She left this world with exemplary resignation. I waited until now to inform you of the sad news, to see what would happen to what she left and to know if it would be necessary to ask you to send me Madame d'Ustou's power of attorney. From the will of the poor deceased lady, I think that her heirs will have something and that Madame d'Ustou should send me her power in due form, so that I may represent her and act in the stead of the lawyer who will represent the absent heirs. I thus suggest, my dear Monsieur Sainte-Gême, that you seize the opportunity of the next ship to send me this power of attorney. Monsieur le Chevalier Hazeur wrote the gloomy news to his niece Madame Latapie.

I think I told you, in one of the letters I sent you last year, about repairs I want to make to our house in the faubourg. A few years ago, I had the roof entirely redone, but the floors downstairs were so collapsed that my good tenants left only to be replaced by rascals who deceived me for several months until I drove them out. Since then, and for such a long time, the house has remained closed. Finally, in August last, I went to the house to make the necessary repairs and found it in such a rotten condition that I had to renounce having it repaired. As I did not want to leave this capital dormant, I decided to have the timber cut immediately on the plantation to build a new one.[2] It is now finished and will give, for a few months, 15 or 16 piastres of rent a month and, in two or three months, 18 piastres, according to the arrangements I made with the people who have already reserved it. It is solid and elegantly built and cost me about 580 piastres, without counting the timber from the plantation. If I can find a buyer

1. Dorville is referring to the death of Hermina's husband.

2. This note, like many others in the correspondence, attests to Dorville's power to make decisions in all of Sainte-Gême's business matters. He really was the keeper of the keys to the big house in Gentilly, but he was clearly much more, which explains his mention, in his January 14, 1830, letter, of the carte blanche he says Sainte-Gême has given him.

who will pay 2,000 piastres, I will sell it immediately. I was offered 1,500 outright and simply refused. My stable is finished as well. It is splendid. It is built in brick tiles with inlays.[3] It is 100 feet long and 24 feet wide. One side will be used for the oxen and the other for the horses. In all, it cost me 150 dollars. The bricks, nails, beams, and battens amounted to 96.43 dollars. The house in the faubourg consumed the money I had reserved for the purchase of eight good horses. My revenues last year were meager. I will barely have enough, next March, to pay for my salary and I need to borrow a couple thousand piastres to cover the expense of the sugar factory, which has already progressed.[4] Four American workers and four nègres that I provided to work with them are working on cutting the timber for the structure. They have already made half of it and I hope everything will be ready sometime in October. My commitment to the contractor is as follows: 300 dollars when the sugar factory is built and covered and 800 dollars when it is finished. I have already come to an agreement for the teams of oxen. It will cost me 250 dollars. The four boilers will cost me another 250 dollars. The bricks, which I will get from my neighbor Darcantel, will cost me 290 dollars, including the tiles for the floor. I will also need 2,000 Pensacola bricks for which I will pay 50 dollars. I will make the lime myself. The sugar factory will be 100 feet long and 77 feet wide, foundry and galleries included. I still do not know how much the machinery will cost. The mill will be horizontal, and a machine called a carrier will be attached to it. It will take the canes from where the cart will unload them and will drive them to the cylinders.[5]

It is too late to think of Messieurs Soniat's house. The youngest purchased the share of the eldest and I know that he also intends to purchase the plantation of Madame Doriocourt who died recently.[6] It will sell before long. For the moment, I have enough cleared land for my eleven nègres and four négresses but when two or three years of success have rewarded my venture, I will do on a grand scale what I have already been doing on a small one. I will clear all the low lands near the river's cypress grove, which will increase by a good third the land cleared on this side. With a workforce, it will not be too difficult. I will dig ditches which will drain the bayou which is lower.

3. The original reads "soles et dez en briques," which is difficult to interpret.

4. Whitten, "Tariff and Profit," 226–233.

5. This long paragraph offers details on building material and techniques, the price of the goods required, as well as the technical devices necessary to sugar production.

6. Felicité Bernoudy d'Oriocourt, born in 1767, died in 1829. She married François d'Oriocourt in approximately 1789. She was the daughter of Anne Dreux and the granddaughter of Mathurin Dreux, the founder of the Gentilly plantation. AANO, Baptisms 1767; Interments 1829.

I have already started planting. I hope to plant about 35 acres[7] and, with my seedlings, I will have more than 40 acres in cultivation.[8] I will process about 35 acres of sugar cane,[9] which should give me, with a low count, 60,000 thousands[10] of sugar. Without mishap and with luck, it can be higher than that, according to the richness of my cane for the past five to six years. I purchased one acre from my neighbor for 50 dollars. I intend to dispose of part of my cattle, since I will use more land than usual. Moreover, I can no longer put them at the Vacherie because many of them have gone maroon in the woods, which might attract the cattle I would put there.[11] These animals have gone wild for three years. I made renewed attempts to bring them back to the plantation without success. I would have to kill them to retrieve them.

I still have not done anything with Martin, although I told him, after receiving your two letters, that I was ready to complete the sale of his two daughters. I do not know how to account for his behavior. Either he does not have enough money, or he finds that you are asking too much from him. We are at the same point we were when I first wrote to you about this matter. As I can have a good nègre for 550 piastres outright, I told him I would deduct 50 dollars from the 600 dollars you asked and that he would pay all the expenses which might amount to eleven or twelve piastres, with the power of attorney you sent me. I also observed that, if he waited too long, I would have to follow your orders by withdrawing the discount of 50 dollars.

My dear Monsieur Sainte-Gême, I cannot promise to write, this time, everything I wish to write to you. Today is Sunday and I take advantage of it because I gave the nègres their day off. Time is running out to get the necessary work done, so they work every Sunday save one a month. I gave them clothes this winter and they have an allowance of meat. If my eyes did not refuse to work by candlelight, I would write at night, but I have been unable to do so for a year.

Poor Monsieur Lambert is not faring well at all. He is always sick. He has been unable to come to the plantation for almost a month because of this. He

7. Literally, "a good forty arpents."

8. Fifty arpents.

9. Forty to forty-five arpents.

10. The original reads "60 000 milliers de sucre," without any precision on the unit, which could be cane plants, barrels of sugar, or even hogsheads. Since he is talking about processing thirty-five acres of sugar, it could also be a unit of processed sugar, which would be molasses, which might strongly suggest gallons. Or it may simply be a mistake, as thousands of thousands is an unexpected way of expressing quantity.

11. "Gone maroon in the woods" is an expression also used to designate runaway slaves.

always asks me not to forget him when sending thoughts to you and Madame, your spouse.

Monsieur Boze is still in good health. He either stays with Monsieur Martel or with Monsieur Eugène Macarty in town.

You may already know that Jackson is president of the United States. He won with a large majority over Adams. Our country that flourishes from one day to the next was almost disrupted by the election. In the wake of the abominable things written by the two Adamite and Jacksonite parties, the inhabitants of Louisiana had been worried that they would witness the horrors of Saint-Domingue renewed here but thank God peace has been restored.[12]

For a long time, you have made me hope that you would come and visit here. If you fulfill this hope, my dear Monsieur Sainte-Gême, I will write in golden letters that the day I see you will be the day in which I have had the most satisfaction in my life. Harboring this sweet hope, I entrust you, my dear Monsieur Sainte-Gême, to give my respectful homages to Madame, your spouse, Mademoiselle Henriette, and the unfortunate Madame d'Ustou, to whom I offer my sincerest condolences. I will be honored if Messieurs, your brothers, accept my distinguished civilities; my young comrades my testimonies of friendship; and you the assurance of the boundless devotion with which I am always, my dear Monsieur Sainte-Gême, your devoted and respectful servant.

Auvignac Dorville

P.S. on the 20th instant

Père Antoine died yesterday.[13] He was placed in the St-François chapel. A king could not ask, before his death, for a more beautiful ceremony than the one

12. Dorville is referring to the Haitian Revolution (1791–1803), which had ended in the proclamation of the Haitian Republic on January 1, 1804. The only successful slave rebellion in the Americas, it sent into exile thousands of whites and free people of color. The fear of seeing this repeated in other slave societies was present throughout the western hemisphere for decades after the proclamation of Haitian independence. Although the fear was generally unfounded, it was so significant that it was sometimes called Haitianism. It was especially strong in New Orleans, which had welcomed more than fifteen thousand former inhabitants of the French colony of Saint-Domingue. For more, see Dessens, *From Saint-Domingue to New Orleans.*

13. Père Antoine was Antonio de Sedella, a Spanish Capuchin friar who was long the leading authority of the Catholic Church of Louisiana. He arrived in New Orleans in 1774 and was appointed pastor of the Church of St. Louis. When the colony was granted a diocese, in 1793, he became rector of the St. Louis Cathedral and remained so until his death on January 19, 1829. He was extremely influential in the Catholic world of New Orleans, although his leadership was contested by Rome, as proven by the appointment of Bishop Louis DuBourg as the apostolic administrator of the diocese

that was carried out for him. The whole city was at his burial. The two chambers of government decided they would have a one-month period of mourning.

Adelin Dreux, who is the executor of his defunct grandmother, told me that he thought she had left debts.[14] We still do not know how much she may owe. A power of attorney is not very expensive, and I suggest that Madame d'Ustou send me hers, for how little she can claim.

All the slaves are faring well.

---

in 1812. Melville, *Louis William DuBourg*. The intrigue between Sedella and DuBourg is detailed in descriptions throughout Melville's book.

14. Guy Adelin Dreux, born in 1804 to François Didier Mathurin Dreux and Maria Françoise Emelia Olivier de Vezin, was the great-grandson of the Gentilly plantation founder Mathurin Dreux and Claudine Françoise Hugot. His grandparents were François Pierre Mathurin Dreux and Jeanne Marie Constance de Lorme. See the opening chapter, "The Gentilly Plantation: A History," for a description of Guy's ancestors.

[MSS 100, Folder 154] Gentilly, January 14, 1830

Duplicate copy

My dear Monsieur Sainte-Gême,

Please, find enclosed a draft of 5247.81 francs for Mesdames Marie Courtade and Marie-Anne Courtade, and Monsieur Dominique Peycheau. In the first letter I sent them, I included the distribution table of this transaction but, since I received a small dividend of 66.46 dollars, I am including the invoice in this letter to you so that they may share it among themselves. You would oblige me if you gave it to them together with the draft. Since the month of September last, I would have taken care of sending them their money if I had had time. But it was impossible.

In four days, it will be exactly one year since I last wrote to you. I could not tell you all the vexations I have experienced since that time. Nevertheless, I made sixteen *boucauds* of sugar, which I estimate at sixteen thousand dollars, maybe more.[1] However, I still have not sold it. Last winter was especially harsh. Periods of freezing and white frost did not finish until April 27th. Then eight months of almost continuous rain made a good share of my cane rot in the soil. The rest has suffered much from weeds, and the last straw was that diseases kept my nègres in hospital a good fourth of the year. All my workers were also ill. One died of yellow fever on the plantation. I finally rolled 17 acres[2] of cane and I kept enough to plant between 25 and 30 acres.[3] I am working at it at present but the rain that keeps falling disturbs me considerably.

I spent much money and I still owe much. In the duplicate copy, I hope to send you the summary of the expenses I made for the sugar factory and talk more at length with you than today.

About two months ago, Mother Sainte-André requested that I come to the convent.[4] I went because she told me she had promised to see me and give me news from you. She seized the opportunity to sing a thousand praises of you

1. A *boucaud* was a measurement of sugar corresponding to between 800 and 1,200 pounds. See *Notice statistique sur la Guyane française,* 134.

2. Twenty arpents.

3. Thirty to thirty-five arpents.

4. Mother Sainte-André was the superior of the Ursuline convent in New Orleans. For a detailed study of the Ursulines in New Orleans, see Clark, *Masterless Mistresses.*

and your amiable family, and she recommended, above all, that I write to you more often than I do. You understand, my dear Monsieur Sainte-Gême, if I write to you about everything concerning you, it will take all my time. No, I do not think so. How is it possible that, one day (oh, why is it not today?), I will not have the satisfaction of having you see with your own eyes if I did well or not since the time you left me entirely in charge, giving me carte blanche?[5] It would suit a happy man, self-assured in his ventures, but not a coward like me, who only has to undertake something for it to fail. Would I confess to you that, until last year, I knew neither the sorrow nor the worries of a man in debt. My hair, until then brown, is changing color and is becoming gray. Now you can judge, my dear Monsieur Sainte-Gême, how happy I would be, now more than ever, if you finally fulfilled the promise you have been making to me for so long, to come once more to see Louisiana.

The succession of the late Madame Dreux is not yet close to being terminated, although all her goods have been sold. The poor old woman had mortgaged her property to Madame Montreuil to guarantee the purchase of Angélie whom Madame Montreuil had purchased from Madame Latapie. However, that mulatto [Angélie] had been given as dowry in Madame Montreuil's marriage contract and could thus not be sold. According to our laws, the goods included in a dowry cannot be sold, the result of which was that the amount from the sale of the land and house will remain in deposit until the matter is settled.

Please offer, my dear Monsieur de Sainte-Gême, to Madame, your spouse, and Madame d'Ustou, as well as to Mademoiselle Henriette, my respectful homages, my civilities to your brothers, my friendship to the young comrades, and receive the assurance of the sincere attachment with which I am still, my dear Monsieur Sainte-Gême, your devoted and respectful servant,

Auvignac Dorville

P.S. the 30th of the instant

I just sold my sugar at 6 and ½ outright. I made 1,043.18 dollars. I still have one *boucault* of bad quality sugar that I hope to make some money from. We made less sugar at the last harvest than at the previous one, even though there are 225 to 230 more sugar plants. I was not the only one to suffer from the worthless year

5. See letter of January 18, 1829, note 2.

that has just passed. The evil was general. I also sold my molasses, but the terms are for 90 days. It amounted to 190 dollars. With the money from the sugar, I already filled many holes, but I am not yet done with it, as you can see now:

Payments made for the sugar mill and outbuildings until the present	3,416.68 dollars
To be paid this year without interests	770.62 dollars
To be paid in March 1831	2,800.00 dollars
Adding the 10% interest	
I have not added to the expenses above the sum of	487.50 dollars

used to buy seven beautiful horses, as well as what I paid in yokes, chains, and many more small accessories necessary to the running of a sugar plantation.

Martin is no longer mentioning to me the purchase of his two children. I am really angered to have told you about the request he pushed me to make.

My two tureens are still here, and I think I will keep them for a long time.

Next time I write to you, I will, I hope, have the satisfaction of giving you a more accurate accounting because my unencumbered head, if I may use this expression, and my heart, already slightly relieved from the burden of owing so much, will enable me to do better than today. Whenever I have some money, I pay those who are in the greatest hurry.[6]

Farewell, my dear Monsieur de Sainte-Gême. I repeat here what I said above for your amiable family and ensure you anew of the affection I always feel when I call myself, my dear Monsieur Sainte-Gême, your very humble and attached servant.

Auvignac Dorville

6. The cost of sugar production, requiring quasi-industrial infrastructures, was higher than the size of the plantation and its manpower permitted. Dorville repeatedly mentions the debts he made to turn the plantation into a sugar plantation. Sugar was a very risky venture and was clearly strongly affected by circumstances, whether climatic or medical. For more information on the production of sugar in Louisiana, see Follett, *Sugar Masters*.

[MSS 100, Folder 186] Gentilly, May 26, 1831

My dear monsieur Sainte-Gême,

On the 12th of this past March, I wrote a letter to you in which I went into circumstantial details about our business here. Nothing has changed since, and my sugar has not yet sold. I could not send it north because the freight this year is 7.50 dollars per hogshead, a huge price to which we would need to add insurance and commission. So, three-fourths of the planters prefer to wait rather than make such great sacrifices.

We only rarely receive news from France; the Louisiana people would be happy to learn that its government is being quietly reestablished. The interest we have for the French makes us desire that for many reasons. Trust would be reborn; business would start again; and we would not see the thousands of boxes of sugar from their colonies exported to the North of the United States and sold there for almost nothing. As a result, the July Revolution is also causing us much damage.[1]

I told you about the railway that was built in the Faubourg Marigny from the river to the lake. It has greatly increased the value of the neighboring properties; I had several proposals for your parcel in the city. I refused 15,000 piastres for it, one fourth to be remitted at closing and the rest with a term of one or two years in two equal payments. The hope of having more makes me wait. I would like you to give me at the earliest the necessary power of attorney to sell it by lots or in one piece specifying in the power that you ratify the sale I could have made before receiving your proxy. I will use the letters in which you give me permission to sell it if need be.

In general, the sugar cane does look good this year. The stocks, in particular, are not in sufficient number, in part because of the excessive cold spells we had last winter. I lost three arpents of my seedlings. This past March we had a deluge, which flooded all our low grounds on the lakeside. The lake cannot spread its

1. The July Revolution, also known as the Trois Glorieuses, or Three Glorious [Days], occurred between July 27 and July 29, 1830, in Paris. It originated in a popular insurrection, which led to the flight of Charles X and the royal family. The liberal members of Parliament, in majority monarchists, brought Louis-Philippe to the throne on August 9, marking the beginning of what is known as the July Monarchy, a constitutional monarchy that ended in another revolutionary bout in 1848. The end of the July Monarchy marked the beginning of the Second Republic. For more, see Dessens, *Creole City,* 126–127. Also see Popkins, *Press, Revolution, and Social Identities.*

waters in our cypress swamps anymore. The railway prevents it as we saw lately and what remains in our cypress swamps only slowly recedes.[2]

I am mourning my young orange trees. They had started last year to give fruit: a large part of them froze to the ground and the others are not worth much. I will not have a single sweet orange this year. Monsieur Boze, who writes to you every month, very often sees Monsieur Lambert to have news of the plantation so that he can transmit them to you in his newsletters.

Next July or August, I will have a small sum to send to Madame d'Ustou but it will be only when we know what the state of business is in France. French newspapers tell us that bankruptcies are multiplying by the day.[3]

Farewell my dear Monsieur Sainte-Gême. Please, be the interpreter of my respectful homages to your dear family and remain assured of the faithful devotion of the one who remains your devoted servant.

Auvignac Dorville

P.S. A word from our old friend Monsieur Lambert. He keeps the habit of holding me company once or twice every week and he kindly requests that I tell you that he still remembers you.

2. Dorville is a firsthand witness to the consequences of human changes to the topography, which were then just beginning to affect New Orleans and vicinity. Depuydt, "The Mortgaging of Souls," 448–464.

3. France had been undergoing a severe economic recession since 1827. See Goujon, *Monarchies postrévolutionnaires,* especially chapter 4, "D'une monarchie l'autre (1828–1832)," 203–256.

[MSS 100, Folder 199] Gentilly, February 28, 1832

My dear Monsieur Sainte-Gême,

Six days ago, I received your letters of October 16th and 31st. My commitment to sell land to Madame Lalaurie was only conditional and I committed only after consulting with several capable people.[1] I thus think that you should seize this opportunity and deal with Monsieur Saint-Avid at 20,000 piastres outright. Madame Lalaurie told me that she would not give 100 dollars more than her offer for it. Last Saturday, I went to town to ask the city surveyor to inform me of the content of the parcel. Because he was already occupied, he was unable to fulfill my request. I went back yesterday despite the rain and dreadful weather that persisted all night and, even then, I was unfortunate enough to have to return to the plantation without what I wanted. I intend to go back the day after tomorrow and I hope to be able to join the map of your property to this letter so that you may sell it more safely. I know it is 90 feet and 6 inches large.

If I had sold the house in the faubourg, I would have informed you and I would have needed your power of attorney. Although the kitchen is in ruin, it gives me a monthly rent of 16 dollars. If we wait a few more years, it cannot but gain in value. As for the plantation, I have the sorrow to tell you that the general opinion is that the land will lose value because the sugar does not sell. We have already had a few examples from the sale of sugar plantations, which were sold for much lower prices than they would have brought four years ago. Seasonal food crops do not yield much, and milk is no longer worth anything. The northern states provide us with hay at ¾ cents a pound and firewood does not offer much. What can people living far away from the city do? I will pursue cultivating sugar until the end. It involves high costs but at least, if the weather is favorable, it enables one to make some money. I will only plant 26 arpents this year. I lost part of my seedlings to the excessive cold we experienced last month. The temperature dropped 16 degrees below freezing. I am, however, among the few who suffered the least. Some planters complain about losing all of their seedlings. We can no longer count on the orange trees. The cold has killed them.

1. Delphine Lalaurie, born Macarty, best known as Madame Lalaurie, from the name of her third husband, was a New Orleans resident (1787–1849) who remained famous (or rather infamous) for torturing and killing many of her slaves. Her house on Royal Street has remained in the annals for being the place where, when the house caught on fire in 1834, several chained slaves were found mutilated, after their mistress had tortured them. For more on her, see Long, *Madame Lalaurie.* For the tradition of violence toward the enslaved, see Hall, *Africans in Colonial Louisiana.*

I sold my 1830 sugar last September, after it lost 1/10, it sold at 4–1/4 cents a pound. I had a few *boucauds* left from February that I sold these past days. Despite all the vexations I experienced last year, my crop will amount to 50 to 55 extra thousand, maybe more. But it is bad. My sugar cane was so tall when the hurricane hit that they were all laid down. I am considering selling it at 4 cents. I am expecting an answer the day after tomorrow. With the money I have left from the sale of the first and what I obtain from the sale of this one, I will pay more than two-thirds of our debt and my heart will be relieved.

I seize this opportunity, my dear Monsieur Sainte-Gême, to send Madame d'Ustou the sum of 495.80 dollars through a draft, made to your order, the amount of which I will indicate in a P.S. I still have not purchased it. The exchange rate will be, I think, 5.15 francs to the dollar. This is her share of the last payment of her late grandmother's succession, as I told you.

We have been charged the sum of 265.7 dollars for the paving. I paid for it last year. In 1818, I had a beautiful *banquette* made.[2] The wood had come from the plantation. I had to purchase only the brick. Nevertheless, it cost me 80.1 dollars. But the city, driven by the council, is very little concerned about the useless and undiscerning expenses it causes to the citizens. As a result, the citizens raised an outcry against the paving and the matter went up to the Supreme Court. The citizens lost.

It is time for me to pay a debt of duty and heart. I am sensitive to the memory of Madame, your spouse, and Madame d'Ustou, as well as that of your amiable family. So, allow me, my dear Monsieur Sainte-Gême, to join here my most admiring thoughts to my respectful homages and to pray you to convey them on my part.

As soon as I have the opportunity, I will hasten to fulfill your friendly commissions. I have been going out only rarely in the past four years and I go to town only when your business and my citizen's duties call me there. So, my relatives and friends are at war with me for not seeing them as often as before. For three or four years, I have not had the luck of enjoying brilliant health, especially since August, as I have not had fifteen days of good health. I had fever and then it relapsed several times. Then I had catarrh in the head, ears, and arms down to the left breast and close to the heart.[3] For a night, I thought you would no longer have news from me directly. I still suffer from one shoulder. I hope the nice season

2. Dorville is writing about the house in town, as *banquettes* were only built in the city.

3. Catarrh is a viral infection causing mucus to build up in the nose, throat, and lungs.

will do me good. I was not the only one to become sick on the plantation. I think I told you that everyone had been ill after the hurricane, to the point that only two were able to prepare the others' infusions.[4] Charles, who had gone to town to get the doctor for me, got drunk and, on his way back, had his arm run over by one of the railroad cars. His arm was broken and damaged but in one and a half month, he healed perfectly without being crippled. Basile has been in the hospital since January 2nd. He suffered from a catarrh that worried me much. Poultice, infusions, and drugs have been ineffective. I applied a vesicant and it fulfilled my aim.[5] Although no longer in danger, he is not working yet. All the others are faring well. Irma is about to give you a young American.[6] She will deliver soon.

Monsieur Lambert has been here since Saturday. The rain that falls incessantly prevented him from leaving yesterday. He prayed me to recall him to your memory and to that of Madame, your spouse. And to let you know that, if you are fond of him, you are not fond of an ingrate. He still has the robust disposition that makes him known as an extraordinary man of his kind.

I do not need to tell you that I was markedly saddened by the accident you had and that, as I was receiving no news from you, I feared that something more unfortunate may have happened to you. So, you may judge, Monsieur Sainte-Gême, what pleasure your letters brought to me. The day after tomorrow, I will go to town for the map and the draft, and I will deposit my letter with the mail of a vessel that, according to what I have been told, must leave shortly for Bordeaux.

I will not end my letter without praying you, once more, to convey, as much as respect commands it, my affectionate feelings to Madame, your spouse, to Madame d'Ustou, and to Mademoiselle Henriette, as well as civilities to Messieurs, your brothers. As for you, my dear Monsieur Sainte-Gême, I am still your devoted and attached servant.

Auvignac Dorville

4. An infusion is a remedy prepared from parts of a plant or herb soaked in liquid. There is no prior mention of the hurricane, but we know that a hurricane hit the city on August 16, 1831, and that a second one hit west of New Orleans on August 28–29. The first caused much damage, including a levee breach and intense flooding, destroyed the fishing village on Grand Isle, and ruined the sugarcane crop on a wide area, as far north as Baton Rouge. Bastian and Meis, *New Orleans Hurricanes from the Start,* 42–44.

5. A vesicant causes blistering.

6. Although the baby will be Dorville's grandson, what he sees is the increase in Sainte-Gême's wealth.

P.S. Included is the draft I mentioned above. The exchange rate is, as I told you, 5.15 francs to the dollar. The vessel is scheduled to depart on the 11th. I managed to have the land plot measured today. It contains less than what you purchased from Monsieur Jacques Pitot.[7]

On the 6th instant: I went to town this morning to have the registers searched to find the titles of the land parcel. I went back to Monsieur Pollock without succeeding. In the deed of sale Monsieur Pitot passed with you, he protected himself from any complaint you may lodge against him concerning the content of this property. I thus think, my dear Monsieur Sainte-Gême, that it would be prudent to sell according to the surveyor's map that I will hopefully include in the present. He promised me I would have it next Saturday. It will be left to the buyer, if the deeds of property can be found, to enjoy the privileges they might offer, if the law allows him.

On the 9th instant: Last night, Irma delivered a dead child. I will wait until she is recovered to make some promises to her, which I will fulfill if she becomes pregnant again and is under my domination.[8]

My sugar sold at 4 cents. I will deliver it by the 25th.

Farewell, my dear Monsieur Sainte-Gême. It is in person that I hope I will say it to you and shake your hand once before I go.

7. Jacques-François Pitot, also known as James Pitot, was New Orleans's second mayor (after Etienne de Boré's resignation), a position he occupied for one year (1804–1805). Among many other appointments, he was probate judge for the Orleans Territory. He died in 1831. Kendall, *History of New Orleans,* chapter 4.

8. The word "domination" is of course a violent one. The use of the first-person pronoun reveals Dorville's position with regard to Sainte-Gême's enslaved people. In an earlier instance, in his letter of July 21, 1819, Dorville wrote that Amazilie was pregnant, adding, "I hope that she will remember the lesson I gave her for her previous miscarriage and that, this time, she will carry her child to term." It seems that, with the same intent of increasing Sainte-Gême's property, he is using a softer incentive with his daughter.

[MSS 100, Folder 210] Gentilly, September 1, 1832

My dear Monsieur Sainte-Gême,

In the past month we have suffered, within eleven days, two horrible weather episodes. One, on the 16th, that lasted for 48 hours. The wind in the east-northeast part blew with such violence and came with such a strong and continuous rain that the two lakes, Bourne and Pontchartrain, became one from the heart of Gentilly to Chef Menteur. Two or three feet of water covered the road from the plantation to the city. There was as much water as during the breach that occurred on Macarty's plantation. The other, speaking of the weather episode, which started on the 18th and ended on the 19th. was not as strong but gave us almost as much water. Everything has suffered considerably. The sugar cane, in particular, was flattened and is still under water at the moment. Three-fourths of 24 arpents of corn and fava beans are also lost. I do not know if I will have enough hay to crush the little cane that will not have been ruined by the water. My animals are in a pitiful condition. The water was corrupted for eleven days and they refused to drink it. The little food I miserably provide them with still sustains them. My intention is to bring them to La Vacherie as soon as the water has improved because now it is still corrupted. The putrification of the vegetables has spread an intolerable stench in the air. All my nègres have been sick but no one was endangered. Today I only have six in the hospital. If it did not make my letter too bulky, I would send you a list of damage incurred in lower Louisiana, up to Baton Rouge. I wrote to you a duplicate letter on the 26th of this past May to have your power of attorney to sell the parcel in the city. Let me tell you that I committed to close the sale as soon as I receive your proxy for the price of 15,000 piastres outright. It is to Madame Blanc, now Madame Lalaurie. If I do not receive the entire sum, I will have 5,000 piastres outright and the rest at the term of one or two years in favorable notes, at the interest of 8% per year. I think that in five or six years, if I live until then, I might have had 18,000 to 20,000 piastres with a term of one, two, three, and four years but many things can happen by then. You forgot to lift the mortgage you had given to Monsieur Jacques Pitot on this property. I had it lifted in the last few days.

You asked me, when we managed to sell the parcel, to send you half of the money and to use the other half to buy nègres. The planters here make such little revenue that I intend, my dear Monsieur Sainte-Gême, to send you the entire sum except for the three thousand and a few hundred piastres that I owe and of which I cannot even pay the interest because I cannot sell my sugar. If this product regains favor, then, with the revenue, I will increase the workforce and then I will think of myself. This is the third year in a row that will finish without my getting my salary. There is smuggling going on in the North that our dear President Jackson and his followers accept without feeling concerned about what is happening to us here. Foreign battery syrup as well as white sugar dissolved in a little water enter all the northern harbors almost without paying duties.[1] These politicians give as a reason for this that the law is not precise enough and, according to them, since the sugar is liquid, it is no longer sugar.[2]

It is the day after tomorrow that I must go into town to deposit my letter in the mailbag of the brick, *Azilia,* leaving for France. At the same time, I will see if the exchange for France is advantageous and I will seize the occasion to send to Madame d'Ustou the sum of 495.83 dollars, which comes from the last payment of the succession of her grandmother.

Please present Madame, your spouse, and all your amiable family the respectful homages of the one that remains, my dear Monsieur Sainte-Gême, your devoted servant.

Auvignac Dorville

P.S. On the 3rd instant

I am in town with a fever. I ran to try to have paper for France. A good place offered me some at 5 francs. This is too low. Another place offered some at 5,15 francs but I fear difficulties. Another boat must leave for France soon and I will take advantage of it to send Madame d'Ustou what I was announcing earlier.

1. Battery syrup is a very concentrated brown cane syrup. "Battery" comes from the name of the last sugar boiler used to produce sugar.

2. As soon as Louisiana became part of the United States, its sugar benefited from the protection of United States tariffs.

[MSS 100, Folder 266] Gentilly, March 22, 1836

My dear Monsieur Sainte-Gême,

Please find enclosed a draft of 3,675 francs from the Union Bank amounting to 700 dollars, which corresponds to the proceeds I have left from last year at 5.25 francs. I would have sent you more but a building I had to have made, containing a kitchen, a hospital, and a servants' bedroom, cost me 521 dollars, 221 dollars more than I thought when I started it. It is 30 by 17 feet, raised 3 feet above the ground, with a front and back gallery, brick between posts, doubled with battens. It is painted bright red with tar and fish oil. I did not neglect anything, making sure it can last a century if it is possible. I had not redone my pathway in 17 or 18 years, and it was much too wide. In November and December, I worked on it, and it cost me almost two months of work. I straightened it as best I could and reduced it to 26 American feet wide, which gained me a good piece of land, and even, at some points, the whole of the old pathway. I had to make stakes, which is no longer easy here, to enclose the property that stretches from Soniat's to the house since the bayou no longer serves as a barrier against animals. It is this part of the plantation, a part that had remained uncultivated since the year you left the country, that I now cultivate. It is already almost entirely seeded and planted with fodder to sell fresh, with sugar cane for the cattle, with sweet potatoes, corn, and many melons. I will also have hay next fall and I will try to plant 300 to 400 cabbages. If I succeed this year, I intend to have a kitchen built in the faubourg. The old one is falling into ruin, and the house only yields 16 dollars a month instead of the 25 dollars it could give me with a good kitchen.

In the last but one season, the Louisiana House and Senate granted a charter to a company incorporated under the name of the Company for the Drying and Clearing of the Low Lands, Etc. Etc.[1] It goes from the city to the nuns' faubourg and down to the fishermen's canal, which means that the whole plantation is included in the sections that must be dried out. Never before, in the United States, has such an unlimited, abominable, and even, according to many, unconstitutional charter as this one been granted. If it was not so voluminous, I would send it to you so that you may judge for yourself. On the 7th of October

1. For a historical presentation of the various attempts made at containing water surges and floods in New Orleans, see Rogers, "History of the New Orleans Flood Protection System."

last, at noon, the engineers of the company started from what once was Madame Haveau's plantation and, drawing a line northward, came out on the plantation and cut a sharp point in it by Soniat's boundary marker. When I saw that, my heart bled, and I was about to stop them when, after thinking about it, I preferred to act in cold blood. The next day, I went to town and protested against them, threatening to sue them for violation of my property and make them pay for the wood they made me cut. Until now, they have made no proposal to me. So, they will soon hear from me. The case is ongoing. People say that the company now renounces drying up down to the fishermen's canal and that it will not go beyond the railroad, which crosses the Darcantel plantation.

The last letters I wrote to you were in June and July 1835. Until now, I still have not received any answer, which makes me fear, my dear Monsieur Sainte-Gême, that you may not be faring well and that it might be your health that has prevented me from receiving what I am still asking you, for the benefit of your interests. It is the renunciation by Madame d'Ustou of her rights to the two properties I sold on your behalf, as well as her rights to Martin's two daughters. Someday, your heirs might be hindered concerning what you bequeath to them. A copy of your agreement with Madame d'Ustou deposited here at the Court of Probate would prevent any difficulty that might arise without this.[2]

I will not go further without telling you about what always gives me the most pleasure. Mademoiselle Henriette must be near you and Madame, your spouse. Please be kind enough to give them a thousand honorable and respectful thoughts from my part and to not forget to send my best to Madame d'Ustou as soon as you see her, as well as to Messieurs, your brothers, to whom I offer my attentive civilities. I am also thinking of the young fellows. The oldest must already be almost a young man. I am sure that, if he were here, he would already know how to manage a horse and a rifle.[3]

I still have not found the occasion to purchase the two young nègres for whom I have 900 dollars from the Union Bank. A man I am acquainted with, who will soon be leaving for the North, has promised to purchase them for me. They will not be superfluous on the plantation. The two Josephs and Bacchus

2. Hermina renounced her rights to the Louisiana property, including the Gentilly plantation. In June 1828, she had given her rights to Gentilly to Sainte-Gême. See power of attorney given to Dorville to sell the Gentilly property in appendix 5.

3. This confirms that although Anatole was to become the godfather of Dorville's son, they did not have any close connections.

are growing old.[4] The latter just came out of the hospital where he stayed four months again after an accident. He dislocated or broke his right foot at the junction with the leg. He is still not entirely healed. Basile went maroon again. It is the third time in fifteen months. The others say he is crazy, although he is clever enough not to get caught. Zaïre also spent three months inside her cabin because of her sea sickness. She has been suffering from it for a year. Clarisse's oldest daughter caught tetanus from a windstorm on the 9th of November last. 90 days of careful treatment put her back on her feet. Finally, measles came to visit the plantation last summer. I came out of it only with lost time. Thank God, everything is going well now.

I do not give you news of Monsieur Boze because I know that he writes to you every day. However, I have never seen him fare as well as he does at the moment. I scrupulously pay him 12 dollars on the 1st of each month, which amounts to 144 dollars a year. Some time ago, he said: "I pray you to give me the favor, when I am ill and dying, of having me carried to the plantation and, after my death, of having me buried in some corner without any expense. Only you will suffice for that." He added: "I am over 83 and it should not be too long." Of course, my dear Monsieur Sainte-Gême, I will not do what he asks.

Poor Madame Dreux is sick and in a condition that will not carry her far. She does not know about it. She will have the satisfaction of leaving her two children recovered from their diseases.

Monsieur Lambert, with his 79 years, still rides his horse to go hunting. He asked me to send you and Madame Sainte-Gême his best.

Last year, I thought I was healed for a month. Unfortunately, it did not last. I am still sick and, when the weather is rainy, I am almost entirely deprived of the use of my right arm and left leg. I will soon take the same medicine that relieved me last year and try to continue it for 40 days. The first time, I could take it only for 12 days, as my stomach could not stand it anymore. My sight is entirely restored.[5] My brother, who is with me a good part of the year, asks me to send you his diligent civilities and to send his respectful homages to Madame, your spouse.

4. There is only one Joseph in the 1814 inventory (see appendix 4). Joseph was thirty-eight at the time and Bacchus was thirty, which means that by this year they were, respectively, sixty-one and fifty-three, which was old for plantation workers, especially at the time.

5. The variety of diseases mentioned in this letter, affecting the slaves, Madame Dreux, and Dorville himself, shows how unhealthy Louisiana was.

Old Monsieur Labatut asks me, every time he sees me, to remind his old friend Sainte-Gême of him. I am fulfilling his recommendation more promptly than I respond to his invitations, although I promised him, 5 or 6 years ago, to go and dine at his place without ceremony every time I am in town.

Farewell, my dear Monsieur de Sainte-Gême.

It is always from my heart that I proclaim myself your attached and respectful servant.

Auvignac Dorville

[MSS 100, Folder 274] Gentilly, March 29, 1837

My dear Monsieur de Sainte-Gême,

Included is a draft for 7,725 francs, which is 1,500 dollars at 5.15 francs per dollar, payable in 90 days. From the low exchange rate and the terms of payment, you can have a good understanding of the state of business here. I would have sent the draft to you two months ago, but my hope of having a bank draft at a higher exchange rate unfortunately made me delay two months before I shipped it. I would then have received 3 ½% and with 30 more days than usual for you to receive the payment in France. It is after obtaining good information that I went to Monsieur J. Mageur, the bearer of the present draft. Before long, it will be impossible to have one cent of exchange with France. We have been turned upside down locally with huge bankruptcies. One will happen or not for six million eight hundred piastres. It concerns Herman Jr Briggs & Co.[1]

The sum belonging to Madame d'Ustou, which I used for your benefit on August 28th, 1830, and I told you about on March 12th, 1831, is 359.12 dollars.

I took 410 dollars from last year's revenues to purchase mules. I lost one of the first I had bought from disease and had to replace it.

The last letter you wrote to me, which was sent from Toulouse, was dated May 1st, 1836. I received it in late December because Monsieur Chotin, who was in charge of delivering it to me, went to French Guiana and sent it to me via Martinique. Before receiving it, I had learned of Mademoiselle Henriette's wedding from Monsieur Labatut. Please live long enough and in good health, my dear Monsieur Sainte-Gême, to see your young children give you still younger ones. I wish it very sincerely. Please do not forget to mention me to your amiable family, especially Madame, your spouse, and Madame Avid.

I will not tell you anything new when I tell you that Monsieur Boze has been with me on the plantation since January 21st last, because you must have learned it already from him. As he has breakfast at nine o'clock and lunch at three o'clock, we do not take our meals together. It would disturb my morning occupations, but, in the morning, one hour and a half before daybreak, it is with happiness that he hears me start my noise, because it means that his cup of coffee will not be long in coming.

1. The United States was experiencing a dire economic crisis, known as the Panic of 1837. Originating in President Jackson's refusal to renew the charter of the Second Bank of the United States, this panic provoked a financial crisis that triggered a major recession lasting well into the 1840s. Europe was faring no better. For an analysis of these Atlantic crises, see Lepler, *The Many Panics of 1837*.

A few years ago, part of the population was overcome with the madness of buying and selling parcels of land here. For a year, the madness slightly abated, but for the past eighteen months, the epidemic has resumed with even more strength. So many lots have been sold that I am afraid to say that all the state's money would not be sufficient to cover half of the sales that have occurred since then. This despite the upheaval that this place is experiencing and that makes many people tremble. Improvements are going on at such a speed that you would no longer recognize the city and the faubourgs. There was word that a railroad would be built from the city to Chef Menteur, but there is no longer any mention of it. All the property owners were supposed to donate free passage and the wood necessary for it. There was also word that a street would be opened from Chevalier Macarty's plantation to the marker at the boundary between our plantation and Soniat's. I gave my consent to it. But it appears that it will not be made any time soon. A charter was granted to a company to open a canal from the lower boundary of Faubourg Marigny to Lake Borgne, via Bayou Bienvenu. There is word that it will start soon. A railroad already leads to the top of the Macarty plantation, where a town called Carrollton is taking shape. The canal of Lake Pontchartrain was completed ten months ago. A railroad that starts at the corner of Canal and Rampart streets, crosses Metairie, the cypress grove, and the meadow in a straight line to Tigouyou. From there, it will cross the lake on stilts, will reach Tangipaho, and then connect with Tennessee. It is already far advanced. Another railroad is soon to be started from Faubourg Marigny to the bottom of Terre aux Boeufs, and more to follow, etc. To this must be added the beautiful buildings that are erected every day in great numbers.[2]

Although the ardor of the land purchasers has strongly diminished, I still think that your Gentilly properties are worth a hundred thousand piastres.

Out of the many years that have passed, only one occurred without any accident among my nègres, those nasty dogs.[3] Since July 1834, Victor slept every night locked up until I freed him on December 24th last. Although in shackles, he fought with Bacchus three days later, on the 26th at noon, armed with a pickaxe handle, while the other had a sugar cane knife. Bacchus had the two bones of his forearm so abominably broken that he had to spend two and a half months in the hospital before completely recovering. This cost me about 50 piastres, his lost time, and the marooning of the other. Until recently, I had no

2. See Dessens, *Creole City*, 71–108.

3. The original reads "chiens de nègres."

news about him, despite all my searches. I think he may have joined Bazile and they are living in some huts. All the others are faring well at the moment. Big Joseph remained in his cabin for some months during these past two winters due to a pain in his right leg caused, I think, by the cold. It swells and bursts at places. His healing always comes once the extreme cold is over. We had a very cold and very rainy winter, which thwarted my activities and made many horned animals die. As for me, I lost two old cows. They had lived their days. And two draft oxen, but they died from indigestion.[4]

Monsieur Boze informed you that poor Madame Dreux had left this world on September 20 last.[5] In the past few days, the buyer of the Philiberts' house asked me to fulfill a commitment I had made to him.[6] I replied that I was expecting to hear from you from day to day about what I promised him and that my delay in respecting my word was due to an illness that kept you bed-ridden for ten months.

The weather has been dry for nine days. In the morning, we perceive distinctly, in the sun, a large black spot. In the evening, we can still see it. I do not know what this announces.

For still more personal news than what I am giving you, I hand over to Monsieur Boze. This is his part.

I will not conclude, my dear Monsieur de Sainte-Gême, without renewing my respectful sentiments to your whole family. And without saying that I remain, my dear Monsieur Sainte-Gême, your devoted and attached servant.

Auvignac Dorville

4. Dorville often refers to the aging enslaved population. The plantation, in general, had also known better days, as this remark suggests.

5. Françoise Emilia Olivier de Vezin Dreux died September 20, 1836. She was the wife of François Mathurin Dreux and sister-in-law to Madame de Sainte-Gême. Her paternal grandfather was Joseph de Lamolère. She was also a relation, by marriage, to Madame Sainte-Gême. AANO, Marriages, October 20, 1795.

6. Adélaïde Philibert was a free woman of color who came to Louisiana from Saint-Domingue with Sainte-Gême in 1809. Philibert and Sainte-Gême had three children together before Sainte-Gême married Marguerite Dreux. After his return to France, Boze was the link between the children and their father, although the son apparently visited his father in France. For more, see Dessens, *Creole City*, 23–26.

[MSS 100, Folder 282] Gentilly, April 27, 1838

My dear Monsieur Sainte-Gême,

I just heard that the brig *Raymond* is leaving for Bordeaux tomorrow or the day after. I seize this opportunity to send five bottles of gumbo filé to Madame Sainte-Gême.[1] In order to ascertain that they reach you safely, I negotiated with one of my acquaintances who is kind enough to address them to you from Bordeaux.

There is nothing new here since the duplicate letter I posted to you on the 7th or 8th instant.

At the beginning of the month, I think, poor Madame Laloire died after giving birth. She leaves a large family behind.

There is word that the banks of the North should resume their cash payments in January 1839. Ours will maybe do the same.

Farewell, my dear Monsieur Sainte-Gême. I gather here all the thoughts that may be pleasant to you and your amiable family. I hope your next letter will tell me that your health is perfect. Hoping that this is the case, I remain, my dear Monsieur Sainte-Gême, your devoted and attached servant.

Auvignac Dorville

1. Gumbo filé is ground young sassafras leaves and stems, used to season and thicken gumbo.

[MSS 100, Folder 285] Gentilly, February 22, 1839

My dear Monsieur Sainte-Gême,

It is with much sorrow that I learnt last week, from a letter sent by Madame Latapie, that your health failed again last October. You are living in a country where there are skilled doctors. Can they not cure you? Your blood always inconveniences you at the same period. Why not forestall the problem one or two months ahead? If I allow myself to give you some advice, you know, my dear Monsieur Sainte-Gême, that it comes from the heart and that nothing could please me more than to learn of your speedy and complete recovery. A father can never live too long for his children, especially when they are as young as yours are.

I would have seized the present opportunity to send you money, had I managed to collect about 200 dollars that are owed to me. I hope to recover it next month and I will then write a lengthier letter to you. I think I informed you that Monsieur Abé Hode is to write to authorize me to receive money on his behalf.[1] The eldest of the Messieurs Sorapura promised to give me some money on Monsieur Abé Hode's behalf next month. I will receive it and will transfer it to him. As he seems to be unhappy, I only require his written permission.

Monsieur Eugène Latapie has been hired as supervisor of a canal that is being built between New Orleans and the Attakapas. He has a good salary. As it was not possible to find a position for Monsieur Labatut, he courageously resolved himself to start a business along the coast with the small but decent capital I lent him. He carried out this exacting trade for six months with relative success. He just went into partnership with a young man from Bordeaux and they purchased a large decked pirogue. They have now opted for coastal navigation. In his hands, 50 cents are worth 1 dollar. If his father could help him, he would not be helping a good-for-nothing and, before long, his son would be capable of paying him back. Before six years, if he continues as he does now and has a little help, he would be well off. Two months after he began peddling, he refused employment in a school, which paid 800 dollars, hoping to go further in his small trade. I only have praises for this young man.

After a two-month wait, Monsieur Azeret obtained employment in a school where he earns 40 dollars a month. As for Monsieur Courot, he came here with the best recommendation anyone can bring when going to a foreign country.

1. The records generally mention AB Hode. Dorville probably spells it as he hears it.

He brought what he needed to work. He is starting upriver, or at least he told me that this was what he intended to do.[2]

I urgently pray you, my dear Monsieur Sainte-Gême, to write two words of news to me, telling me what you are doing to heal. If you do not write, I address my prayer to Madame your spouse. Please give her and all your amiable family the most honorable and pleasant thoughts that can be addressed and remain assured of the sincere and respectful friendship of the one who still is, my dear Monsieur Sainte-Gême, your devoted and attached servant.

Auvignac Dorville

2. Sainte-Gême probably recommended him, as he had several inhabitants from the vicinity of his village in southwestern France over the years, which gives information on the migratory circuits to New Orleans in the nineteenth century.

[MSS 100, Folder 288] Gentilly, March 15, 1841

My dear Monsieur Sainte-Gême,

Please, find enclosed a draft for 12,941.47 francs. Allow me, before I start discussing business matters with you, to talk about your amiable family.

I cannot tell you how worried I am each new year because it is always when the cold starts that your health starts failing. I would give anything, every year, to receive news from you as my New Year gift. There are none I would receive with more pleasure. I very sincerely wish that the fears you had about your youngest son's illness may have been unfounded. And I hope that the news you will give me will let me know that you are all faring well. It will happen if God grants your family the good health which I pray him to give you all.

I am deeply saddened to have to tell you that poor Delmas was no longer with us when the letter addressed to him arrived.[1] He died on December 27th last. Last summer, he had come to New Orleans to be examined by doctors. Doctor Guesnard, who treated him, had managed to make him feel so appreciably better that, in the fifteen days he had spent with me on the plantation, we had hoped to see him entirely recovered. I did what I could to keep him for two months, but the love of his family was stronger than my insistence and he returned home. Unfortunately, imprudence led him to his grave. He leaves behind, with no fortune, a large and charming family—his wife who is the mother to his five young daughters (the two eldest are married) and three sons, the two eldest are already men. The youngest, Armand, is sixteen. Madame Delmas sent him to me so that I might find him a position. After one month of waiting, I managed to place him with a cotton broker.

I could have sent you a long time ago the money you are receiving now, but the exchange rate was so unfavorable for the buyer that I hoped it would increase, which did not happen. I purchased this draft at 5.7 francs to the dollar, which is slightly more than the par value. The 800 dollars for Irma are included. On October 26th, 1840, Monsieur M. Cucullu sold her to me,[2] three or four days after receiving the power of attorney. And 1,553 dollars of the ordinary revenue, which was, in 1840, substantially lower than that of 1839. Here is a comparative table:

1. Madame Sainte-Gême's brother.

2. The original reads "m'en a passé la vente." As Irma was Dorville's daughter as well as Sainte-Gême's slave, this sale made her her father's property.

1839	sugar cane	1,028.50 dollars	
1840	"	841.81 ¼ dollars	186.68 ¾ dollars less
		186.68 ¾ dollars	
1839	melons	732.31 ¼ dollars	
1840	"	559 dollars	175.31 ¼ dollars less
		175.31 ¼	
1839	fava beans	150 dollars	
1840	"	16 dollars	134 dollars less
		" 134	
Total for 1840			496 dollars less

The cause of this decrease is not diminished labor. I had as much sugar cane last year as the year before, but because my sellers cannot sell all of it, they keep bringing what is unsold back to me. Because of that, I lost much of it. The melons were so abundant that we almost had to give them away. The fava bean crop failed everywhere. It was devoured by millions and millions of bugs and what I collected was unsellable. Instead, I used it to feed the animals. Above all else, the problem is the currency. What we—the food crop planters[3]—used to sell for a picaillon and an escalin now brings 5 and 10-cent coins. That accounts for the 20% loss I incurred in the beginning of the year. Now I trade the 5-cent coins for bank paper at 18 per piastre with retailers. But the 10-cent ones are still at 10 per piastre. I think my estimate would be too low if I said that I lost 150 dollars last year.

In 1839, my orange trees gave me 137 oranges. In 1840, I counted them in money. I made 48.70 dollars for a start. Although they suffered an icy frost last Saturday, their blossoms were sufficiently advanced to avoid any damage. Last year, I sold cattle for 110 dollars and sheep for 18 dollars. As I wrote to you already, before the winter, I took 38 cows to the cowshed I had closed in on one side. I am afraid a good part may have died. The winter has been excessively and generally harsh for the animals. It is not that it was very cold, but rain fell almost incessantly from December 29th to late February. During this time, we have not had two consecutive days of nice sun. The roads thus became impassable and

3. The original reads "habitants journaliers," that is, planters producing daily crops, the equivalent of today's truck farmers.

what annoyed me most was that it made me one month late in my labor. Let's hope the drought now does not do us as much damage as the rain has. Then we can forget the past.

You asked me if you could advantageously dispose of the property in the faubourg. The time when we could have obtained between 4,000 dollars and 4,500 piastres is no longer. Today, its price is 2,500 dollars. There is so much financial difficulty here that I do not even know if we could be paid for it outright. Everybody complains about poverty here and most expect the new president William H. Harrison to do wonders. As for me, although he did not get my vote, I would be very grateful if he managed to make the over-abundant paper money that poisons us disappear, especially the municipal bonds, much of which are counterfeit. Lucky are those who do not get any.

I asked Dobevil Dutillet to send me minute details about his family. I intend to join his letter to this one if he fulfills the promise that he made to me to send one.

I always scrupulously transmit the messages of friendship you entrust me with, my dear Monsieur Sainte-Gême, without forgetting what you ask me to tell your slaves. I congratulate myself with not having had a single one fall sick during the bad winter that just ended. It was not the case before. Nérisse and Zaïre remained for a relative long time (and too long) in their cabin. On December 7th last, Ben, one of my best laborers, walking by a ditch that was not even one foot deep, slipped and fell standing straight on his right leg. He sprained his knee, and it was not until January that he started working again. Another, Henry, was quarantined for dysentery. My accounts with the doctor and the pharmacist amounted to 55 dollars and 1 escalin. I had not paid so much in a long time. I see the Philiberts from time to time. They are faring well. The young man, who got married, sometimes comes to visit me. I think I already wrote to you about it. He is well behaved.[4]

God has forgotten that Monsieur Boze is down here. Everything has grown a little older in him except his meanness and the ridiculous obsessions no other man has ever had. I assure you he is a heavy burden for me for the fear I have that he may set fire to the house at any moment, as almost happened already several times. I would prefer to die rather that lose your papers. I have almost fallen out with him for the past two months or so, because I took away from

4. The boy, referred to as Gême in Boze's letters, was the youngest of Sainte-Gême's three children with Adélaïde Philibert. See Dessens, *Creole City,* 14–15.

him two lamps that he absolutely wanted to have during the night. Now I no longer have to get up every time he feels like visiting his room, candle in hand.

When I write to you, I am like the gourmand at the table who always keeps the best for the end. That is why I finish, my dear Monsieur Sainte-Gême, by what fills most my heart, praying you to offer Mesdames, your spouse and daughters, my respectful and sincere friendship, Messieurs, your brothers and sons, my attentive civilities, and to receive, for yourself, the insurance of the boundless devotion of the one who calls himself forever, my dear Monsieur Sainte-Gême, your devoted servant.

Auvignac Dorville

P.S. No news from the two maroons.[5]

My brother, who almost never stays with me anymore, asked me to properly respond to your agreeable thoughts and prays Madame Sainte-Gême to accept his respectful homages.

Please oblige me by opening the enclosed letter and sending it to the address indicated after adding what is missing.

5. Victor and Bacchus, letter of March 29, 1837.

[MSS 100, Folder 289] Gentilly, March 17, 1842

Second

My dear Monsieur Sainte-Gême

Included is a draft of 7,175 francs that I wish I could have sent to you earlier but, since the exchange rate for francs, until the last few days, had lost 7 ½% of its value, I did not think it appropriate to hurry. It was not without apprehension, however, that I waited until now. The people were in such a state of turmoil that it could be feared that, like the Tennesseans, they might perpetrate violent acts against the banks. The little money I have was at the Citizens' Bank from which I obtained the above-mentioned draft. Congress has just passed a strict bill in order to maintain the integrity of these institutions. Four of them have collapsed. At this point, the plantation has lost 20 dollars. Now, we hope that trust will be renewed, and business will recover little by little.

Everything, really everything, is doing badly here. For a few years, I have been wishing, and still more today, that one of your sons would come and spend a year here to see for himself the point we have reached. As early as last July, I estimated, without being mistaken, that there would be no profits for the year.[1] I told you so at the time. Deducting from the draft the 200 dollars that came from selling Martin's two daughters and the 237.50 dollars for one of the tureens, there is only 962.50 dollars left of the net produce of the plantation.[2] That is far from enough to cover the losses I incurred last year. More than half of my orange grove is lost, and the rest will not yield anything at the next crop, or at least very little. Although thwarted by rain since New Year's Day, everything I planted looks relatively good. We will see if this will be sacrificed, as in the past, or if we will have more luck. My horned livestock is increasing. But it is so worthless at the moment that I wait until circumstances change to sell any of them. These days, I am having repairs made to the house in the faubourg. It will cost me at least 80 dollars and, what is more, I have been obliged to decrease

1. The depression following the Panic of 1837 continued to plague the country. Rezneck, "Social History of an American Depression, 1837–1843," 662–687.

2. We do not know if it was Martin who purchased his two daughters. The sum mentioned here is only one-third of the six hundred dollars Sainte-Gême demanded in 1828. Perhaps Sainte-Gême's reduced fee was a consequence of the continuing depression. Dorville had been trying to sell the two tureens for six hundred dollars. It seems that this sale, although it concerned only one of tureens, eventually brought him close to what he was asking for.

the monthly rent by two piastres. For many other things, I refer to the letter I had the pleasure of sending you on December 5th, 1841.

I have been without news from you for six months, even indirectly. It is with impatience that I await some news this season.

I could never be too insistent, my dear Monsieur Sainte-Gême, in praying you to convey to your amiable family, and in particular to Madame Sainte-Gême, marks of the sincere and respectful friendship I still have for all of you. Adieu, farewell, and so long. It is from the bottom of my heart that I call myself, my dear Monsieur Sainte-Gême, your devoted and attached servant.

Auvignac Dorville

P.S. Monsieur Boze will see the end of the world. Several times, he went maroon, and I had to chase after him.

One of our elders, Madame widow de Fléchie, died these past days. My aunt Labarre as well, 4 or 5 months ago.

[MSS 100, Folder 290] Gentilly, April 9, 1845

Dear Monsieur, dear friend,

I send you herewith Monsieur Hommey's receipt for the business you asked me to complete with him. I will narrate this business from beginning to end since the time you left, to let you know exactly how I completed it. The day after your farewell letter, I went to the elder cousin of Saint-Avril who gave me the letter for Monsieur Hommey (and who told me that, this time, you had really gone). Having learned that the mail was not reliable along the coasts, I contacted Rivarde who was kind enough to have the letter delivered to Hommey's address. Several days later, I received a letter from Monsieur Hommey asking me to set an approximate date to complete your order. To be perfectly safe, I told him that it would be the following July. I was surprised, yesterday, at midday, to see him arrive at the plantation to ask for the money or, if not, to obtain a draft from me. At last, after much supplication on his part, I gave him a promissory note payable during the month of July next, for a sum of 125.35 dollars, which represents, in French money, the 659.5 francs that you are expecting. I must add that I notified Monsieur Hommey that he would lose something on my note and that you would immediately recover your funds. In spite of everything, he was content.[1] You will say that this represents many words for a trifle. Well, I could not tell the story in less. I still have your books on the plantation. Twice, I talked to Monsieur Saint-Avril about it. He wants to entrust them to the care of some acquaintance leaving for Le Havre, so that the fees you will pay might not be too heavy.

The charlatan who has attempted to cure William has failed. Doctor Alpuente is now seeing him. I fear he might not succeed either. I am still very happy about the last nègres you gave me. Only one was sick. It is the one who can do anything. Caroline is still, from what they say, without a male. There is thus no chance that her belly will swell.

On the Wednesdays of the 19th and 26th of last month, we experienced severe cold. The first was a cold rain that looked like ice, with some black ice for ten or twelve hours. Fortunately, my orange trees did not suffer from it. They are beautiful this year.

If you are not with Madame, your mother, and your amiable family, Messieurs, your uncles included, when you receive the present letter, please transmit

1. Dorville was persistent. It took him twenty years to resolve the matter.

to them, on the first occasion, my respectful feelings. As for you, dear Monsieur and friend, it is with all my heart that I call myself your devoted and attached servant.

Auvignac Dorville

The 22nd instant

Since the 10th, I would have sent you the present letter, but that very day, Irma took to the bed with a catarrh, which, for eight days, gave me much concern. Thanks to Doctor Guesnard and to my care for ten days and nights, she is better today, and I hope that she will recover from it and that, tomorrow, I will be able to leave her, without risk, to go to town to mail my letter. At the moment, Caroline's child is very sick. For three or four months, maybe more, that bitch has been pregnant, and she was still breastfeeding her child.[2] Fortunately, I noticed it last week. If I had not, she would have entirely poisoned it. Poor old Catherine is also sick and is very often in the hospital.

Since the affair of the Vassant succession, Feuillas[3] has had all the world's volcanoes in his head. For several days, however, he has been calmer. He obtained almost $900.00 for the efforts and care he displayed, for I do not know how many years. He asked me to remind you of him.

These past days, Gilbert Léonard, Hortense Lacoste's husband, was killed in a duel due to the elections.[4]

On the 25th, in the afternoon,
Ten minutes after two o'clock, Irma's poor little girl died after four days of sickness.[5]

2. The offensive language is a direct translation of the French. This paragraph shows how Dorville alternates between actual concern for the health of some of the enslaved and offensive remarks that reveal his inherent contempt for them.

3. Feuillas François Dorville was Auvignac's brother. Born in 1790, he died in 1850. AANO, Interments, March 19, 1850.

4. Eulalie Hortense Lacoste, the daughter of Pierre Casimir Lacoste, was the granddaughter of Pierre Lacoste and Pélagie Dreux. She was born on December 25, 1821. AANO, Baptisms, March 11, 1823.

5. This was not in the first letter but was added to the duplicate. There is no previous mention of Irma's pregnancy or delivery in the extant letters.

[MSS 100, Folder 296] Gentilly, February 16, 1846

My dear friend,

Included is a bill of exchange of 4,670.30 francs. According to the information I had from Madame Cavelier, the bearers are good. I went to the Albert Company, or rather to its representative, who wanted to give me only 32 ¼. I had 33 ¾ with Messieurs Heine Frères. The present 875 dollars added to the 125 dollars that I sent you in the past month of May add up exactly to 1000 piastres.

I will be more than brief today because my letter must be at the post office by ten o'clock so that it does not miss the first steamboat to Europe. But in my second letter I hope to make amends for it at length. In the meantime, if you are close to your amiable family, please give them, on my behalf, all the most agreeable thoughts you may gather.

Farewell, and receive testimonies of the sincerest attachment from your servant and friend.

Auvignac Dorville[1]

March 4, 1846[2]

As I promised in my first letter I will not be as terse this time and I will open by speaking of last year's crop.

My sweet potato crop was not successful. In general, that has been the case. I made only 140.55 dollars with them. The beans have given me 62.60 dollars. My fava bean crop has also been unsuccessful. The fodder has been in small quantities because of the drought. I made 150 dollars and a few piastres in fruit. Only melons have produced relatively well. They brought me 422.65 dollars. My sugar cane was beautiful, but I still have most of it because it did not sell. They have never sold as bad as this past season. I made only 503.25 dollars. I hoped for at least 800 dollars.

The fence between your property and that of Hopkins has been built and will hold for a long time. A beautiful slave cabin is finished, and another one will be soon.[3]

1. This letter bears a manuscript inscription reading "To Anatole." Anatole was the son of Henri de Sainte-Gême. This is the second letter of the archived correspondence written after Henri de Sainte-Gême's death.

2. This was added to the duplicate letter.

3. Gould, "'The House That Was Never a Home.'"

Concerning extraordinary expenses, I made two, but they were absolutely necessary. One was for a plow horse, 45 dollars, and the other for two milk cows, 50 dollars. I have not been successful with the latter. After 15 or 18 days, one of them died . . . The slaves are all faring well. In this past month of May, Victor walked off again: a silk stocking that I gave him as a present made him lose half his reason. Zaire again and again takes her *ganave.*[4] I wrote to you in the past that Caroline had almost killed her child by breastfeeding him while she was a few months pregnant. The poor little devil went through many ordeals. Now he is beginning to run everywhere. That bitch gave birth to a beautiful daughter on the 14th of September, but the baby died suddenly in the night of the 27th to 28th of September. I strongly suspected her of having stifled her baby in her sleep.[5] I told you in the past about the precautions I had taken to prevent that kind of thing from happening. So, if I had not feared God, I would have made her wear manacles until she gave me another weaned one.[6] Your Caroline will enrich you before long with one more slave. I must warn you beforehand that I will claim half of it because this is the work of my house servant Charles, and it would not be fair if you collected the entire amount.

The drought of last summer made us suffer much and the winter was rainy and cold, cold like we had not seen for many years, which made me one month late in my labors. This year I only planted four arpents of cane. I do not know if they will yield, the ice having spoiled much of it under the straw.

My two poor little orphans are growing every day, more in malice than in anything else. Your godson asks me every day why his godfather "pi oule vini encore," which translates as does not want to come here again.[7]

If I send my letters to Saint-Gaudens instead of Paris it is because I thought you may have succeeded in your plans and not be in France. If I send them to Saint-Gaudens, Madame, your mother, can read them and respond to them.

4. The original reads "Zaïre prend sa ganave souvent et souvent." We have been unable to discover what *ganave* means.

5. At the time, there was no knowledge of sudden infant death syndrome, which led many planters to believe that enslaved women killed their babies.

6. We note the use of the first-person pronoun again.

7. This is the first time Dorville mentions his children in the whole correspondence. He switches to Creole to quote his son's words. It attests to the use of the Creole language on the plantation, including by Dorville. The use of the word "encore" also suggests that Anatole had visited Louisiana and shows the proximity in the relationships between the Sainte-Gêmes and Auvignac Dorville. The familiarity with which the latter addresses Anatole, and the phrasing which indicates that Anatole knew about his sons, suggests that there might have been a parallel correspondence between Dorville and Anatole.

The good Monsieur Saint-Avid is as well as his asthma will permit. I see him from time to time.

I was about to forget to tell you that I planted 880 plum trees of three different qualities, to avoid having the plums all at the same time.[8]

I put William in the hands of a nègre doctor.[9] It will cost me only his food in case he does not heal. If he heals, I will have to spend 60 dollars.

On the 12th instant: It is only the day after tomorrow that I will bring my letter to the post office. I hope it will reach the north by the end of the month. You have to plan in advance because it takes 14 to 15 days from here to New York. The roads have been damaged by the bad weather. Until now we still have rain that prevents us from working the land. Farewell, thousands of friendly thoughts for you. Please, mix them with enough respect to share some of them to your amiable family.

Your devoted servant.
Auvignac Dorville

8. Although the number seems surprisingly high, this is what the original reads.

9. The medical knowledge of people of African descent is well known, and this remark shows that the Creoles trusted these Black doctors.

[MSS 100, Folder 297] Gentilly, May 20, 1846

My dear friend,

On the 6th instant, I received the letter in which you requested the second of the drafts I sent you in February last. As I addressed the second draft fifteen days after the first one, I think you had it in your hand before I received your request. That is why I did not hasten to reply earlier, expecting the departure of Monsieur Eugène Latapie who is going to join his daughter and who, since he will go through Paris, is supposed to hand the present letter to you. He is leaving tomorrow evening. If he happens to need a recommendation, I pray you to be agreeable to him. Doing this, you know that I would not be the only one to be obliged to you.

I wrote to you on April 30, via Madame Sainte-Avid, about the poor condition of our crop. Monsieur Latapie will tell you what he saw. If I still have some hope, it is with my melons. My first corn is not looking good. The second is passable. I do not know if I will be able to produce as much of it as usual. It will depend on the weather. Feuillas sends his best.

I address you a thousand farewell wishes. I shake your hand and I am your devoted servant.

AD

P.S. We are at war. You must have heard the news of the beating that the Americans gave to the Mexicans.[1]

In your last letter, you mentioned letters I have not received.

1. We believe that Dorville is referring to the Battle of Palo Alto of May 8, 1846. The war against Mexico, triggered by the annexation of Texas by the United States, had then just started. It lasted until 1848 and ended with the Treaty of Guadalupe Hidalgo that gave the United States the territory north of the Rio Grande.

[MSS 100, Folder 313]

Part of an incomplete letter[1]

Your latest letter is that of September 21, 1847, posted from Florence [Italy]. It has been with extreme impatience that I have been expecting, until now, your reply to the one I sent you on September 3 last. When I finished selling my sugar cane, I managed to exchange many 5 and 10 cent coins which were worth three or four hundred piastres for bank paper. I am seizing this opportunity to send a draft to Madame, your mother, in which I included the 91.60 dollars that is in your favor. I think, my friend, that you wrote to Madame, your mother, about this. My obligation is to also tell her about it today.

If you have some leisure time, write to me, acknowledging receipt of the drafts I am sending you. This is my fourth letter and I have no news about the others. My sheet of paper is so small that I have to shorten my letter. My duplicate will be a longer one.

Farewell

From my heart, please receive my esteem. Your devoted servant
Auvignac Dorville

P.S. We are still expecting Madame Sainte-Avid

The room above L. Thomas is rented at 12 dollars a month.

1. Incomplete letter (the upper part of the first page is missing), dated in pencil "January 48." The address page bears a note written in ink, which includes no date and is incomplete, though it deals with money and, for Auvignac, with the funds of Madame Sainte-Gême for Anatole. The upper half of the page has clearly been cut off. On the back of this lower half of the page, we can read "Last. Farewell. I shake your hand as a friend. Auvignac Dorville."

[MSS 100, Folder 315] Gentilly, July 8, 1849

Monsieur Anatole de Sainte-Gême

Duplicate

My dear friend,

You will find included 246 dollars in one draft of 1,279.20 francs. Our current account is included as usual. This account gives you the detail of the draft and will show you that the exchange rate produces loss rather than benefit.

The tenant George Nebar, who is in financial difficulty, had asked me last February to cancel his lease or to transmit it to a man called John Hoffman who manages a refreshment stand. As I did not know the latter, I asked for time to put him to the test. I was satisfied with him and, since June 1st, everything is on his account.

Jean Gélali, the fruit seller, warned me that he was about to leave me from one moment to the next. The poor man has incurred loss after loss in the past six to seven months because of cholera. The floor of the store he is leaving is rotten and the walls are so decrepit that I do not know if, in the bad season we are in at the moment, we will find a tenant immediately.

I take the present opportunity to write to Madame, your mother, and send her money. I am still without any news from you.

Feuillas sends his best. Big Head, your godson, is a bad subject and I have to rule him with an iron rod. I fear I will never succeed in managing him. As far as health is concerned, everything is fine on the plantation. As far as the weather is concerned, it is the contrary. Rain, always rain, which made me lose my melons, one of the main branches of my revenue. Farewell. Write to me to give me news. I shake your hand.

Auvignac Dorville

[MSS 100, Folder 316] Gentilly, August 2, 1850

Monsieur Anatole Sainte-Gême

My dear friend,

I wrote to you a few days ago to say that I had completed the sale of the plantation to Monsieur McDonogh. As I said, I am in a difficult situation since I have not received any instructions from you on how to dispose of the 13,250 dollars that I cashed from Monsieur McDonogh. I hope that in the first days of October next, at the latest, I will have received your reply on this matter.

Yesterday, I negotiated with Monsieur Eugene Rochereau and Co, for a draft of 259.20 dollars. Tomorrow, I will include it in this letter, together with our current account. I am actively taking care of closing all the plantation accounts that concern you. It will soon be done, and you will know how much money I have for you.

Monsieur McDonogh does not want me to leave the plantation. Until now, I have not settled anything with him. I can tell you that, if I work for him, my conditions will be such that I will be freed from this enslavement, so to speak, which has been a burden to me for almost thirty-six years.[1]

If you experience some delay in the reception of your funds, it will be compensated, I hope, by the benefit we will have on next October's drafts. As October is still at the tip of my quill, you know that this is our critical month I do not need to remind you of it. How happy will I be, my friend, to be able to complete this business in whole or in part. It worries me maybe as much as you.

As per your recommendation, I have been taking care of finding a position in a distillery for Caze, though I did not know that he was trying to be employed in the same place. He was swifter than I was. I asked the person who was helping me to see the owner of the distillery, whom he knows well, so he could transmit to him all the good recommendations this young man brought here with him.

Farewell, my friend, please give my best to your amiable family. I cordially shake your hand.

Auvignac Dorville

1. Dorville negatively describes the year he managed the plantation for the city commission. He implies that during the years he managed the plantation for the Sainte-Gêmes he was too involved, but that leasing it from the McDonogh estate will free him from his burden.

[MSS 100, Folder 317] Gentilly, January 10, 1851

Monsieur Anatole Sainte-Gême

My dear friend,

The city councils that had been stopped in their passing of a law during the past session of the legislature, were just granted this law by a decision of the Supreme Court. The first municipality set the 1850 tax on property at 1 and ⅞%. It will cost me 375 dollars for you and will add to the special tax of 66.65 dollars that I have already paid. Having learned that this tax would not be claimed until the end of February or the beginning of March next, I can give you today the included draft of 2,301.26 francs, corresponding to the balance of your rents of last month and the whole of those of this month. I say whole because, when I took the draft, I forgot to deduce my ordinary commission, as you will see in our current account included. I will settle this omission next month.

I am about to leave Gentilly forever or to stay here for two more years. Before finishing my letter, I think I will be able to let you know which one it will be. Until then, please give my best to your amiable family and believe in the friendship of your devoted servant,

Auvignac Dorville

P.S. I hope my latest letter of December 16 reached you without trouble.

12th instant: I just learned that the executors of the McDonogh succession have accepted my request of having the plantation and all it contains for two years at a thousand piastres net per year which I will give them each year on January 15. These gentlemen asked me to send them an application. I wrongly thought that it was to set the price they could ask. But not at all, since they did not accept applications that offered one third more than mine. So, my friend, here I am for two more years in Gentilly, if God blesses me.

[MSS 100, Folder 318] Gentilly, March 6, 1851

Monsieur Anatole Sainte-Gême[1]

My dear friend,

I acknowledge receipt of your three letters of December 24, 1850, and of January 14 and 18, 1851. Before pressing forward, I must let you know that February ended without my writing to you because I wanted to settle the matter of the outrageous taxes the city makes us pay. The paying population of New Orleans rebelled against them. I think that when the press echoed their sentiments, it kept the council at bay. Consequently, it asks of us only ⅞ piastre per cent, for the moment, on the value of our property. That is added to the ⅓ we paid last year for the special tax. The rumor has it that we will have something more to pay this year. I hope to God that these are only rumors! May the Devil take all the malicious aldermen.[2] The mistake I made in the account I sent you can be claimed on these taxes that put me in such a bad mood. As the owner of two poor houses on Esplanade and on Claiborne, I paid 13.35 dollars for the improvement of Levee, Charters, Conti, and Royal streets. I would not consider that amount to be so much if I had not lost, between last year and today, almost 300 dollars because of my inability to rent these houses.

Please find included a draft for 1,504.25 francs that one of my comrades gave me at 5.10 francs per dollar payable on demand after three days. Everywhere else, I could have an exchange rate of only 5.05 francs. If business continues as it has since last year, I do not know if we will continue to find exchange rates at any price. Included is the duplicate of my account of January 10 last for your rents of December, as well as the one for your rents of January and February instant.

The drafts I received from the late Monsieur McDonogh for the plantation are to his own order and endorsed by him.

The young man Cazes is working in a distillery of the first municipality where he earns, I think, 15 to 20 dollars a month.[3] As for the Medan brothers, I am still expecting a reply to the letter of their father and mother, as well as to mine. They will most likely never write to me. They are said to be real . . .

1. This folder contains two letters and two envelopes. The two envelopes are addressed to Monsieur Anatole de Sainte-Gême, St. Gaudens, France. One of them specifies "Per Boston Steamer Via England," and the other "Per New York Steamer Via England." The two letters are identical.

2. In English in the original.

3. This shows that, comparatively, the lease Dorville had to pay on the plantation was high.

however you might want to describe them. I hope your poor France will not be as shaken as you feared. The *French people*[4] are too enlightened today, and so, if anything happens in France, it will be something important. For the rest, let us hope that a long period of tranquility will lighten the heavy taxes they pay. May God want it so. I see with pleasure that you have decided to terminate with Monsieur Languille. Nothing could have pleased me more than this determination on your part. When I gave these gentlemen an account of the 6,000 dollars you owed them, they wrote on the body of the draft that it had been reduced to 2,263.58 dollars. I wrote to you, on December 16 last, that there had been an error of 21.96 dollars on this payment. And that it had been extended to July 31, 1851. Moreover, I have another genuine receipt for my draft on the Bank of the State of Louisiana to the order of these gentlemen that they endorsed without being able to cash the amount. On the day I finish paying these gentlemen, I will have the mortgage on your property immediately lifted. I acted for you in this matter as I would have acted for myself, as custom sanctioned it. When I sued Amad, I sued him only for the two months of rent that he owed me, reserving the right to sue him later for as long as he keeps my lease. I am expecting the Supreme Court's decision before acting since, at the moment, there is nothing I can do. As for Gelale,[5] I will have to write off the 30 dollars he owes. He is in utter destitution.

Concerning the investment Madame, your mother, is considering for the capital she has here, I consulted with several capable persons who told me that it could be invested, with all possible guarantees at 9%. I wrote to you, some time ago, that Monsieur McDonogh reserved the right to pay only half the taxes for 1850 when I sold him the plantation. This has not been difficult on my part because it is the custom. I will pay this half of the taxes with the rent of the house in the faubourg without spending any of the reserve I kept for the trial of the 3rd municipality against the planters of Gentilly. Once this is paid, I will include the balance of this rent in the first draft I will send you. One of your three houses is occupied by a married man. Each time his wife sees me, she complains that she cannot use this little piece of balcony without risking falling through it and asks me, as if it was indispensable to the functioning of her household, to have it rebuilt. I always reply that you do not intend to spend any money but that I will write to you about this. This is how I always attempt to save myself.

4. Underlined in the original.

5. Elsewhere spelled Gelali.

I am not sure I have replied to all your requests. I will re-read your letters and will fulfill your desires in my next letter.

Farewell. Please, give a thousand flattering and agreeable thoughts on my part to your amiable family. I shake your hand with friendship.

Auvignac Dorville

P.S. Having paid the tax to the city (which is always in a hurry to receive money) as soon as they were ready to receive it, they granted me an account of 2.5% on 175 dollars, which reduces the tax to 170.65 dollars and makes us recover 4.35 dollars.

I wrote to you some time ago that I had leased the plantation. The term I proposed for the lease was largely reduced by the executors who did not want or could not commit themselves beyond 10 and a half months. I accepted this short term, following the advice of one of these gentlemen, who is a lawyer and told me that he did not think that the succession would be settled before four or five years. If any misfortune brings you to the shores of the Mississippi River when I am still in Gentilly, please come, you will always be welcome.

Epilogue

Auvignac Dorville managed the plantation for the Sainte-Gêmes until 1850, when John McDonogh purchased it. Since McDonogh died shortly after signing the sales agreement to purchase the plantation, the city appointed a commission to oversee it. In turn, the commission leased it to Dorville, an arrangement that was new to Dorville and not to his advantage. In his letter of March 6, 1851, he explained the arrangement to Anatole de Sainte-Gême. He wrote that the lease negotiated by the commission was for ten and a half months, although, according to Dorville, "[McDonogh's] succession would not be settled before four or five years." In the letter he wrote in October of the same year, he mentioned to Anatole that he was near the end of his lease, adding that he had made no new arrangement with the McDonogh executors but that if he remained on the plantation, and if the coming year was no better than the current one, he would not make a fortune.[1] Despite the unfavorable terms, Dorville remained there for the next four years.

Looking back, we can see that Dorville was facing an uphill battle. It seems that his situation soured after the commission took control. He had to answer to a group of unsympathetic men only interested in the profits he turned. The commission had no interest in him or in the plantation, its crops, or its bondspeople, only in profits, which were in decline and unacceptable to everyone. There are signs that the Sainte-Gêmes were also in a holding pattern. Dorville was clearly exasperated with them. He had not received a reply to any of his questions con-

1. October 12, 1851, Ste-Gême Family Papers, MSS 100, folder 323.

cerning the plantation and its ongoing business matters.[2] Obviously frustrated, he wondered if the Sainte-Gêmes had lost all interest in the plantation after it had been sold, as their lack of response suggested. The Sainte-Gêmes were not alone in their disinterest, and Dorville progressively lost faith in his ability to succeed. The slave force had grown older, the plantation less profitable. For more than five years, Dorville repeatedly wrote to Anatole de Sainte-Gême asking what he should do with the documents Henri de Sainte-Gême had left on the plantation in 1818.[3]

So why did Dorville remain there, trying to salvage something from the plantation after it was sold? He probably believed that he could make a profit from the arrangement, maybe even make a better profit than he had under the Saint-Gêmes. After all, by 1850, New Orleans was one of the biggest port cities in the world. Further, the Sainte-Gême plantation had been his home, not the Sainte-Gêmes', for thirty-two years.[4] He had been there for his entire adult life, and by 1850, in poor health, he most likely assumed he would die on the plantation.

In addition, during the years he leased the plantation, Dorville's duty to the commission and his loyalty to the Saint-Gêmes put him squarely in the middle between the two parties. In April 1851, he reminded the Saint-Gêmes that the McDonogh heirs were having difficulty paying the mortgage on the plantation. It amounted to $13,250, which was no small change.[5] Dorville was also repeatedly forced to remind Anatole that Madame Sainte-Gême still owed taxes on the plantation. In another letter, written in September 1852, Dorville informed the Saint-Gêmes that the executors of the McDonogh succession still had not paid the amount mentioned and were once again unable to meet the deadline, which probably explains why they wanted Dorville to continue to manage the

2. Ste-Gême Family Papers, MSS 100, folders 341, 351, 352.

3. Ste-Gême Family Papers, MSS 100, folder 339. Although we do not have Anatole's reply, if any, we know that in June 1862, during the Civil War, he expressed his fears about having so many valuable papers in his house because of the threats against the city and because the banks no longer offered to safeguard boxes (folder 393). In October of the same year, he informed Anatole that he had placed Madame Sainte-Gême's papers with the French Consul because he feared something might happen to them or to him (folder 396).

4. Although he was probably already living on the plantation when the Sainte-Gêmes left for France, since he writes in November 1822 that he was in New Orleans "after 41 years and 3 days in Gentilly." Ste-Gême Family Papers, MSS 100, folder 354.

5. Ste-Gême Family Papers, MSS 100, folder 319.

plantation.[6] It appears that as long as he was there and the plantation continued to be self-sufficient, both the commission and the Sainte-Gêmes were determined to play the waiting game.

By 1854, however, Dorville had come to realize that life on the Gentilly plantation was no longer tenable for him. He was increasingly dissatisfied with his situation, and for good reason. The Sainte-Gêmes had paid him to manage the plantation whether it made a profit or not, and it appears that he usually had side ventures that supplemented his income. But the executors of McDonogh's estate required him to pay rent to continue in his managerial position, even though the plantation was not more profitable, and was probably less so, than it had been in the previous decades.

Dorville wrote thirty-one letters to the Sainte-Gêmes during the years he leased the plantation from the commission. In these letters, he failed to mention the plantation, its crops, or its livestock, and only on a rare occasion did he mention the bondspeople. Yet comparison of the names and ages of the slaves listed in the McDonogh sale with the list contained in the 1814 Inventory of the Late Louis Leufroy Dreux suggests that seven of the enslaved adults present on the plantation in 1814 were still there: Charles (56), Bacchus (68), Augustin (47), Nérisse (57), Zaïre (50), the younger Catherine (58), and Honoré (45, maroon).[7] To this list must be added Victor (also maroon), most probably the young man referred to by Dorville as the "Spanish gentleman," who was born one year after the 1814 inventory was made. All of them would have been known to Madame Sainte-Gême, but it seems that Dorville understood that the Sainte-Gêmes, and especially Madame Sainte-Gême, had lost interest in the plantation and its enslaved people.

At first sight, their disinterest is puzzling. Of course, the Sainte-Gêmes no longer owned the slaves, but the Gentilly plantation had been home to Marguerite Sainte-Gême for fifteen years before she left for France, and according to what Dorville wrote over the years, she had expressed a special interest in them. Throughout his earlier correspondence, he often wrote that he was giving news of the slaves at the request of Madame Sainte-Gême, who wanted to know how they were faring. She had known the older ones, had lived with them, and was apparently eager to hear about them. The letters often conveyed

6. Ste-Gême Family Papers, MSS 100, folder 328.

7. The two documents are reproduced as appendixes 4 and 6.

the impression that this was more than a simple business interest on the part of Madame Sainte-Gême, and even on Dorville's part. From the moment the plantation became part of McDonogh's estate, however, the slaves were rarely mentioned, which suggests that the interest she had earlier expressed was not personal; their lives and well-being were of no concern to her.[8]

Dorville mentions Victor once, in 1854, when he reports that he had been jailed in 1850 and that the sum of $35.50, which was owed to him by the city for Victor's labor, had only just been paid.[9] The information he gives is thus monetary. In his letter of May 1855, he wrote that two of the slaves had died earlier that year. Zaïre, he reported, "died of her drunkenness. She had a stroke that left her paralyzed." He added that two other slaves, who are not even named, had had varicella (chicken pox); one had died and one had been in the hospital for three months.[10]

These are the only two times the Gentilly slaves can be found in the correspondence after the sale. Even so, those reports make it clear that at least some of the enslaved, if not all, remained on the plantation after the sale, which also might have been inferred from the situation, since Dorville would have been unable to show a profit without the benefit of their labor. What happened to them after he left the plantation in 1855 is a mystery as the last listing we found was the one included in the 1850 sale. Dorville never even alluded to them in the later extant letters, which suggests that the Sainte-Gêmes were not the only ones who had lost any interest in the Gentilly slaves.

By March 1855, five years after Dorville had signed his first lease, he complained that he was so tired of living at Gentilly that he hoped he would no longer be there by the next January. Again, in May of the same year, he complained that "Gentilly lies heavy on me," adding that the revenue from his crops did not cover the amount of his lease and that he would have to pay from his own savings, hopefully only an extra two hundred or three hundred dollars.[11]

8. There have been recurrent historiographical debates about planter/slave relationships and indication, at least in the planters' own words, that their relationship was more than a business relationship. Dorville's letters confirm this impression. The silence subsequent to the sale, while news of the enslaved had been proportionally frequent in the earlier letters, confirms that the interest Madame Sainte-Gême manifested was for their economic value rather than for the individuals themselves.

9. Ste-Gême Family Papers, MSS 100, folder 335.

10. Ste-Gême Family Papers, MSS 100, folder 347.

11. Ste-Gême Family Papers, MSS 100, folder 347.

Upon getting ready to leave the plantation, he explained that the final amount he owed was actually six hundred dollars.[12]

The leasing fees he owed to the city were not the only financial problems he faced. From his first days on the plantation in 1818, Henri de Sainte-Gême had remunerated him for his role as manager. Anatole continued the obligation. However, beginning in 1848, Anatole failed to compensate him even though Dorville repeatedly reminded him that the sum (initially $1,024.10) continued to grow, especially since it carried a 9 percent interest rate. In December 1852, Dorville nudged Anatole again, reminding him that the back fees he owed had grown.[13] In September 1854, he asked Anatole to at least pay him the interest.[14] By September 1855, Dorville's financial situation had become so dire that he wrote that he had deducted eight hundred dollars from Madame Sainte-Gême's earnings to build a house so he could move away from the plantation. In a postscript to the same letter, he suggested that Anatole settle the debt directly with his mother. Still deferential, he wrote, "I cannot tell you the huge service you would render me if you settled the debt with your mother."[15] Eventually, his advancing age, his declining health, and his inability to make a profit or collect on debts induced him to leave the plantation.

In May of the same year, he had told the Sainte-Gêmes that he had just purchased a piece of land in Faubourg Tremé, and although he said that the location was not favorable, as there were no banquettes and no streetlights, he expressed his relief at the prospect of settling in his own house, entirely built of wood, which he expected would be finished by the following November.[16] When Dorville wrote his last letter from the plantation, on October 26, 1855, he explained that he was expecting two carts that would carry all his belongings to New Orleans and that he would then relinquish the keys to the big house to the McDonogh heirs. A month later he wrote to say that he had left the plantation after forty-one years and three days.[17]

His departure, however, did not interrupt his loyalty to the Sainte-Gêmes. During the next ten years, from November 20, 1855, to May 25, 1865, while

12. Ste-Gême Family Papers, MSS 100, folder 351.
13. Ste-Gême Family Papers, MSS 100, folder 330.
14. Ste-Gême Family Papers, MSS 100, folder 339.
15. Ste-Gême Family Papers, MSS 100, folder 351.
16. Ste-Gême Family Papers, MSS 100, folder 347.
17. Ste-Gême Family Papers, MSS 100, folder 354.

Dorville lived in New Orleans, he wrote fifty-six letters to Anatole. In them, he mostly kept the Saintes-Gêmes updated on their urban property and financial assets, on the conditions of the houses and stores they owned in the city, on the rents he received for Anatole, on the repairs he had to make. He also commented on the events that occurred in the city, as well as the economic and political situation during the Civil War. After he moved to his last home, a farm in St. Bernard Parish, he wrote sixty-seven more letters to Anatole, dated from October 27, 1865, to September 12, 1873. He continued to update the Sainte-Gême family on their urban real estate, and he often included personal news of interest to them and news of the city during Reconstruction.[18]

His final departure from the plantation, which he had managed for more than half his life, scarcely preceded the end of the plantation world as he knew it. Yet his move was perhaps fortuitous. The plantation system based on slavery had been under attack by abolitionists and Free Soilers for decades. By the time of Dorville's departure from the plantation in 1855, southern slaveholders and northern abolitionists were passionate about the issue of slavery. Both sides had reached the boiling point. In a letter dated November 3, 1860, Dorville wrote:

> I don't know if your newspapers in France mentioned the agitation that reigns in the United States about the [election] of a president. This capital question will be decided next Tuesday. It is unfortunately probable that it will be a black Republican, that is to say an abolitionist, who will occupy the seat of the presidency. All the slave states are upside down and the question of disunion is already being discussed. How will this end? Only God knows. A civil war would completely ruin the United States.[19]

Dorville rightly predicted that a Republican would be elected. Abraham Lincoln was elected sixteenth president of the United States on November 6, 1860. Politically, Lincoln's opposition to the spread of slavery into the territories of the United States provoked outrage in most of the South. A little more than a month after his election, representatives from South Carolina held a Secession Convention, and on December 22, South Carolina seceded from the United

18. Although these late letters are part of Dorville's story and of a larger narrative of the history of New Orleans, they were not included in the selection contained in the present volume as its focus is on the Gentilly plantation, which is entirely absent from them.

19. Ste-Gême Family Papers, MSS 100, folder 387.

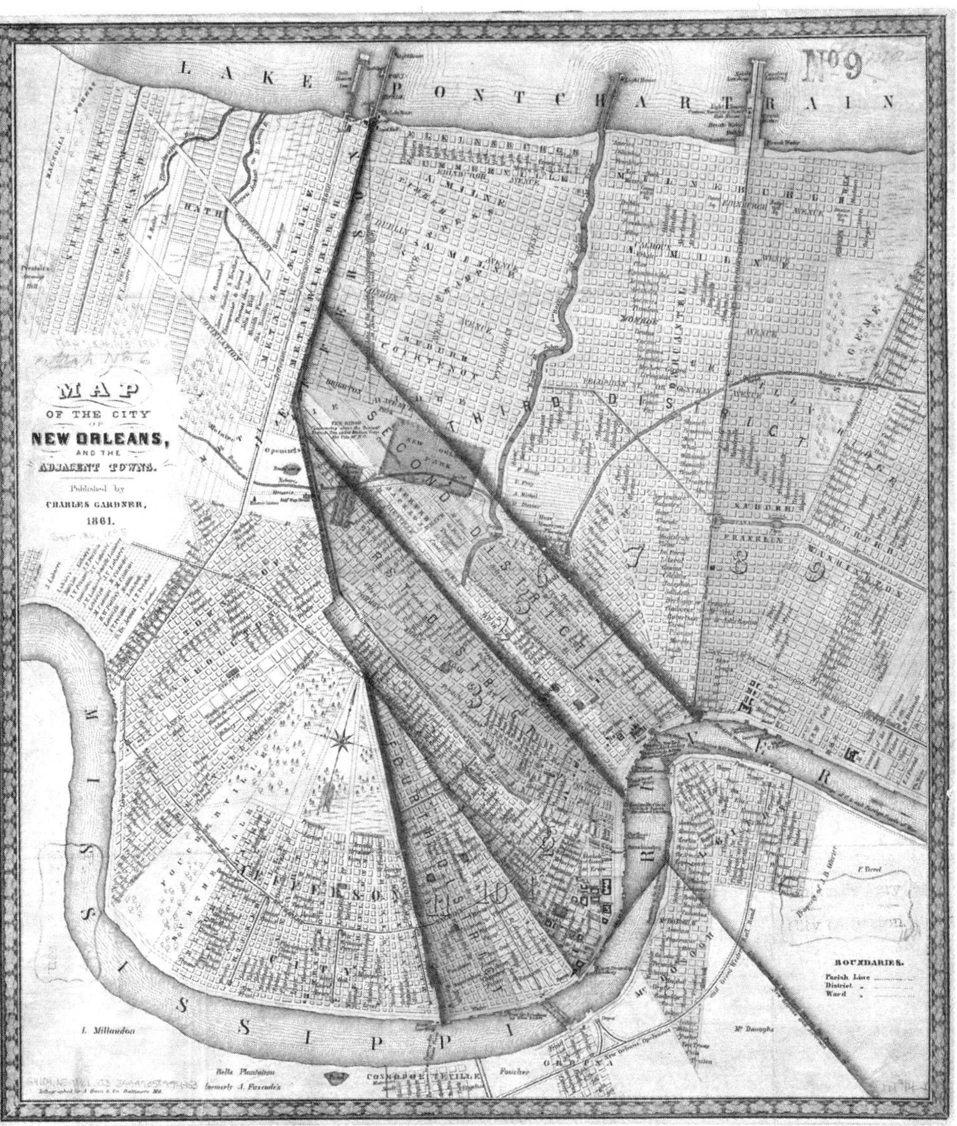

Map of the City of New Orleans, and the Adjacent Towns (1861), by Charles Gardner. This map still indicates "St. Geme," but the land bearing the name of the former owner is now a diminutive triangle enclosed between two urbanized sectors of the Gentilly Ridge. Norman B. Leventhal Map Center, Boston Public Library.

States. Louisiana seceded the following month; it was the sixth state to join the confederacy.

In February 1861, Dorville expressed his fears again:

> We are not far from March the 4th, the day when Abraham Lincoln is to take the reins of what is left of the American union. Whether it is right or not, people say he has bellicose intentions. If this is true, he will have much to do because six states have already withdrawn from the confederation and Texas will do the same before long. Other states have not said anything definite, but they will inevitably be obliged to join the secessionists.[20]

A year later Union forces captured New Orleans. Writing soon after the city fell, in June 1862, Dorville, whose political convictions aligned perfectly with the sentiments of the Confederacy, penned a few nostalgic lines. Mourning the election of Lincoln and the occupation of New Orleans, he called Lincoln's government "the government of the saber." He complained about the lack of freedom of speech, since "no one can, without risking being jailed, write or speak too loudly one's mind," adding that "the city is teeming with spies."[21] The world the slaveholders had made, the world of plantation slavery, was gone, to Dorville's deepest regret, even if he was no longer part of it and no longer the holder of the keys to the Gentilly plantation. By then, the plantation, which had been an integral part of the history of New Orleans for almost a century and a half, had been erased—symbolically erased from the narrative Dorville had built through his correspondence and literally erased from the New Orleans landscape.[22]

20. Ste-Gême Family Papers, MSS 100, folder 389.

21. Ste-Gême Family Papers, MSS 100, folder 393.

22. By the 1850s, the urbanization that had begun to overtake the plantations in and around New Orleans had started spreading northward. Campanella, *Bienville's Dilemma,* 148–150. Although, when Dorville left Gentilly, engineers were building a rudimentary drainage system meant to drain water toward Lake Pontchartrain, the city suffered from periodic floods and the back of town remained a landscape of ooze. Richard Campanella best describes the area: "The uninhabitable backswamp seemed to most New Orleanians to produce little more than miasmas, mosquitos, and mud, while inhibiting urban growth and travel. Residents and visitors dreaded the hydric landscape, anthropomorphizing it as ugly and evil" (219–220). In the 1890s, developers familiar with hydrology began to dig canals, install drainage pumps, and build levees along the lake, allowing for the development of the Gentilly neighborhood in what had once been cultivated fields and pastureland (220–222).

APPENDIX I

Auvignac Dorville's Letter of July 18, 1822

Gentilly le 18 juillet 1822

Je viens d'apprendre, mon cher monsieur Ste Gême, qu'il doit partir un bâtiment demain pour Le Havre, je profite du court moment que j'ai pour vous confirmer l'envoi[1] de traites que je vous ai fait le 21 de mai dernier, et vous dire le plaisir que vous me feriez de m'en accuser la réception au plus tôt, si vous les avez reçues.

Plus d'occasion de Bordeaux ici, et d'ici à Bordeaux ; d'après la tournure des choses, il n'y en aura pas de longtemps, alors si vous m'écrivez je vous engage à faire passer vos lettres au Havre à quelque personne de votre connaissance qui à son tour me les acheminera. Je ne saurais trop vous dire combien votre présence ici serait nécessaire pour vos intérêts. Je me rappelle vous avoir entendu dire quelques fois, mon cher monsieur Ste Gême, que l'œil du maître engraisse le cheval. Personne plus que moi n'est de cet avis ; c'est ce qui peut me permettre de vous engager à faire, pour quelque temps, le sacrifice des liens qui vous retiennent en France, et à vous rendre à mes demandes, ou plutôt à vos intérêts.

Mdme Vve Dreux, Mr Dreux et sa dame m'ont chargé de mille amitiés pour vous, madame votre épouse et mademoiselle Hermina. Mdme Desbois leur fille ne tardera pas je crois à leur faire verser encore bien des larmes. Cette malheureuse jeune personne est dans le même état qu'était sa sœur Mdme Bermudez, et les médecins pour elle ont déjà épuisé leur savoir. Par mes lettres du 21 mai je

1. The letter has been transcribed as faithfully as possible, though capitalization, punctuation, and some basic spelling mistakes have been corrected. Here, for instance, the noun "envoi" had been spelled "envoie."

vous ai mandé que le pauvre Basile est poitrinaire ; il ne va pas mieux quoiqu'il ne souffre qu'à peine de la poitrine, mais il a les jambes, les pieds et les bras tout enflés. Tous les autres esclaves se portent bien; Clarisse et Amazilie sont toutes deux grosses, et avancées. Nous avons eu ces jours derniers un coup de temps très fort ; j'avais 23 arpents de beau maïs, prêt à être plié, qui a été abimé.

Je vous prie, mon cher monsieur Ste Gême, de vouloir bien offrir de ma part à votre aimable et intéressante famille, les choses les plus honnêtes et les plus respectueuses, et me croire, mon cher monsieur Ste Gême, votre sincère et dévoué serviteur

Auvignac Dorville

P.S. Depuis que je vous ai écrit, je n'ai pas eu de nouvelles de Mr Boze.

Source: Sainte-Gême Family Papers, MSS 100, folder 61.

APPENDIX 2

Detailed Account Sent by Auvignac Dorville to Henri de Sainte-Gême, 1818–1819

1818		Credit[1]
March 3 to April 3	Oranges	345.3
March 12 to April 21	Milk	18.15
March 13	One ox	40
April 4	Hay remaining from 1817 account	36
April 17	Two months of rent of Jean-Louis	35
April (whole month)	Milk	36.4
May 22	Rent of the faubourg house (March and April)	24
May 23	One cypress tree	5
May (whole month)	Milk	83.3
		623.35[2]
June (whole month)	Milk	126.2
July (whole month)	Milk	132.4
August	Rent of the city house (1st trimester)	150
August (whole month)	Milk	65.75
September 2	Rent of the faubourg house (1st trimester)	45
September 10	Melons	73.15
September 24	Potatoes	3
		595.7
September 24	Pomegranates	1.1
September (whole month)	Milk	79.45
September (whole month)	Butter	15.4

1. All sums are in dollars.

2. None of the totals and subtotals are correct. The difference is generally a few cents, but in some cases it amounts to one or two dollars. This is true throughout the account (debit as well as credit). The figures have been left as in the original.

October 13	Dog Cupidon	60
October 14	28 of rent of Jean-Louis (owed since May 15)	17.6
October 14	Payment of the bill of Mr. Henry the lawyer	40
October (whole month)	Milk	80.1
November 14	Rent of the city house (2nd trimester)	150
		444.05
November 23	100 giraumon pumpkins	6
November 29	100 green giraumon pumpkins	2.4
November (whole month)	Milk	81.5
December 7	Potatoes and melon squash	6.3
December 10	1000 oranges	20
December 14	800 oranges	16
December 21	Rent of the faubourg house (3rd trimester)	45
December 27	1 month of Clarisse's rent	12
December (whole month)	Milk	95
		284.4
1819		
January 14	Cabbage, lettuce, and melon squash	9
January 15	One barrel of pecan	18
January 30	100 giraumon pumpkins	6
January (whole month)	Milk	107.1
February 2	One month of Clarisse's rent	12
February 9	Rent of the city house (3rd trimester)	150
February 11	50 giraumon pumpkins	3
February 11	Cabbage and lettuce	4.3
February (whole month)	Milk	96.3
March 6	Sorrel horse	110
March 6	50 melon squash	4
March 6	200 oranges	4
1818		
Sept 28 to March 17, 1819	Firewood	1,019.4
		1,543.3
	Total	3,491.2
Credit from previous page		3,491.2
March 18	One month of Clarisse's rent	12
March 18	600 oranges	9
22	700 ditto	10.4
24	1000 ditto	15
25	900 ditto	13.4
26	890 ditto	13.3
27	950 ditto	14.2

	29	1,000 ditto	15
	30	800 ditto	12.5
	31	700 ditto	10.4
	whole month	Milk	93.35
			3,710.95
April	1	800 oranges	12
	2	800 ditto	12
	3	900 ditto	13.4
	5	900 ditto	12.2
	6	800 ditto	14
	7	800 ditto	14
	8	700 ditto	12.2
	10	800 ditto	14
	11	corn grinder owed by Mr. Terrance Le Blanc	16
	12	800 oranges	14
	12	400 ditto moldy	8
	13	800 ditto	14
	14	1000 ditto	17.4
			173.4
April	15	600 ditto	10.4
	19	100 ditto moldy	3
	19	One month of Clarisse's rent	12
	20	250 oranges	7.4
	21	800 hampers of fava beans	200
	whole month	Milk	91
May	1	Rent of the city house (4th trimester)	150
	1	rent of the faubourg house (3rd trimester)	45
	14	Picking of hay[3]	356
	23	One month of Clarisse's rent	12
	24	Rent of the faubourg house (4th trimester)	45
	whole month	Milk	84.15
June	4	100 hampers of fava beans	25
			1,041.15
June	7	One dictionary of the French academy in 2 vol.	14
	15	8 months of Clarisse's rent (t see note)	96
	27	One month of ditto ditto	12
	whole month	Milk	83.5
July	9	Butter	11.1

3. There is a hardly legible name in the margin (possibly Dubmassau?), which suggests he was picking hay for someone and getting paid for it.

	16	4 cypress trees	8
	16	One month of Clarisse's rent	12
	whole month	Milk	88.65
August	4	Melons	7.1
	11	Rent of the city house	150
	17	160p of 5/6 timber at 10 each p	16
			498.6
		Total	5,423.7

(t) Shortly after Alexandre received négresse Clarisse, he left for a journey that kept him away from New Orleans 3 or 4 months. Upon his return, I could not obtain what he owed me. Having had difficulty with him on this topic, I retrieved the négresse after 8 months and rented her to herself. Finally, it is only after this long period of 7 months and a half that I managed, by trickery, to obtain payment of this sum of $96.

1818		Debit	
March	17 and 18	For the food of the servants in the city after your departure	1.5
	20	Augers	1.1
March	13 to 31	My food	8.5
	27	7 ewes 5 of them with their young	42
	27	1 goat	12
April	3	1 crate of soap	3.05
	4	The rest of my salary (+)	275
	8	Repairs to the city house	.2
	14	7 letters from your family withdrawn from the post office	0.75
	20	35# sugar	5
			389.5
	24	1 barrel of sugar (1)	22.2
	24	1 act of which you received a copy (by Mr. de Armas)[4]	25
	24	Legalization of said act by the Spanish Consul	2
	24	Repairs on one watch	6
	30	1 plowshare	22
	whole month	My food (2)	16
May	4	Payment to the jail to retrieve Bacchus	1.2
	4	2 tinplate cans	5
	5	1 rope to guide a cart	0.15
			99.55

4. The original reads Harmas but de Armas was a New Orleans notary, and it is probable Dorville misspelled his name.

	8	2 lottery tickets[5] to Mr. Garidel	10
	8	Paper offcuts to Mr. Yves Tapissier	5.4
	8	The 1815 state tax for the property of Mr. Morlot (3)	11.3
	11	½ ream of common paper	2
	20	6 pickaxes	5.4
	21	1 container bottom	0.3
	25	1 bottle of Madeira wine (4)	1.3
	30	2 container padlocks	0.4
	Whole month	My food	15.25
			51.75
June	3	1 measure to sell the milk	0.25
	5	The making of 6 shirts and two dresses for Irma	2.4
	5	1 bottle of Madeira wine	1.3
	5	2 letters at the post office	0.15
	5	12 hampers (baskets)	1.6
	13	Sewing thread	0.2
	19	1 barrel of tar	1.6
	20	Given to Nérisse for her trip to the other side of the lake	2
	23	A pair of wheels reconditioned	11
	23	35# sugar	5
			26.1
		Total	565.3

(+) I had already received $25 before you left.
(1) It is the first one you received.
(2) Included in these expenses 5 cents every Sunday for the half-day of the milk seller considering that I do not provide him with clothes. The same applies to all months to come.
(3) When he left for Havana, I gave Mr. Boze the receipt I had from Mr. Longpré so that he may recover the sum by presenting it, as expected, to Mr. Morlot.
(4) This one, like the following, has been purchased for the composition of a remedy for Nérisse.

Debit reported from previous page			$565.3
June	Whole month	My food	18.45
July	2	36 barrels of corn	75.6
	9	State taxes for the year 1819	51.4
	9	Parish taxes for the year 1819	20.65
	18	2 bottles of rum for Jn Louis	1

5. There is a shortened word here, *Pés,* which could be *payés,* that is, "paid to Mr. Garidel."

	27	1 passport for Nérisse (when she went to the other side of the lake)	2.2
	29	One pair of wheels put back on their rims	9
	31	Laurent to have one tooth pulled out	1
	31	One flannel shirt for Jn Louis	1.45
			746.6
July	Whole month	My food	17.4
August	1	Catherine's delivery	4
	13	City taxes for the year 1819	11.5
	13	Mr. Dreux balance (+)	8
	13	Repairs on two containers	1
	15	Jn Louis's burial and his coffin	7
	17	1 pair of guides for the cart	0.4
	19	Repairs on two pairs of wheels	9
	19	3 pots of grease	3
	24	1 gallon of fish oil and 5# lard	2.2
			63.7
	24	4 locks for the city house (1)	10.4
	26	1 wheel repaired	1
	Whole month	My food	15.65
Sept.	2	1 well[6] and some repairs to the faubourg house	15.6
	2	Fees for 12 scythes and the customs duties	5.3
	24	4# of cabbages	0.6
	Whole month	My food	17.75
Oct	5	12# coffee	4
			71.1
	11	Balance to the old M[ie] Louise for her to buy clothes	4
	14	Construction of 118 feet of banquette	84.05
	15	1 bucket[7] patched up and bottom covered[8]	0.5
	21	35# sugar	5
	26	8 pots of grease	8
	29	Fees for the security of négresse Anna	7.4
	Whole month	My food	20.65

6. The word is difficult to read but is most probably *puits*; hence the translation choice here.

7. It is most likely a bucket. The word in the original is *sceau,* which means "seal," but Dorville probably made a spelling mistake and wrote *sceau* instead of *seau,* which means "bucket."

8. The word used is *foncé,* a verb usually used in French to indicate that something has been put on the bottom of a container, generally a baking pan. Hence the choice here.

Nov	21	6 empty barrels	3
			133
	21	4 & ½ gallons tafia	3.75
	25	1 padlock, hasp, and 2 clamps	0.7
	29	20-day's rent of 3 nègres	31.7
	Whole month	My food	17.25
Dec	19	Given to Zaïre mandated by you	2
	26	Customs duties on imported products	.55
	Whole month	My food	18.75
			75.5
		Total	1,090.35

(+) Sum he had lent you to complete the payment of big Joseph.
(1) For the courtyard pavilion and some repairs on the house servants' bedrooms

Debit reported from previous page			$1,090.35
1819			
Jan	2	New Year's present to old Mie Louise	1
	11	Making and supplies for 3 camisoles for Irma	6.65
	11	Zaïre's food allowance for her month of apprenticeship	2
	14	2 pairs of shoes for Irma	2
	25	1 file for pit saw	0.3
	25	1 padlock	0.2
	Whole month	My food	.75
Feb	2	Alignment and leveling of the banquette, city house	3
	2	Zaïre, health bureau	1.4
	9	12# coffee	4.15
	9	1 No[9] for the city house, rue de la Levée	0.4
	11	Balance to Mr. Jambu for various remedies year 1818	12.3
	18	1 barrel of tar	.6
	21	Zaïre's food allowance	2
			1,148.5
	24	Zaïre's apprenticeship, first month	4
	Whole month	My food	17.45
March	2	1 month rent of Bambara, Mr. Dreux's nègre	18
	9	30# sugar	4

9. Abbreviation is difficult to decipher and to interpret without context.

	9	61# grease	7.5
	9	1 ham	0.75
	14	Given to Zaïre to have a tooth pulled out	1
	Whole month	My food	19.1
April	8	2 locks and 2 pairs of hinges	3
	16	1 crate of prunes (see note) (1)	2
	19	1 churn for milk	1.6
	21	Zaïre's apprenticeship, 2nd month	4
			83
	21	Zaïre's food allowance (2)	1
	22	1 swage[10] (3)	2
	Whole month	My food	17.25
May	1	Balance to Mr. Dreux's forge for the work of 1819 and 18	39.6
	4	12# Coffee	4.4
	4	Putting tires back to the wheels of the milk cart	6
	14	Balance to Mr. Dreux for interests (for the rest, see bank book)	207
	15	1 watering can	2.4
	15	639# sugar at 10/00 (4)	63.7
	15	1 barrel of salt	3.4
	16	Zaïre's apprenticeship (3rd month)	4
	16	Zaïre's food allowance	2
	3	Balance to the jail to retrieve Basile Cuba	1.2
	Whole month	My food	17.5
			372.25
		Total	1,603.75

(1) The elder Mr. Turpin asked me $2 for this crate of prunes that you took, he says, shortly before you left New Orleans and that you forgot to pay to him.
(2) Zaïre not having had her tooth pulled out, the gourde I had given her for that served for half of her monthly food allowance.
(3) You had forgotten to pay Mr. Wils for it.
(4) It is the one of which I sent you 529# via Captain Davis. I kept the rest of the barrel for my use.

Debit reported from previous page			$1,603.75
June	7	Advance on my salary	326
	15	The rest of my salary	74
	19	3 tubs for the milk	1.4

10. The word in French is *étampe.* A swage is a tool used to shape metal by hammering.

	20	Zaïre's apprenticeship (4th month)	4
	20	Zaïre's food allowance	2
	Whole month	My food	16.75
July	1	Consultation of Doctor Martin, for Colas	4
	9	6 days of rent of a négresse (Thérèse)	4.6
	12	Zaïre to have a tooth pulled out	1
	13	Expenses for Colas (he was at the faubourg at Mr. Dreux's)	3
			2041.1
	16	Zaïre's apprenticeship (5th month)	4
	16	Zaïre's food allowance	2
	21	1 crate of soap	3.4
	23	1 grindstone	3.55
	23	Other expenses for Cola's treatment	2.4
	Whole month	My food	18.05
August	4	15#1/2 Coffee	5
	11	5 gallons of eau de vie	5
	11	1 No[11] for the city house, rue du Quartier	0.2
	12	Colas's burial and his coffin	7
	16	Zaïre's food allowance	2
			53
			2,094.1

Source: Sainte-Gême Family Papers, MSS 100, folder 615. Translation by volume editors.

11. See note 9. It is the same abbreviation.

APPENDIX 3

Louis Leufroy Dreux's Last Will and Testament, 1813

Before Michel de Armas, notary public residing in New Orleans, state of Louisiana, United States of America, and in the presence of the witnesses hereafter named and undersigned.

Is present Sieur Louis Leufroy Dreux, resident of Gentilly and present in this city at the house of Madame Widow Dreux, his mother, on rue Bourbon, where said notary and witnesses have found said Sieur Louis Leufroy Dreux in a bed, unhealthy in body but of sound mind as he appeared to said notary and witnesses; said Sieur Dreux, in the sight of death and fearing to meet it without leaving his last wishes, requested said notary to receive his will that he dictated as follows:

I am the legitimate son of late Sieur François Dreux et Dame Marie Hazeur, my father and mother, and I am native of this country and about forty-four years old;

I declare that I am married to Demoiselle Marguerite Delmas, of which marriage I have two children, a daughter named Marie Hermina aged nine and a half and a son named Henry aged four;

In case my wife remarries, I want the guardianship of my children to be withdrawn from her and entrusted to Monsieur François Dreux, my brother, or, if impossible, to Monsieur Louis Hazeur Delorme;

I want my executor to proceed to all the necessary steps, all fees being paid by my succession, so as to give, two years after my death, freedom to my nègre Martin, aged about forty-two years, in reward of his good and faithful services to me;

I declare that I have made to my wife the present of the carriage and horse we are using at the moment;

I give and bequeath to my wife the whole furniture that now garnishes our house in Gentilly so that she may enjoy it as she estimates proper;

I appoint as my executor François Dreux, my brother, whom I beg to grant me this last token of friendship and I authorize him to act in whatever is related to my succession without any intervention of justice as far as possible and I give him referral of my possessions for the year and half.

I cancel and revoke all the testaments and codicils I may have written before the present one which is the only one containing my last wishes;

This testament was thus dictated by the testator in the presence of said witnesses to said notary who wrote it down immediately and without diverting to other acts, all in the presence of said witnesses. This testament was read by said notary to the Sieur testator who declared hearing it and understanding it properly and persevering;

I want the property of my children to be maintained in nature, except in absolute necessity.

Done and acted in New Orleans, in the house of said Madame Dreux, on the sixth day of the month of October of the year one thousand eight hundred and thirteen, the thirty-eighth year of the American Independence, in the presence of Sieurs Henry de Ste-Gême, Pierre Roger, Jean Joseph Blache, Charles Louis Blache, all four witnesses expressly required for this and residents in this city. And the Sieur testator has signed with said notary and witnesses after the whole was read.

Louis Leufroy Dreux
Signed Roger, H Ste Gême, Jn Jh Blâche, Ch L Blâche, Michel de Armas

Source: Louisiana Court of Probates, Will Book 2, 95. Translation by volume editors.

APPENDIX 4

Inventory of the Estate of the Late Louis Leufroy Dreux, 1814

STATE OF LOUISIANA

PARISH OF ORLEANS COURT OF PROBATES

REGISTER OF WILLS OFFICE

Inventory of the Estate of the late Louis Leufroy Dreux deceased

Today, the twenty-fourth day of the month of May of the year eighteen fourteen of our Lord and the thirty-eighth of the independence of the United States of America, eight o'clock in the morning, at the request of Mr. François Dreux, testamentary executor of the late Sieur Louis Leufroy, we, Jean Baptiste Marc Brierres, Deputy Register of the wills for the City and Parish of New Orleans, transported ourselves to a plantation sited in the Gentilly neighborhood, distant by about one league and a half from this city, to proceed to a descriptive and estimative inventory of the movable and immovable property coming from the succession of the aforesaid late Sieur Leufroy Dreux, where, upon arriving, we found Sieur François Dreux, testamentary executor of the deceased, Dame Marguerite Dreux, the widow of Louis Leufroy Dreux, natural guardian of her minor children named Marie Hermina and Henry Dreux, and Jean Latapie, surrogate guardian of the aforesaid minor children, and have, in their presence and in that of the Sieurs Paul Darcantel and Pierre Colson, neighbor planters and appreciators chosen by the testamentary executor, who took with us the oath to estimate in good conscience, and according to their best judgement, everything that would be presented to them to be inventoried as coming from the aforesaid succession, to which we proceeded as follows. Here Mr. François

Dreux declared to us that, at the time of the death of the aforesaid Sieur Louis Leufroy Dreux, they had not had seals affixed on the movable effects which were concerned, as the furniture was bequeathed in its entirety to the widow of the aforesaid deceased, of which he requested due acknowledgement, which we duly acknowledged, and he signed.

Signed François Dreux.

First, in a bedroom, on the righthand side upon entering, we found what follows:

A wardrobe in walnut wood, at the opening and examination of which we found what follows:

Sixteen good or bad shirts, estimated by the aforesaid appreciators ten piastres	10
Twelve pairs of trousers from Nankin, Bazin, and other effects estimated ten piastres	10
Fifteen white and colored handkerchiefs estimated six piastres	6
Three Cirsaca jackets estimated eight piastres	8
Two black suits and a gray serge frock coat with a pair of casimir trousers together estimated twenty piastres	20
A hat estimated by the same three piastres	3
Three wool blankets and two cotton counterpanes estimated together twenty-five piastres	25[1]
Three pairs of assie bed sheets estimated twenty-five piastres	25
Two cotton mosquito nets and two linen ones estimated forty piastres	40
Five dozen good and bad finely worked napkins and four tablecloths ditto estimated twenty-five piastres	25
A silver watch estimated ten piastres	10
Aforesaid wardrobe in walnut wood estimated twenty piastres	20
A mounted walnut bed furnished with a Spanish moss mattress and a bolster estimated fifteen piastres	15

1. A subtotal was included here ($82). Likewise, a subtotal was indicated at the bottom of every page and then repeated at the top of the next page. They are suppressed here for the sake of clarity.

A broken mirror and a pair of candlesticks	
estimated two piastres	2
Iron fire tongs and a pair of andirons	
estimated one piastre fifty	1.50
A pair of silver brace buckles	
estimated one piastre	1
A pair of razors and their case	
estimated six piastres	6
A single-shot gun	
estimated fifteen piastres	15
Twelve dark straw chairs and an armchair	
estimated twelve piastres	12
Which is everything that was in the aforesaid room.	

In the room on the righthand side:

Two medium-sized tables in walnut wood	
estimated nine piastres	9
A large dinner table in walnut wood	
estimated two piastres	2[2]
Which is everything that was in the aforesaid room	

In the pantry, at the bottom of the house:

Six silver pieces of cutlery and a large silver spoon	
estimated thirty-four piastres	34
Twelve common stemmed glasses	
estimated one piastre fifty cents	1.50
Four dozen dinner plates and a dozen soup plates and eight earthenware dishes of various sizes	
estimated together ten piastres	10
A hundred empty bottles	
estimated eight piastres	8
Three empty demijohns	
estimated three piastres	3
Two earthenware jars from Provence, a large and a small one,	
estimated together twenty piastres	20
Which is everything that was in the aforesaid pantry.	

In the kitchen:

Twelve iron boilers of various sizes several of which are cracked or patched up	
estimated four piastres	4

2. Subtotal here of $265.50.

Two frying pans
estimated two piastres 2
A pair of iron andirons
estimated three piastres 3
A grill
estimated fifty cents .50

In the stable at the bottom of the house:
A cabriolet with its harnesses
Estimated the sum of a hundred piastres 100[3]
Here Dame Marguerite Delmas, Widow Leufroy Dreux, declared to us that half of the cabriolet we just inventoried belongs to her, for having paid it with her own money, reason why she made all reservations of rights, of which she required acknowledgement, granted to her, and she signed.

Signed Widow Leufroy Dreux

In the courtyard:
Two iron hooped tubs
Estimated three piastres 3
Three small tubs
estimated one piastre 1
Which are the movable objects presented to us as belonging to the aforesaid succession to be inventoried.

Documents:

A bundle containing five items, maps or property titles referenced by us, initialed on the first and last page of the documents, by us inventoried under reference a number 1. Which are all the documents that were presented to us to be inventoried.

After what we proceeded to the inventory and estimation of the slaves in the succession as follows:

Slaves
Joseph, Creole, nègre aged about thirty-eight years,
suitable for all the works of a plantation,
estimated five hundred piastres 500[4]
Bazile, Creole, aged about thirty-five years,
suitable for all the works of a plantation,
estimated 500 piastres 500

3. Intermediate total of $451.50.
4. Intermediate total of $955.50.

Bacchus nègre of the Maninga nation, aged about thirty, estimated four hundred piastres	400
Bazile nègre from St. Domingue, aged about twenty-four to twenty-five, field slave estimated five hundred piastres	500
Charles Senegal nègre, aged about eighteen to nineteen, domestic and house slave, estimated six hundred piastres	600
César nègre of Congo nation, aged about sixty years, field nègre, estimated three hundred piastres	300
Hector nègre of Maninga nation, aged about thirty-eight, for the field, estimated four hundred piastres	400
Télémaque of Congo nation, aged about sixty years, with his sight affected and crippled, estimated one hundred piastres	100
Catherine, creole négresse, aged forty-five years, with her child négrillon named Augustin aged seven, said négresse attacked with asthma, estimated with her négrillon six hundred piastres	600
Nérisse, creole négresse, aged 20 years, domestic, estimated five hundred piastres	500[5]
Amazilie creole négresse aged eighteen, Domestic, estimated five hundred piastres	500
Zaïre, creole négresse, aged thirteen to fourteen, domestic, four hundred piastres	400
Colas, creole négrillon, aged ten, estimated three hundred piastres	300
Noisette, creole mulâtresse from St Domingue, aged about nineteen, with her two children, one named Valsin, quarteron, aged about four and a half, and Herminaque, quarteronne, aged about one year, the mother and the two children together estimated nine hundred piastres	900
One négresse named Catherine of Higbou[6] nation, aged about twenty-four, unskilled, estimated four hundred piastres	400

5. Intermediate total of $4,855.50.

6. Igbo, misspelled.

Azor, Congo nègre,
maroon for two years, currently in the woods,
handicapped with a hernia, aged thirty,
estimated fifty piastres 50

Sieur François Dreux has declared that there was also a négrillon named Honoré, aged five years, verbally given by the late Sr. Louis Leufroy Dreux when he was alive to his son Henry Dreux, as well as a négritte named Féliciane aged about fifteen months, who was given by the same and in the same way to his daughter Marie Hermina Dreux, all of which he requested us to duly act, act to him granted and signed.[7]

Signed François Dreux

Dairy cows
A cow named Clarisse with its young
estimated thirty piastres 30
Another cow named La Rousse with its young
estimated thirty piastres 30
Another cow named Sophie
estimated thirty piastres 30
A cow named Mignonette with its young
estimated thirty piastres 30
A cow named Maniche
Estimated thirty piastres 30
A cow named Rosette with its young
estimated thirty piastres 30
Another cow with its young named Sophie
estimated thirty piastres 30
A cow named Aimée with its young
estimated thirty piastres 30
Another cow named Mignonette with its young
estimated thirty piastres 30
Another cow named Jacqueline
estimated thirty piastres 30
Another cow named Moutarde with its young
estimated thirty piastres 30[8]
Thirteen cows without young whose names
follow
Bellote, Barrière, Labiche, Fanchonnette,
Doucette, Jeune Bellote, Vermillon, Rosalie,
Bonfouca, Vieille Rosalie, Caillette, Sanson,
Larouge estimated three hundred and twenty-five piastres 325

7. Intermediate total of $7,405.50.

8. Intermediate total of $7,735.50.

Eight heifers[9]	
estimated fifty piastres	50
Four young steers not yet tamed	
estimated sixty piastres	60
Oxen	
Vigoureux and Couteaux	
estimated forty piastres	40
Vermeil and Papillon	
estimated forty piastres	40
Bruner and Jambart	
estimated forty piastres	40
Laurier and Janvier	
estimated forty piastres	40
Barbouillier and Jeanbon	
estimated forty piastres	40
Capita and Créole	
estimated forty piastres	40
Février and Fringin	
estimated forty piastres	40
Vaillant and Taupin	
estimated forty piastres	40
Mutin without its pair	
estimated twenty piastres	20

After what were presented to us several horses, mares, female and male mules tamed and untamed[10] whose names follow:

A riding and work horse, named Petit Rouge	
estimated thirty piastres	30
A riding and work horse, named Caster	
estimated fifty piastres	50
A black untamed ditto	
estimated twenty-five piastres	25
An untamed bay ditto	
estimated fifty piastres	50
An untamed brown bay ditto	
forty piastres	40
A small foal	
estimated fifteen piastres	15
An untamed black mare	
estimated twenty piastres	20

9. The original reads "torailles," which probably means young cows.
10. Intermediate total of $8,510.50.

Draft male and female mules

A male mule named Mars	
estimated forty piastres	40
Another male mule named Berger	
estimated forty piastres	40
Another male mule named Ardent	
estimated forty piastres	40
Another male mule named Souris	
estimated forty piastres	40
Another male mule named Sanitte	
estimated forty piastres	40
After what we were presented	
a flock of sheep of fifty heads	
estimated a hundred and sixty-two piastres	162
We were also presented three oxen carts, with iron axles,	
their bow, legs, and yokes	
estimated each the sum of twenty piastres,	
together[11] sixty piastres	60
A cart with wooden axles	
estimated fifteen piastres	15
A hand cart with its chain	
estimated thirty piastres	30
Three diane chains	
estimated together eighteen piastres	18
Two pairs of brand new cart wheels	
estimated twenty piastres	20
A horse cart with its saddlery	
estimated forty piastres	40
A cart with iron axles	
estimated twenty-five piastres	25
A grindstone estimated ten piastres	10

Tilling tools

A horse harrow estimated five piastres	5
An oxen harrow garnished in iron	
estimated ten piastres	10
Two plows in bad condition	
estimated fifteen piastres each, together thirty piastres	30
A pit saw estimated six piastres	6
Twelve axes	
estimated twelve piastres	12

11. Intermediate total of $9,102.50.

Nine iron piles estimated eight piastres 8
Eight pickaxes and two hoes
estimated four piastres 4
One hollow adz
estimated one piastre 1
Which are the only tilling tools to be inventoried.

After what we proceeded to the inventory and estimation of the plantations included in said succession.[12]

Plantations

First the plantation on which we are proceeding, sited one league and a half from the city, containing thirty to thirty-two arpents on both sides of the Bayou Sauvage, marked out in the west by the property of Messrs Edmond and Jules Dreux, and in the east by the properties of Mr Pellerin, and in the depth on the north side by the cypress groves of Lake Pontchartrain, and at the bottom by those of the river, on which plantation is an old half-timbered mansion raised seven feet above ground in bad condition as well as a kitchen,[13] a dovecote, a cow shed, with brick poles, eleven slave cabins, and a shed to shelter the carts, all together with the buildings as they stand, estimated by above-mentioned appreciators, considering the circumstances, ten thousand piastres 10,000

Another land property in the same district of Gentilly, one league from the present one, seventy-five arpents long on both sides of Bayou Sauvage, twenty arpents deep on each side of the Bayou, about 60 arpents of which have been cleared, marked out, in the west, by Mr Guy Dreux's property, in the east by that of Mr Lafont, in the north by the cypress groves of Lake Pontchartrain and in the south by those of the river, said property estimated four thousand piastres 4000

$23,396.50

And considering that nothing else was presented to us to be inventoried as coming from the said succession of the late Louis Leufroy Dreux, of which Sieur François Dreux swore under oath that he had not misappropriated or led to misappropriate anything, or had knowledge anything had been misappropriated, we above-mentioned and undersigned Deputy Register have ended and closed the present inventory, and, having read it, have found the amount of the inventory to be twenty-three thousand three hundred ninety-six piastres fifty cents, which have remained in the charge and under the responsibility of said

12. Intermediate total of $9,396.50.

13. The original French reads "cuisine sur saule," which would translate as "kitchen on willow."

François Dreux, executor, who acknowledged it, took charge and signed with us and the other parties of witnesses, each in their respective capacity, the same day, month and year as noted above, and then we withdrew.

Signed Widow Leufroy Dreux, François Dreux, Paul Darcantel, Latapie, Colson, Brierre Deputy Register

Source: Sainte-Gême Family Papers, MSS 100, folder 626. Translation by volume editors.

APPENDIX 5

Mandate Given to Auvignac Dorville for the Sale of the Gentilly Plantation

In the year eighteen hundred and fifty and on May the seventeenth, in the town of Saint-Gaudens, administrative seat of the arrondissement, in the department of Haute-Garonne,

Before us, Jean-François Labatut, lawyer-notary, in residence in said town, undersigned, assisted by the witnesses hereafter named, have appeared:

Madame Marguerite Delmas, widow of Monsieur Jean-François Henri de Saintegême, proprietor residing in Bagen, municipality of Sauveterre, canton of Saint-Bertrand, arrondissement of St. Gaudens, department of Haute-Garonne,

> Acting on her own initiative
> On the grounds of the community that existed between her and Monsieur Louis Leufroy Dreux, her first husband,
> And as heir of Monsieur Henri Dreux, her son,
> And finally on the grounds of the community that existed between her and Monsieur Saintegême, her second husband

Monsieur Henri Marie François Gabriel Anatole de Saintegême, proprietor residing in the same premises of Bagen, municipality of Sauveterre.

Monsieur Bertrand Henri Joseph Armand de Saintegême, proprietor residing in Payssous, same canton, arrondissement, and department.

Madame Françoise Eléonore Henriette de Saintegême, spouse of Monsieur Jean Joseph Sidney de Meynard, proprietor, assisted and authorized by him for the present, residing together in Orleix, department of Hautes-Pyrénées.

And Madame Marie Antoinette Céleste Ovide de Saintegême, spouse of

Monsieur Bernard Marie Adrien Marcellier de Gayac, proprietor, assisted and authorized by him for the present, residing together in Lombez, department of Gers.

Messieurs de Saintegême and Mesdames de Meynard et de Gayac, brothers and sisters, heirs of said Monsieur Jean François Henri de Saintegême, their father, deceased in the municipality of Sauveterre on the twentieth of July of the year eighteen hundred and forty-two, who declared that they jointly designate as their authorized representative Monsieur Auvignac Dorville, proprietor residing in Gentilly, in the vicinity of La Nouvelle-Orleans, state of Louisiana in the United States of America.

To whom they give power, for them and in their name, to sell irrevocably and in perpetuity, to Monsieur John MacDonogh, proprietor residing in La Nouvelle Orléans, the properties of the plantations said of Gentilly and la Vacherie that the settlors jointly own in the Gentilly neighborhood, in the vicinity of La Nouvelle Orléans, state of Louisiana, with all the nègres, livestock, and tilling tools that are placed in it, and generally all their belongings in the outbuildings, with no other exception than the reserved furniture, for the price of fifty-three thousand piastres, that is two hundred and eighty thousand francs payable in quarters, one quarter upfront, another quarter in one year, the third quarter in two years, and the last quarter in three years, all of which from date of signature of the act; to set the date of the enjoyment by the buyer; to submit the settlors to all the guarantees of the right; to reserve the privilege of the coursers as well as the right of resolution of the sale until integral payment of the price; and to make, concerning said sale, all the other stipulations and conventions he will judge proper; to declare that the properties concerned belong in totality and indivisibility to the constituents, that is Madame widow Saintegême born Delmas, according to the rights resulting from the communities that existed successively between her and her two husbands, and as heir of Henri Dreux, her son, and to her four children named hereunder as sole heirs of Monsieur Jean François Henri de Saintegême, their father, who had all the rights of Madame Marie Hermina Dreux, their uterine sister, on the properties concerned, according to the contract we reported on the sixteenth of June eighteen hundred and twenty-eight, duly recorded.

To receive the amount of said sale as the payments are made, give receipt and valid disclaimer of it, once granted all mentions and any subrogation which will be made, give discharge of all inscriptions of office or others.

Finally, to pass and sign all acts and to generally perform all that he will deem useful or necessary to the interests of the constituents, promising to incorporate and ratify it if required.

The constituents nonetheless reserve the possibility of sharing between them the amount of said sale as payments are sent by their representative, in the proportion of their respective rights which will be determined at a later date, without intending to bring with this reservation any restriction to the powers hereunder conferred to their representative.

Duly acknowledged.

Established and read to the constituents in the presence of Sieurs Joseph Leyraud and Dominique Villeneuve, town bailiffs, residents of Saint-Gaudens, who signed with the constituents and us, notary.

De Saintegême née Delmas,
De Gayac née de Saintegême,
Maynard née de Saintegême,
Ale de Saintegême
And de Saintegême,

S de Maynard, A Marcellier de Gayac, Leyraud, Villeneuvre and Labatut notary Signed immediately

Registered in Saint-Gaudens on May the eighteenth of eighteen hundred and fifty, folio three recta, cases

Source: Jean-François Labatut, notary, Saint-Gaudens, France, May 17, 1850. Included in the act of sale of the plantation, July 19, 1850, act 249, vol. 117, NONA. Translation by volume editors.

APPENDIX 6

Act of Sale of the Gentilly Plantation to John McDonogh

UNITED STATES OF AMERICA
STATE OF LOUISIANA—CITY OF NEW ORLEANS

Be it Known, That on this nineteenth day of July in the year of our Lord one thousand eight hundred and Fifty and the Seventy Fifth of the Independence of the United States of America,

Before me, **Henry Paul Caire**, Notary Public in this City and Parish of New-Orleans, and (State of Louisiana) duly commissioned and sworn,

Personally came and appeared,

Mr. Auvignac Dorville residing in this city; herein acting as attorney in fact of the following persons viz

1 Mrs. Marguerite Delmas widow by her first marriage of Mr Louis Leufroy Dreux, and by her second marriage of Mr. Jean François Henri de Sainte-Gême, residing at Bagen in France

2 Mr. Henry Marie François Gabriel Anatole de Sainte-Gême, residing also at Bagen (France)

3 Mr. Bertrand Henri Joseph Armand de Sainte-Gême, residing at Payssous (France)

4 Mrs Françoise Eléonore Henriette de Sainte-Gême, wife duly authorized of Mr Jean Joseph Sidney de Meynard residing both at Orleix (Htes-Pyrenees-France)

5 Mrs Marie Antoinette Céleste Ovide de Sainte-Gême wife duly authorized of Mr Bernard Marie Adrien Marcellier de Gayac, residing both at Lombez (France)

By virtue of the procuration which they granted unto him per act passed before Mr Jean François Labatut notary at St Gaudens (France) under date of the seventeenth of May eighteen hundred and fifty; an authorized copy of which power of attorney duly legalized, is and remains hereto annexed for reference,
Which appeared Mr Auvignac Dorville acting as aforesaid, declared that he does by these present, grant, bargain, sell, convey, transfer, assign, abandon and set over under all lawful guaranty

Unto Mr John McDonogh residing at McDonoghville, on the right bank of the river Mississippi, here present and accepting purchases for him, said McDonogh, his heirs and assigns and acknowledging delivery and possession thereof the following properties and slaves, viz

1 A certain plantation known under the name Gentilly, situated, lying and being at Gentilly (in this Parish) measuring in French measure thirty three *arpents* three *toises* front to the Bayou Sauvage, & on each side of said Bayou, by twenty *arpents* deep also from each side of the Bayou, bounded on one side by the plantation of James Hopkins, on the other by that of Mr Joseph Soniat Dufossat according to a particular plan drawn by Mr Louis Bringer surveyor general of this state, on the twenty eighth July Eighteen hundred & twenty seven which plan has been given by Mr Dorville to Mr McDonogh who acknowledges the receipt thereof together with all the buildings and improvements existing thereon, in a master house, a kitchen, an hospital, store, stable, sugar-house furnished with a mill & three sugar boilers, dover house, cart, ploughs, axes, mattocks, shovels, keys, coulters, nippers, and also two horses, six mules, four oxen, six wild oxen, twenty four cows, fifteen calves, twelve small bulls, two fine wild bulls, making altogether seventy one.

2. The following slaves attached to said plantation

Names	Men	Years
Ben	negro man	50
Augustin	" "	47
Grand Henry	" "	47
Frank	" "	25
Petit Henry	" "	25
Henry Goye	" "	47
Petit John	" "	23
Charles	" "	56
Grand John	" "	47
Achilles	" "	26
Abel	" "	26
Bacchus	" "	68
Victor	" "	36
Bazile	" "	45
Honoré	" "	45

Those two slaves, Bazile and Honoré are runaway since about twelve years; & though there is very little hope still to find them; they have been comprised in the present sale.

Names	Women	Years
Nerisse	negro woman	57
Zaïre	negress	50
Catherine	"	58
Caroline (Creole)	"	27
Caroline (American)	"	23
	Children	
François (alias) mulatre	negro boy	6
Henriette (alias) Caninine	negro girl	3
A young girl not yet named	negro girl	7 months
All three of the above are the children of Caroline (Creole)		
Virginia	negro girl	4
Josephine	negro girl	2
Adèle	negro girl	6 months
All three are the children of Caroline the American		

The whole of what proceeds according to an inventory made by the parties and which has been left in the hands of Mr McDonogh who acknowledges the receipt thereof

> 3rd Another plantation known as the Vacherie situated, lying and being at Gentilly (in this Parish) having in French measure seventy five arpents front on each side of the said Bayou Sauvage by twenty arpents also deep from each side of the Bayou according to a particular plan drawn by Carlos Trudeau surveyor, on the twenty sixth April of the year eighteen hundred and entered upon record number three page three the eighth of October Eighteen hundred and seven which plan has been given by Mr Dorville to said Mr McDonogh who acknowledges the receipt thereof.

Source: Henry Paul Caire, Notary Public in the City and Parish of New Orleans, July 19, 1850, act 249, vol. 117, New Orleans Notarial Archives, New Orleans.

BIBLIOGRAPHY

Archival Material

Archives of the Archdiocese of New Orleans

Sacramental Records

Archives Départementales d'Indre-et-Loire

Baptêmes, Mariages, Sépultures

Archives Nationales d'Outre-Mer, Aix-en-Provence

Archives des Colonies, series G1
Fonds Louisiane, series C13

The Historic New Orleans Collection, Williams Research Center, New Orleans

Ste-Gême Family Papers, MSS 100 (849 Items)

Louisiana State Museum

Louisiane, Recensements
Records of the Superior Council

Missouri State Archives

Census of 1766, Spanish Louisiana Territory, Records and Archives

New Orleans Notarial Archives

Andres Almonaster y Roxas archives
Narcisse Broutin archives
Henry Paul Caire archives

Michel d'Armas archives
Juan B. Garic archives
Adolphe Mazureau archives
Carlos Ximenes archives

New Orleans Public Library

Census rolls, Louisiana Division
Louisiana Court of Probates, Will Book 2
Marriage Indexes, Louisiana Division
New Orleans City Directory
New Orleans (La.) Office of the Mayor, Indentures, 1809–1843, AA660/661, vol. 3, Louisiana Division
Succession Records, 1846–1880, Louisiana District Court (Orleans Parish)

The University of New Orleans

State of Louisiana (State of Maryland Intervening) v. Executors of John McDonogh and City of New Orleans, 8 La. Ann. (1853), Louisiana Supreme Court Cases, Earl K. Long Library

Printed Primary Sources

Adkins, John. *A Voyage to Guinea, Brazil, and the West Indies.* 1735. London: Forgotten Books, 1970.

American State Papers: Documents, Legislative and Executive, of the Congress of the United States, part 8, vol. 6. Published by the United States Congress. Washington, DC: Gales and Seaton, 1860.

Cabildo Archives, *Louisiana Historical Quarterly* 3, no. 1 (January 1920).

Caillot, Marc-Antoine. *A Company Man: The Remarkable French-Atlantic Voyage of a Clerk for the Company of the Indies.* Ed. Erin M. Greenwald. Trans. Teri F. Chalmers. New Orleans: Historic New Orleans Collection, 2003.

Chandler, R. E., ed. "Ulloa's Account of the 1768 Revolt." *Louisiana History: The Journal of the Louisiana Historical Association* 27, no. 4 (Autumn 1966): 407–437.

Darby, Jonathan. "Account of Jonathan Darby." *Records of the American Catholic Historical Society of Philadelphia* 10 (June 1899).

Gordon, Harry. "New Orleans and Bayou Saint John in 1766, Journal of Captain Harry Gordon." In *Travels in the American Colonies,* ed. Newton Dennison Mereness. New York: Macmillan, 1916.

Labat, Jean Baptiste. *Nouvelle relation de l'Afrique occidentale: contenant une description exacte du Sénégal et des Païs situés entre le Cap-Blanc et la Rivière de Serrelionne, jusqu'à a plus de 300 lieues en avant dans les Terres. L'Histoire naturelle de ces Païs, les différentes Nations qui y sont répandues, leurs Religions et leurs et leurs mœurs.* 5 vols. Paris: Guillaume Cavelier, 1728.

Laussat, Pierre Clément de. *Memoirs of My Life to My Son during the Years 1803 and after, Which I Spent in Public Service in Louisiana as Commissioner of the French Government for the Retrocession to France of That Colony and for Its Transfer to the United States.* Ed. Robert D. Bus. Trans. Agnes-Josephine Pastwa. Baton Rouge: Louisiana State University Press, 1978.

LeMoyne d'Iberville, Pierre. *Iberville's Gulf Journals.* Trans. and ed. Richebourg Gaillard McWilliams. Tuscaloosa: University of Alabama Press, 1991.

Maduell, Charles R., Jr. *The Census Tables for the French Colony of Louisiana from 1699 through 1732.* Baltimore: Clearfield, 2008.

McDonogh, John. *The Last Will and Testament of John McDonogh, Late of MacDonoghville, State of Louisiana: Also, His Memoranda of Instructions to his Executors, Relative to the Management of His Estate.* New Orleans: Job Office of *The Daily Delta,* 1851.

McWilliams, Richebourg Gaillard, ed. *Fleur de Lys and Calumet: Being the Pénicault Narrative of French Adventure in Louisiana.* Tuscaloosa: University of Alabama Press, 1988.

Miller, Branch W. *Louisiana Reports: Cases Argued and Determined in the Supreme Court of the State of Louisiana.* New Orleans: Gaston Brusle, 1834.

Notice statistique sur la Guyane française: extrait des Notices statistiques sur les colonies françaises, imprimées en 1838, par ordre de M. le Ministre de la Marine et des Colonies. Paris: Firmin Didot Frères, 1843.

Rowland, Dunbar, and Albert Godfrey Sanders, eds. *Mississippi Provincial Archives, 1704–1743: French Dominion.* Vol. 3. Jackson: Press of the Mississippi Department of Archives, 1930.

Secondary Sources

Allain, Mathé. *"Not Worth a Straw": French Colonial Policy and the Early Years of Louisiana.* Lafayette: Center for Louisiana Studies, University of Southwestern Louisiana, 1988.

Allen, William. *The Life and Work of John McDonogh.* Baltimore: Press of I. Friedenwald, 1886.

Arthur, Stanley Clisby, George Campbell, and Huchet de Kernion. *Old Families of Louisiana.* New Orleans: Harmanson, 1931.

Atherton, Lewis E. "John McDonogh—New Orleans Mercantile Capitalist." *Journal of Southern History* 7, no. 4 (November 1941): 463–472.

Baptist, Edward E. *The Half Has Never Been Told: Slavery and the Making of American Capitalism.* New York: Basic Books, 2014.

Bastian, David F., and Nicholas J. Meis. *New Orleans Hurricanes from the Start.* Gretna, La.: Pelican Publishing Company, 2014.

Bauer, Craig A. *Creole Genesis: The Bringier Family and Antebellum Plantation Life in Louisiana.* Lafayette: University of Louisiana at Lafayette Press, 2011.

Beauchamp, Michael K. *Instruments of Empire: Colonial Elites and U.S. Governance in Early National Louisiana 1803–1815.* Baton Rouge: Louisiana State University Press, 2021.

Beckles, Hilary. "Black Female Slaves and White Households in Barbados." In *More Than Chattel: Women and Slavery in the Americas,* ed. Barry David Gaspar and Darlene Clark Hine, 111–125. Bloomington: University of Indiana Press, 1996.

Berlin, Ira. *Many Thousands Gone: The First Two Centuries of Slavery in North America.* Cambridge: The Belknap Press of Harvard University, 2003.

Campanella, Richard. *Bienville's Dilemma: A Historical Geography of New Orleans.* Lafayette: Center for Louisiana Studies, University of Louisiana at Lafayette, 2008.

Cañizares-Esguerra, Jorge, Matt D. Childs, and James Sidbury, eds. *The Black Urban Atlantic in the Age of the Slave Trade.* Philadelphia: University of Pennsylvania Press, 2013.

Chasteen, John Charles. *Americanos: Latin America's Struggle for Independence.* New York: Oxford University Press, 2009.

Christovich, Mary Louise, Sally Evans, Roulhac Toledano, and Betsy Swanson. *New Orleans Architecture.* Vol. 4, *The Creole Faubourgs.* Gretna: Pelican Publishing, 1995.

Ciravolo, G. Leighton. *The Legacy of John McDonogh.* Louisiana Life Series 12. Lafayette: Center for Louisiana Studies, University of Louisiana at Lafayette, 2002.

Cizeck, Eugene D., John Lawrence, and Richard Sexton. *Destrehan: The Man, the House, the Legacy.* Destrehan, LA: River Road Historical Society, 2008.

Clark, Emily. *Masterless Mistresses: The New Orleans Ursulines and the Development of a New World Society, 1727–1834.* Chapel Hill: University of North Carolina Press, 2007.

———. *The Strange History of the American Quadroon: Free Women of Color in the Revolutionary Atlantic World.* Chapel Hill: University of North Carolina Press, 2013.

Clark, Emily, Cécile Vidal, and Ibrahima Thioub, eds. *New Orleans, Louisiana, and Saint-Louis, Senegal: Mirror Cities in the Atlantic World, 1659–2000s.* Baton Rouge: Louisiana State University Press, 2019.

Cody, Cheryl Ann. "Cycles of Work and of Childbearing: Seasonality in Women's Lives on Low Country Plantations." In *More Than Chattel: Black Women and Slavery in the Americas,* ed. Barry David Gaspar and Darlene Clark Hine, 61–78. Bloomington: University of Indiana Press, 1996.

Colten, Craig E., ed. *Transforming New Orleans and its Environs: Centuries of Change.* Pittsburgh, PA: University of Pittsburgh Press, 2000.

Conrad, Glenn. *First Families of Louisiana.* Baton Rouge: Claitor's Publication Division, 1970.

Davis, William C. *The Pirates Laffite: The Treacherous World of the Corsairs of the Gulf.* San Diego: Harcourt, 2005.

Dawdy, Shannon Lee. *Building the Devil's Empire: French Colonial New Orleans.* Chicago: University of Chicago Press, 2008.

———. "Scoundrels, Whores, and Gentlemen: Defamation and Society in French Colonial Louisiana." In *Coastal Encounters: The Transformation of the Gulf South in the Eighteenth Century,* ed. Richmond F. Brown, 132–150. Omaha: University of Nebraska Press, 2007.

Decker, William Merrill. *Epistolary Practices: Letter Writing in America before Telecommunications.* Chapel Hill: University of North Carolina Press, 1998.

Depuydt, Peter. "The Mortgaging of Souls: Sugar, Slaves, and Speculation." *Louisiana History: The Journal of the Louisiana Historical Association* 54, no. 4 (Fall 2013): 448–464.

Dessens, Nathalie. *Creole City: A Chronicle of Early American New Orleans.* Gainesville: University Press of Florida, 2015.

———. "Cultures plurielles et hybridation: Fêtes et célébrations à La Nouvelle-Orléans (1803–1840)." In *Interculturalités: La Louisiane au carrefour des cultures,* ed. Nathalie Dessens and Jean-Pierre Le Glaunec, 137–164. Québec: Presses de l'Université Laval, 2016.

———. *From Saint-Domingue to New Orleans: Migration and Influences.* Gainesville: University Press of Florida, 2007.

———. "New Orleans between Atlantic and Caribbean: Reinterpreting the Saint-Domingue Migration." In *Mobility and Coercion in an Age of Wars and Revolutions,* ed. Jan C. Jansen and Kirsten McKenzie, 153–172. Cambridge: Cambridge University Press, 2024.

Downs, James. *Maladies of Empires: How Colonialism, Slavery, and War Transformed Medicine.* Cambridge, MA: Harvard University Press, 2021.

Dubois, Laurent. "The Haitian Revolution and the Sale of Louisiana." In *Empires of the Imagination: Transatlantic Histories of the Louisiana Purchase,* ed. Peter J. Kastor and François Weil, 93–113. Charlottesville: University of Virginia Press, 2009.

Dunn, Richard S. *A Tale of Two Plantations: Slave Life and Labor in Jamaica and Virginia.* Cambridge, MA: Harvard University Press, 2014.

Eccles, William J. *France in America.* Rev. ed. East Lansing: Michigan State University Press, 1990.

Ellis, Scott S. *The Faubourg Marigny of New Orleans. A History.* Baton Rouge: Louisiana State University Press, 2018.

Faber, Eberhard L. *Building the Land of Dreams: New Orleans and the Transformation of Early America.* Princeton, NJ: Princeton University Press, 2016.

———. "The Passion of the Prefect: Pierre Clément de Laussat, 1803 New Orleans, and the Bonapartist Louisiana That Never Was." *Louisiana History: The Journal of the Louisiana Historical Association* 54, no. 3 (Summer 2013): 261–291.

Follett, Richard. *The Sugar Masters: Planters and Slaves in Louisiana's Cane World, 1820–1860.* Baton Rouge: Louisiana State University Press, 2005.

Fortier, Alcée. *A History of Louisiana: The American Domination.* Part 1, *1803–1861.* Baton Rouge: Claitor's Publishing Division, 1985.

Freiberg, Edna B. *Bayou St. John, 1699–1803.* New Orleans: Harvey Press, 1980.

Gayarré, Charles. *History of Louisiana.* Vol. 3, *The Spanish Domination.* Gretna, LA: Pelican Press, 1974.

———. *History of Louisiana.* Vol. 4, *The American Domination.* Gretna, LA: Pelican Press, 1974.

Gerber, David. "Epistolary Ethics: Personal Correspondence and the Culture of Emigration in the Nineteenth Century." *Journal of American Ethnic History* 19, no. 4 (Summer 2000): 3–23.

Gibson, Campbell. *Population of the 100 Largest Cities and Other Urban Places in the United States: 1790 to 1990.* United States Census Bureau, https://www.census.gov/library/working-papers/1998/demo/POP-twps0027.html.

Giraud, Marcel. *Histoire de Louisiane Française.* Vol. 1, *Le règne de Louis XIV.* Paris: Presses Universitaires de France, 1953.

———. *Histoire de la Louisiane Française.* Vol. 3, *L'Époque de John Law (1717–1720).* Paris: Presses Universitaires de France, 1966.

———. *A History of French Louisiana: The Company of the Indies, 1723–1731,* ed. Brian Pearce. Baton Rouge: Louisiana State University Press, 1987.

Goujon, Bernard. *Monarchies postrévolutionnaires, 1814–1848.* Paris: Le Seuil, 2012.

Gould, Virginia Meacham. "Bienville's Brides: Virgins or Prostitutes? 1719–1721." *Louisiana History: The Journal of the Louisiana Historical Association* 59, no. 4 (Fall 2018): 389–408.

———. "A Chaos of Iniquity and Discord: Slave and Free Women of Color in the Spanish Ports of New Orleans, Mobile, and Pensacola." In *The Devil's Lane: Sex and Race in the Early South,* ed. Catherine Clinton and Michelle Gillespie, 233–246. New York: Oxford University Press, 1997.

———. "Creoles." In *Encyclopedia of the United States in the Nineteenth Century,* ed. Paul Finkleman. New York: Charles Scribner's Sons, 2001.

———. "'The House that Was Never a Home': Slave Family and Household Organization in New Orleans, 1820–1850." *Slavery and Abolition: A Journal of Slavery and Post-Slave Studies* 18, no. 2 (August 1997): 90–103.

———. "'If I Can't Have My Rights, I Can Have My Pleasures: And If They Won't Give Me Wages, I Can Take Them': Gender and Slave Labor in Antebellum New Orleans." In *Discovering the Women in Slavery: Emancipation Perspectives on the American Past,* ed. Patricia Morton, 179–201. Athens: University of Georgia Press, 1996.

———. "In Full Enjoyment of Their Freedom: Free Women of Color of the Gulf Ports of New Orleans, Mobile, And Pensacola." Unpublished PhD diss., Emory University, 1991.

———. "Urban Slavery—Urban Freedom: The Manumission of Jacqueline Lemelle." In *More Than Chattel: Black Women and Slavery in the Americas,* ed. David Barry Gaspar and Darlene Clark Hine, 298–314. Bloomington: University of Indiana Press, 1996.

Hall, Gwendolyn Midlo. "African Women in French and Spanish Louisiana: Origins, Roles, Family, Work, and Treatment." In *The Devil's Lane: Sex and Race in the Early South,* ed. Catherine Clinton and Michelle Gillespie, 246–261. New York: Oxford University Press, 1997.

———. *Africans in Colonial Louisiana: The Development of Afro-Creole Culture in the Eighteenth Century.* Baton Rouge: Louisiana State University Press, 1992.

Hoffman, Paul E. *A History of Louisiana before 1813.* Baton Rouge, LA: LSU Bookstore, 1996.

Hoyt, William D., Jr. "John McDonogh and Maryland Colonization in Liberia, 1834–1835." *The Journal of Negro History* 24, no. 4 (October 1939): 440–453.

Ingersoll, Thomas. *Mammon and Manon in Early New Orleans: The First Slave Society in the Deep South, 1718–1819.* Knoxville: University of Tennessee Press, 1998.

Johnson, Jerah. "La Coutume de Paris: Louisiana's First Law." *Louisiana History: The Journal of the Louisiana Historical Association* 30, no. 2 (Spring 1989): 145–155.

Johnson, Rashauna. *Slavery Metropolis: Unfree Labor in New Orleans during the Age of Revolutions.* New York: Cambridge University Press, 2016.

Johnson, Walter. *Rivers of Dark Dreams: Slavery and Empire in the Cotton Kingdom.* Cambridge, MA: The Belknap Press of Harvard University Press, 2013.

———. *Soul by Soul: Life in an Antebellum Slave Market.* Cambridge, MA: Harvard University Press, 1999.

Kastor, Peter. *The Nation's Crucible: The Louisiana Purchase and the Creation of America.* New Haven, CT: Yale University Press, 2012.

Kastor, Peter, and François Weil, eds. *Empires of the Imagination: Transatlantic Histories of the Louisiana Purchase.* Charlottesville: University of Virginia Press, 2009.

Kendall, John. *History of New Orleans.* Chicago: Lewis Publishing Company, 1922.

Kidder, Tristram R. "'Making the City Inevitable': Native Americans and the Geography of New Orleans." In *Transforming New Orleans and its Environs: Centuries of Change,* ed. Craig E. Colten, 7–21. Pittsburgh, PA: University of Pittsburgh Press, 2000.

Kilcer VanHuss, Laura, ed. *Charting the Plantation Landscape from Natchez to New Orleans.* Baton Rouge: Louisiana State University Press, 2021.

King, Grace. *Creole Families of New Orleans.* New York: Macmillan, 1921.

Kolb, Frances. "The New Orleans Revolt of 1768: Uniting against Real and Perceived Threats of Empire." *Louisiana History: The Journal of the Louisiana Historical Association* 59, no. 1 (Winter 2018): 5–39.

Kukla, John. *A Wilderness So Immense: The Louisiana Purchase and the Destiny of America.* New York: A. A. Knopf, 2002.

Lachance, Paul. "The Foreign French." In *Creole New Orleans: Race and Americanization,* ed. Arnold R. Hirsch and Joseph Logsdon, 101–130. Baton Rouge: Louisiana State University Press, 1992.

———. "To train them to habits of industry and usefulness." In *Children Bound to Labor: The Pauper Apprentice System in Early America,* ed. Ruth Wallis Herndon and John E. Murray, 94–120. Ithaca, NY: Cornell University Press, 2009.

———. "Were Saint-Domingue Refugees a Distinctive Cultural Group in Antebellum Louisiana? Evidence from Patterns and Strategies of Property Holding." *Revista/Review Interamericana* 29, no. 1–4 (1999): 171–192.

Law, Robin "The Original Manuscript Version of William Snelgrave's 'New Account of Some Parts of Guinea.'" *History in Africa* 17 (1990): 367–372.

Le Glaunec, Jean-Pierre. "'Grand Dieu quand serais-je Délivré de ces tracasseries': The Lost World of Jean-Michel Fortier, Citizen and Merchant of Louisiana, as Seen through His Correspondence, 1801–1804." In *Haïti, regards croisés,* ed. Nathalie Dessens et Jean-Pierre Le Glaunec, 95–113. Paris: Le Manuscrit, 2007.

———. "Slave Migrations in Spanish and Early American Louisiana: New Sources and New Estimates." *Louisiana History: Journal of the Louisiana Historical Association* 46, no. 2 (Spring 2005): 185–209.

Lepler, Jessica M. *The Many Panics of 1837: People, Politics, and the Creation of a Transatlantic Financial Crisis.* Cambridge: Cambridge University Press, 2013.

Long, Carolyn Morrow. *Madame Lalaurie, Mistress of the Haunted House.* Gainesville: University Press of Florida, 2012.

Marler, Scott P. *The Merchants' Capital: New Orleans and the Political Economy of the Nineteenth-Century South.* New York: Cambridge University Press, 2013.

Martin, François Xavier. *The History of Louisiana, from the Earliest Period.* 1882. Gretna: Firebird Press, 2000.

Massey, Doreen. *Spatial Divisions of Labor and Space, Place, and Gender.* Minneapolis, MN: University of Minneapolis Press, 1994.

McGowan, James Thomas. "Creation of a Slave Society: Louisiana Plantations in the Eighteenth Century." Unpublished PhD Diss., University of Rochester, 1976.

Melville, Annabelle M. *Louis William DuBourg: Bishop of Louisiana and the Floridas, Bishop of Montauban, and Archbishop of Besançon, 1766–1833.* Vol. 2, *Bishop in the Two Worlds, 1818–1833.* Chicago: Loyola University Press, 1986.

Mertas, John, Serge Daget, and Michelle Daget. *Répertoire des expéditions négrières françaises au XVIIIe siècle.* Paris: Société Française d'Histoire d'Outre-Mer, 1984.

Mintz, Sidney W. *Caribbean Transformations.* Chicago: Aldine Press, 1974.

Moore, John Preston. *Revolt in Louisiana: The Spanish Occupation, 1766–1770.* Baton Rouge: Louisiana State University Press, 1976.

Morris, Christopher. "Impenetrable but Easy: The French Transformation of the Mississippi Calley and the Founding of New Orleans." In *Transforming New Orleans and its Environs: Centuries of Change,* ed. Craig E. Colten, 22–42. Pittsburgh, PA: University of Pittsburgh Press, 2000.

Morrow Long, Carolyn. *Madame Lalaurie, Mistress of the Haunted House.* Gainesville: University Press of Florida, 2012.

Nuhrah, Arthur G. "John McDonogh: Man of Many Facets." PhD Diss., Tulane University, 1950.

O'Neil, Charles F. "The Louisiana Manifesto of 1768." *Political Science Reviewer* 19 (Spring 1990): 247–289.

Paquette, Robert. "Revolutionary Saint-Domingue in the Making of Territorial Louisiana in 1800." In *A Turbulent Time: The French Revolution and the Greater Caribbean,* ed. Barry Gaspar and David Geggus, 204–225. Bloomington: University of Indiana Press, 1997.

Pargas, Damian Alan. *The Quarters and the Fields: Slave Families in the Non-cotton South.* Gainesville: University Press of Florida, 2010.

Pearson, Sarah M. S. *Atlantic Families: Lives and Letters in the Later Eighteenth Century.* Oxford: Oxford University Press, 2008.

Petitjean Roget, Jacques. *La Société d'Habitation à Martinique: Un demi-siècle de formation, 1635–1685.* 2 vols. Lille: Librairie Champion, 1980.

Plater, David D. *The Butlers of Iberville Parish, Louisiana: Dunboyne Plantation in the 1800s.* Baton Rouge: Louisiana State University Press, 2015.

Popkins, Jeremy. *Press, Revolution, and Social Identities in France, 1830–1835.* Philadelphia, PA: Penn State University Press, 2001.

Powell, Larry. *The Accidental City: Improvising New Orleans.* Cambridge, MA: Harvard University Press, 2013.

Price, Jacob M. *A History of the French Tobacco Monopoly, 1674–1791, and of its Relations to the British and American Tobacco Trades.* Ann Arbor: University of Michigan Press 1973.

Pritchard, James S. *In Search of Empire: The French in the Americas 1670–1730.* Cambridge: Cambridge University Press, 2007.

Rezneck, Samuel. "The Social History of an American Depression, 1837–1843." *American Historical Review* 40, no. 4 (July 1935): 662–687.

Rodriguez, John Eugene. *Spanish New Orleans: An Imperial City on the American Periphery, 1766–1803.* Baton Rouge: Louisiana State University Press, 2021.

Rogers, J. David. "Chapter Four: History of the New Orleans Flood Protection System." Climate Change and Public Health Law Site, LSU Law Center. https://biotech.law.lsu.edu/katrina/ILIT/report/CH_4.pdf.

Rushforth, Brett. "'A Little Flesh We Offer You': The Origins of Indian Slavery in New France." *William and Mary Quarterly* 60, no. 4 (October 2003): 777–808.

———. "'Next Stop, Honoré Beaugrand': Connections, Relocations, and Redirections." In *French Connections: Cultural Mobility in North America and the Atlantic World, 1600–1875,* ed. Robert Englebert and Andrew Wegmann, 245–250. Baton Rouge: Louisiana State University Press, 2020.

Scarborough, William K. *Masters of the Big House: Elite Slaveholders of the Mid-nineteenth-century South.* Baton Rouge: Louisiana State University Press, 2003.

Schafer, Judith Kelleher. "New Orleans Slavery in 1850 as Seen in Advertisements." *Journal of Southern History* 47, no. 1 (February 1981): 33–56.

Seck, Ibrahima. *Bouki fait Gombo: A History of the Slave Community of Habitation Haydel (Whitney Plantation), Louisiana, 1750–1860.* New Orleans: University of New Orleans Press, 2014.

Sexton, Jay. *The Monroe Doctrine: Empire and Nation in Nineteenth-Century America.* New York: Hill and Wang, 2012.

Spear, Jennifer. *Race, Sex, and Social Order in Early New Orleans.* Baltimore: Johns Hopkins University Press, 2009.

Starr, Wilbur. "In Search of Royalty: The Dreux Family." *New Orleans Genesis* 29, no. 114 (1990): 125–128.

Texada, David Ker. *Alejandro O'Reilly and the New Orleans Rebels.* Lafayette: Center for Louisiana Studies, University of Southwestern Louisiana, 1970.

Trask, Benjamin H. *Fearful Ravages: Yellow Fever in New Orleans, 1796–1905.* Lafayette: Center for Louisiana Studies, University of Louisiana at Lafayette, 2005.

Tregle, Joseph George. *Louisiana in the Age of Jackson: A Clash of Cultures and Personalities.* Baton Rouge: Louisiana State University Press, 1999.

Usner, Daniel H. *American Indians in Early New Orleans: From Calumet to Raquette.* Baton Rouge: Louisiana State University Press, 2018.

———. *American Indians in the Lower Mississippi Valley: Social and Economic Histories.* Omaha: University of Nebraska Press, 2004.

———. *Indians, Settlers, and Slaves in a Frontier Exchange Economy: The Lower Mississippi Valley before 1783.* Chapel Hill: University of North Carolina Press, 1992.

Vidal, Cécile, ed. *Caribbean New Orleans: Empire, Race, and the Making of a Slave Society.* Chapel Hill: University of North Carolina Press, 2019.

———. *Louisiana: Crossroads of the Atlantic World.* Philadelphia: University of Pennsylvania Press, 2014.

Villiers, Baron Marc de. "A History of the Foundation of New Orleans (1717–1722)." *Louisiana Historical Quarterly* 3 (April 1920): 157–253.

Wade, Richard. *Slavery in the Cities: The South, 1820–1860.* New York: Oxford University Press, 1965.

Wegmann, Andrew N. *An American Color: Race and Identity in New Orleans and the Atlantic World.* Athens: University of Georgia Press, 2022.

Whitaker, Arthur P. "Antonio De Ulloa." *Hispanic American Historical Review* 15 (May 1935): 155–194.

White, Sophie. *Voices of the Enslaved: Love, Labor, and Longing in French Louisiana.* Williamsburg, VA: Omohundro Institute of Early American History and Culture, and Chapel Hill: University of North Carolina Press, 2019.

———. *Wild Frenchmen and Frenchified Indians: Material Culture and Race in Colonial Louisiana.* Chapel Hill: University of North Carolina Press, 2012.

Whitten, David O. "Tariff and Profit in the Antebellum Louisiana Sugar Industry." *Business History Review* 44, no. 2 (Summer, 1970): 226–233.

Wilson, Samuel, Jr. "The Plantation of the Company of the Indies." *Louisiana History: The Journal of the Louisiana Historical Association* 31, no. 2 (Spring, 1990): 161–191.

Winston, James E. "The Cause and Results of the Revolution of 1768 in Louisiana." *Louisiana Historical Quarterly* 15 (April 1932): 181–213.

Websites

"Afro-Louisiana History and Genealogy, 1719–1820," https://www.ibiblio.org/laslave

Louisiana Digital Library, https://louisianadigitallibrary.org

Trans-Atlantic Slave Trade Database, https://www.slavevoyages.org/voyage/database

INDEX

Note: Page numbers of images are indicated by italics.